Principles of Microeconomics

Bassim Hamadeh, CEO and Publisher
Carrie Montoya, Manager, Revisions and Author Care
Kaela Martin, Project Editor
Jess Estrella, Senior Graphic Designer
Natalie Piccotti, Director of Marketing
Kassie Graves, Vice President of Editorial
Jamie Giganti, Director of Academic Publishing

Cover image copyright © 2014 Depositphotos/Merfin.
Interior image copyright © Depositphotos/romvo79.

Printed in the United States of America.

ISBN: 978-1-5165-2067-1 (pbk) / 978-1-5165-2068-8 (br) / 978-1-5165-4512-4 (al)

cognella® | ACADEMIC PUBLISHING

SECOND EDITION

Principles of Microeconomics

Mehmet Serkan Tosun

University of Nevada, Reno

Pavel Yakovlev and **Antony Davies**

Duquesne University

BRIEF CONTENTS

——

PART IV   Market Structures

DETAILED CONTENTS

ABOUT THE AUTHORS

Mehmet Serkan Tosun

Dr. Tosun is the Barbara S. Campbell Distinguished Professor of Nevada Tax Policy at the University of Nevada, Reno. He is also a Professor of Economics and Chairman of the Department of Economics. He is a research fellow at the Institute for the Study of Labor (IZA) in Bonn, Germany, an affiliate research fellow at the Oxford Institute of Population Ageing at the University of Oxford, and a research fellow at the Economic Research Forum (ERF) for Arab Countries, Iran and Turkey. Dr. Tosun received his Ph.D. in Economics from the Maxwell School of Citizenship and Public Affairs at Syracuse University. His research interests and expertise include public finance, economics of population and demographic change, international political economy, regional economics and economic growth. He has been a consultant for the International Monetary Fund, the World Bank, the United Cities and Local Governments (UCLG), the United Nations Development Fund for Women (UNIFEM), and the United Nations Economic and Social Commission for Western Asia (UNESCWA), among others. Dr. Tosun has received Dean's Research Professorship Award from the UNR College of

Business in 2013. He was recognized as the Best Researcher of the Year in 2009 by the Nevada Alpha Chapter of Beta Gamma Sigma, an international honor society for business studies. He was the recipient of the Middle East Economic Association's Ibn Khaldun Prize in 2005.

Pavel Yakovlev

Pavel Yakovlev is associate professor of economics at Duquesne University and Mercatus Affiliated Scholar. Pavel teaches microeconomics, macroeconomics, and public economics courses at Duquesne University. He has written numerous journal articles and book chapters on a diverse set of topics ranging from taxation to armed conflicts. He joined Duquesne University in 2007, after earning his doctorate degree from West Virginia University in 2006 and completing a year of post-doctoral research in the Bureau of Business and Economic Research at WVU. Pavel also has an M.A. in economics from West Virginia University and a B.S. in economics and business administration from Shepherd College. Pavel is a recipient of the WVU Foundation Distinguished Doctoral Fellowship in Social Sciences.

Antony Davies

Antony Davies is associate professor of economics at Duquesne University. Davies co-hosts *Words & Numbers*, a weekly podcast on economics and policy. He has written books on statistics, economics, and government, and has co-authored hundreds of op-eds for, among others, the *Wall Street Journal*, *Los Angeles Times*, *New York Daily News*, *Huffington Post*, and *Washington Post*. His YouTube videos on economics, government, and policy have garnered millions of views. In addition to his academic work, Dr. Davies was Associate Producer at the Moving Pictures Institute, Chief Financial Officer at Parabon Computation, founded several technology companies, and is co-founder and Chief Academic Officer at FreedomTrust, a non-profit educational institution. Davies earned his B.S. in Economics from Saint Vincent College, and Ph.D. in Economics from the State University of New York at Albany.

AKNOWLEDGEMENTS

We would like to thank our former professors and students for inspiring us to write this textbook. Some students also helped with the preparation of the book. We would like to thank specifically Adam (AJ) Davis and Rattaphon Wuthisatian, both former graduate students at the University of Nevada, Reno, for their help with finding data and other information used in some of the examples in the book. Our former professors and faculty mentors played an important role early in our careers when we were still students. Mehmet Tosun would like to thank in particular Gunar Evcimen and the late Demir Demirgil from Bogazici University, Turkey, and Donald Dutkowsky, Douglas Holtz-Eakin, and Mary Lovely from Syracuse University, U.S.A. who were all great role models, and mentors.

PREFACE

Economics is everywhere in our lives. We live in an increasingly interconnected and complex world that continues to evolve. As a social science, economics studies human behavior and its consequences. While individuals may seem at times irrational and unpredictable, humans as a group exhibit certain behavioral patterns that can be systematized and analyzed. In this book, we present the theories that explain those behavioral patterns. We aim to provide insight into the behavior of three important economic agents, individuals, firms and the government, and the interaction between these agents in a market economy.

We believe the students will benefit from a more concise textbook that is rich in real world examples and applications. In this textbook, we are providing a breadth of interesting examples that span different topics such as economics of superstars, the Arab Spring, Scotland independence vote, rising inequality, minimum wage, decline in entrepreneurial activity, oil cartel, and marijuana legalization to name a few. They also traverse different geographies such as the United States, Europe, Middle East, South America, and Asia. We hope that these will make economics more applicable, useful, and enjoyable to students.

PART 1

Introduction to Microeconomics

1 Introduction, Basic Concepts, and Definitions

On December 17, 2010, Mohamed Bouazizi, known by his friends and family as "Basboosa," was selling produce in the streets of Sidi Bouzid in Tunisia, as he had been since he quit school to work full-time in his late teens. This day was also not out of the ordinary in that Basboosa had his wheelbarrow of produce confiscated by local police officers followed by a humiliating beating. The harassment had been occurring for years, but Basboosa had no other way of supporting himself and his family. The one thing that was different about December 17, 2010, was that Basboosa decided to go to the governor's office to seek retribution. When he was denied a meeting with the governor, he was quoted as saying, "If you don't see me, I'll burn myself." He obtained a can of gasoline from a nearby gas station, returned to the governor's office, and then screamed, "How do you expect me to make a living?" When again he was ignored, he soaked himself in gasoline and lit a match. This event is thought to be the trigger that ignited the uprisings and a democratization process in the Arab world that is now referred to as the "Arab Spring." While Basboosa's story is tragic, it is an example of how economics is behind many facets of life. *Economics* is essentially the study of how rational agents choose to maximize their objectives in the face of scarcity and constraint. Basboosa wished to maximize the happiness of himself and his family by trying to provide them with a "decent living" in the face of his limited education and income. When deprived of even the modest quality of life provided by his produce cart, Basboosa resorted to extreme measures, set himself on fire, and died about two weeks later on January 4, 2011.

This chapter introduces the basic concepts and definitions that we use in what we call "economics" today. It is important to start with a formal definition of economics and microeconomics.

What Is Economics?

Alfred Marshall, the influential British economist, who is also one of the founders of neoclassical economics, defines *economics* as the study of wealth and man's (or human) actions. Marshall puts the emphasis on the study of man's actions or behavior. Hence, a very important part of economics is the study of behavior. *Microeconomics* can then be defined as the study of individual behavior and decisions, and how those decisions determine market outcomes within an economic system. In this definition *individual decisions* refer to decisions made by consumers, firms, and the government, which are the main economic actors we will study in this book.

ECONOMICS OF SCOTTISH INDEPENDENCE   Economic factors played a critical role in the 2014 Scottish Independence Referendum. Starting with some of the arguments in favor of independence, proponents argued that independence would give Scotland ability to keep its own revenues from such key economic sectors as oil, gas, other alternative energy (such as wind/tidal) sectors, tourism, food and drink, and financial services. This could obviously have significant positive economic and fiscal impacts for Scotland. With a relatively small population of little over 5 million, an independent Scotland could enjoy a high income per capita and become a prosperous small state within the European geography. Independence would also give Scotland power to decide on its own economic and government policies, including policies to reform taxes, transfer and social insurance programs.

   Opponents of independence also raised some important issues. One important argument is that an independent Scotland would be leaving the United Kingdom (UK) which could expose the country to serious risks both internally and externally. Externally, Scotland might have to leave the protective security, currency and trade umbrella the UK provides. While current oil and gas revenues look attractive, that may not be so in the future, especially if both oil production and prices fall significantly in the future. Internally, Scottish government would have to deal with rising health and social security payments due to aging of their population. They would no longer rely on the social insurance protection from the UK pension system.

   While Scotland voted against independence at the end, it was interesting to see the important role played by economics factors in the discussions.

Microeconomics versus Macroeconomics

Microeconomics and macroeconomics are the two main branches in the study of economics. Simply put, while *microeconomics* is the study of the small, *macroeconomics* is the study of the large. By "large" we mean the entire economy, as opposed to individual decision-making units (consumers, firms, and the government). Macroeconomics studies economy's aggregates, such as the output level, economic growth, unemployment rate, and inflation. The examples below present typical microeconomic and macroeconomic news we read about or watch in the media.

ALFRED MARSHALL (1842–1924)   British economist and one of the founders of neoclassical economics. He made an important contribution to economics teaching with his use of demand-and-supply diagrams in his renowned book Principles of Economics, which was first published in 1890.

Essential Concepts in Microeconomics

At the heart of microeconomics is individual choice and rational decision making. A rational decision maker must choose from numerous alternatives and weigh the costs and benefits of making a particular decision. To understand the mechanism behind individual decision making, we will go through four essential concepts. These are scarcity and trade-offs; incentives; voluntary trade; and the distribution of income and wealth. These concepts are key in the sense that they help explain the behavior of economic agents, such as consumers, firms, and the government, and thereby the functioning and consequences of the market system.

Concept 1: Scarcity and Trade-Offs

One of the most basic and important facts of life is that resources are limited. The scarcity of resources leads to one of the most important concepts in economics, trade-offs. This is also the concept behind the expression "there is no free lunch." We always need to give up something in order to get something else. Good examples are the decision to go to college or the decision to study a certain field in college. A young basketball star would have to decide between going to college and playing in the NBA. He knows that he can't do both at the same time. A typical student would have to decide which field he or she wants to study. While universities allow dual majors, a student still needs to choose from a number of possible fields of study. A decision to study economics, for instance, would mean that the student won't be able to study many other fields (physics, engineering, anthropology, etc.). These examples have one particular thing in common: time is limited. The scarcity of the resource (in this case, time) forces the individual to make a choice. Another common example of a trade-off is related to our spending. We have limited income, and we can't simply buy unlimited amounts of everything. This means that we have to choose between the different goods and services we buy. Buying a new TV set in a given month would mean that the consumer would have to buy less of many other things (CDs, books, etc.). The same thing is also true for firms when they are purchasing inputs for their production of goods or services, and also the government, which needs to spend based on a limited budget in any fiscal year. In the example on spending, trade-offs faced by consumers, firms, and the government come from the scarcity of the financial resources, mainly money.

EXAMPLES OF MICROECONOMIC NEWS

- "Electric-car maker Tesla Motors said it expects to ship 35,000 of its Model S sedans in 2014, up 55 percent from a year earlier" (from Bloomberg Businessweek, http://www.businessweek.com/articles/2014-02-19/teslas-stock-remains-electric-on-higher-sales-forecast).
- "Strong global demand and stagnant production in other countries has led to increased exports of U.S. dairy products in recent months, generating more money for dairy farmers but resulting in likely price hikes of 10-20 percent at the retail level in some markets, according to analysts" (from Reuters, http://www.reuters.com/article/2014/02/19/us-usa-milk-prices-idUSBREA1I1N820140219).

EXAMPLES OF MACROECONOMIC NEWS

- "Real gross domestic product—the output of goods and services produced by labor and property located in the United States—increased at an annual rate of 0.2 percent in the first quarter of 2015, according to the "advance" estimate released by the Bureau of Economic Analysis. In the fourth quarter of 2014, real GDP increased 2.2 percent" (from the Bureau of Economic Analysis [BEA], http://www.bea.gov/newsreleases/national/gdp/gdpnewsrelease.htm).
- "The Consumer Price Index for All Urban Consumers (CPI-U) increased 0.2 percent in March (2015) on a seasonal adjusted basis, the U.S. Bureau of Labor Statistics reported today. Over the last 12 months the all items index declined 0.1 percent before seasonal adjustment" (from the Bureau of Labor Statistics [BLS], http://www.bls.gov/news.release/cpi.nr0.htm).

Concept 2: Incentives

Incentives are the rewards that drive us to make a decision. In a market economy, prices play a key intermediary role by delivering incentives, where all decision makers, consumers, firms, and the government respond to those incentives. Incentives are critical when we are weighing the costs and benefits of making a decision.

Superstar Economics

In 2006, Viacom, the parent company of Paramount Pictures, decided to end its fourteen-year relationship with Tom Cruise's production company. The decision announced by Viacom's CEO, Sumner Redstone, received quite a lot of media attention, as it went against the spirit of what is called "superstar economics." Economics of superstars, as explained by the late University of Chicago economist Sherwin Rosen, refers to "the phenomenon of Superstars, wherein relatively small numbers of people earn enormous amounts of money and dominate the activities in which they engage.'" Because there is no doubt that Tom Cruise was at the time and still is a superstar, one wonders why Viacom decided to let him go. Media rumors were pointing to his erratic behavior in some TV shows and his association with Scientology, but this is largely about incentives in economics. We expect that Viacom indeed weighed the costs and benefits of continuing with Tom Cruise.

Concept 3: Voluntary Trade

Voluntary trade refers to free exchange of goods, services, and factors of production between economic agents in a given market. While a market is thought be a physical location, it could very well be a virtual place as well. It is also important to note that trades should be voluntary and not forced. Each party should be willing to buy or sell what it has. That means that each party weighs the costs and benefits of that trade. Apparently, people find a lot of trades with net benefits, as we see millions of trades happening in any given day. With improvements in computer technology, and especially since the invention of the Internet, the volume of trades has expanded tremendously through electronic trades in virtual markets.

---

1   *Sherwin Rosen, "The Economics of Superstars,"* American Economic Review 71 (1981): 845–858.

Concept 4: Distribution of Income and Wealth

Distribution matters. Economists often talk about increasing the size of the economic pie, which really means economic growth (growth in the real GDP per capita, to be precise). While growing the economy is critical for the overall welfare of residents and progress in society, the distribution of income and wealth is also very important. Some level of inequality is always expected as economies grow, but inequality can have serious negative consequences. History is full of revolutions, social unrest, and many other social transformations, and it is thought that a high degree of inequality might have played a role in these events. At the same time, economists do not agree on an optimal level of inequality, and income distribution and inequality vary significantly even among more developed economies with strong democratic institutions. Figure 1.1 shows the average real income of people at the top 10% and the bottom 90% of the income

distribution in the U.S. There is a clear upward trend in the average income of people at the top10% group. While there is also some increase for the bottom 90% group, that trend is much less pronounced. This is one graph that points to rising income inequality in the U.S. over a long period of time. The income gap between the high income and the lower income groups seems to have risen consistently over time. Figure 1.2 shows that income inequality measured by the Gini coefficient (or Gini index) varies quite significantly across the Organization for Economic Cooperation and Development (OECD) countries, which is a group of relatively higher income countries. A higher Gini coefficient indicates higher income inequality. It looks like some countries like Mexico, Turkey and the United States experience a significantly higher degree of income inequality than other relatively higher income countries.

Positive versus Normative Economics

Positive economics is about how economic agents choose their actions and how those actions are affected by changes in policy. *Normative economics* is about the evaluation of policies and the choice of optimal policy, which is the policy that meets a certain objective, such

as maximizing overall welfare in society. Normative economics is about value judgments, whereas positive economics refrains from that. Examples of positive and normative statements are as follows:

SUPERSTAR ECONOMICS   Sherwin Rosen explains in one of his most notable papers, "The Economics of Superstars," that "in certain kinds of economic activity there is concentration of output among a few individuals, marked skewness in the associated distributions of income and very large rewards at the top."[2]

SOME QUESTIONS TO CONTEMPLATE: Does a Superstar guarantee success? Do people see a movie for its cast?

POSITIVE ECONOMIC STATEMENT: The federal minimum wage rate is $7.25 per hour of work as of January 1, 2015.

NORMATIVE ECONOMIC STATEMENT: The federal minimum wage rate should be higher than $7.25.

Source: http://topincomes.g-mond.parisschoolofeconomics.eu/

---

2   Sherwin Rosen, "The Economics of Superstars," American Economic Review 71 (1981): 845–858.

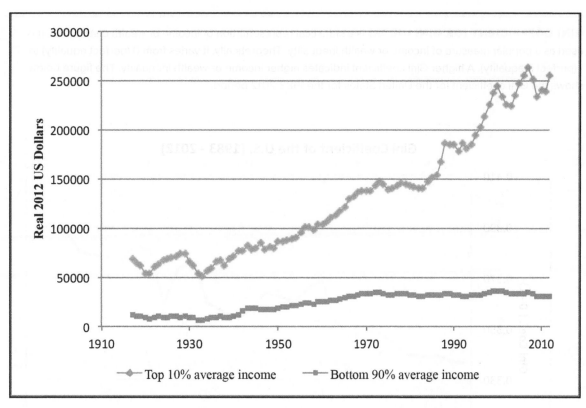

FIGURE 1.1 Average Real Income of People at the top 10% and the bottom 90% in the U.S.

Source: http://topincomes.g-mond.parisschoolofeconomics.eu/

We see both positive and normative analysis in economics. While economists largely agree on positive economic issues, they largely disagree on normative issues because their values differ quite extensively.

Who Is an Economist, and What Does an Economist Do?

Formally, we define an *economist* as a professional in the social science discipline of economics. This is an individual who develops or applies theories typically to economic issues. However, an economist is much more than that. An economist would most likely have studied economics at least at the undergraduate level. A good number would have studied economics at the graduate level (the master's or doctoral level) as well. But who is an economist? How does she or he think? Here is a short list.

An economist is a person who:

- Always thinks in terms of alternatives
- Weighs the costs and benefits of different choices
- Develops models to analyze the relationships between different events
- Occasionally makes predictions about the future of the economy

GINI COEFFICIENT (OR GINI INDEX) is a statistical representation of income or wealth distribution. It is used as a popular measure of income or wealth inequality. Theoretically, it varies from 0 (perfect equality) to 1 (perfect inequality). A higher Gini coefficient indicates higher income or wealth inequality. The figure below shows the Gini coefficient for the United States for the 1983-2012 period.

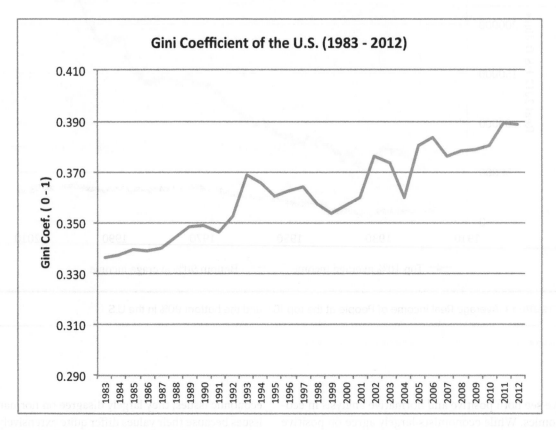

Sources: Source: http://www.oecd.org/statistics

Of course, these are broad generalizations. Economists differ a lot in terms of the specific work they do. How they differ depends, to a large extent, on where they work and what type of work they do. We see economists in both the private sector and the public sector. Within the public sector, we see economists in all three branches of government, executive, legislative, and judicial. For example, the secretary of the Treasury in the United States plays a key role in economic and fiscal policy and acts as the key economic advisor to the president. Alexander Hamilton, who was the first Treasury secretary, also proposed the creation of a national bank that would act as a stabilizing force for a fragile economy and financial system after independence from Britain. After two short-lived national banks, the Federal Reserve System was founded on December 23, 1913. The Chairperson of the Federal Reserve Bank has become one of the most visible economists in the United States. Janet Yellen was recently confirmed as the new Federal Reserve chair. She is the first woman to hold the top job at the Fed. There are many other examples of influential economists in both the public and the private sectors.

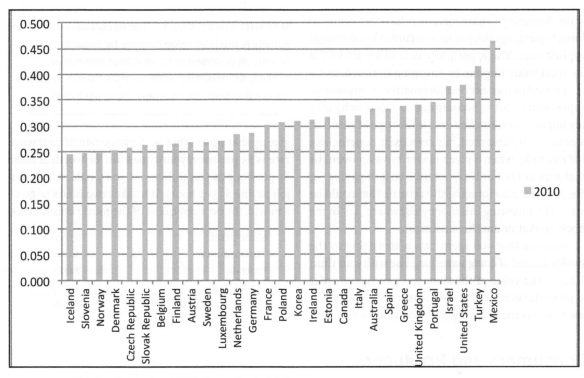

FIGURE 1.2 Gini Coefficient for OECD Countries in 2010

Basic Model Definitions: Cost, Economic Agents, and the Market

In the final section of this chapter, we provide definitions of basic economic concepts and also the key economic players and the environment that economic transactions take place, which we refer to as a *market*.

Economic Cost

Whenever economists speak of "cost," they mean *economic* cost, not *accounting* cost. *Accounting* cost is the explicit cost of undertaking an activity. *Economic cost, which is also called opportunity cost,* is accounting cost *plus* the implicit cost of not undertaking other activities. For example, suppose you go to the movies. Your accounting costs are as follows:

Movie ticket:	$7.00
Transportation:	$2.00
Popcorn:	$4.00
Accounting cost of the movie:	$13.00

Source: http://www.oecd.org/statistics/

Now, suppose that instead of going to the movies, you could have done something else with your time, such as hiking, working, studying, visiting, and so on. Because you have foregone the opportunity of doing something else, you have incurred an additional implicit cost. The *opportunity* cost of an activity is the total value forgone by engaging in that activity as opposed to its next best alternative. Economic or opportunity cost is accounting cost (explicit) plus any implicit cost. Implicit cost is the type of cost that is not directly observed, but does exist nonetheless. For example, when a pizza maker buys an oven, he or she incurs not only the explicit cost of paying for the oven but also forgoing the returns that could be earned by investing this money elsewhere (i.e. in the stock market or another business).

Suppose that you spent two hours going to the movies instead of doing something else with your time. What is the value of the time you gave up in order to go to the movies? A good measure of the value of one's time is the price that one is willing to accept to

---

OPPORTUNITY COST The opportunity cost of an activity is the total value forgone by engaging in that activity as opposed to its next best alternative.
TOTAL ECONOMIC (OR OPPORTUNITY) cost is accounting (explicit) cost plus any implicit cost.

---

give up that time—that is, the wage rate. If your wage rate is $5 per hour, your time must be worth at most $5 per hour to you (otherwise you wouldn't accept a job paying $5 per hour). If it takes two hours to go to a movie, the economic cost of the movie is as follows:

Movie ticket:	$7.00
Transportation:	$2.00
Popcorn:	$4.00
Cost of time:	$10.00
Economic cost of the movie:	$23.00

Consumers and Producers

All economic interactions occur between consumers and producers. It is common to think of consumers as people and of producers as firms. This is not, however, always the case. Who plays the role of consumer and who plays the role of producer varies depending on the product in question. In the case of shoes, the consumer could be a person and the producer would be a firm. In the case of labor, the reverse is true: the consumer is the firm and the producer is a person. In the case of electricity, both the consumer and producer could be firms, or the consumer could be a person and the producer could be a firm. Because the roles vary depending on the product in question, we shall avoid using terms like "firm" and "person" and instead say "producer" and "consumer." Regardless of who plays each role, the producer is *always* the one offering the product, and the consumer is *always* the one desiring the product.

"Producer" does not necessarily mean the same thing as "manufacturer." If we consider the wholesale

---

A CONSUMER is one who desires a product.
A PRODUCER is one who offers a product.

---

market for televisions, the producers are television manufacturers, such as Zenith, Sony, Magnavox, and so forth. The consumers are retail outlets, such as Wal-Mart, Sears, K-Mart, and so on. If we consider the retail market for televisions, the producers are retail outlets and the consumers are people. In the retail market for televisions, Wal-Mart, Sears, and K-Mart are considered producers (they are the ones offering the product for sale), even though they are not the manufacturers (they did not make the product). You can think of Wal-Mart, Sears, and K-Mart as firms that buy a factor (televisions) and produce a product that is identical to the factor (televisions).

Economic Interactions

Economists are interested in economic interactions—what happens when consumers and producers come together. When producers and consumers of a particular product come together, we call the interactions between them a *market*. A *market* is the total of all interactions between consumers and producers concerning a particular product.

In order for any two people to interact, each person must behave in a certain way. So, before we can describe the interactions of consumers and producers, we must examine how each group behaves independently of the other. The behavior of consumers is summarized by what we call *demand*. The behavior of producers is summarized by what we call *supply*. Demand tells

---

A MARKET *is the total of all interactions between consumers and producers concerning a particular product.*

---

us under what conditions consumers are willing to purchase various amounts of a product. Supply tells us under what conditions producers are willing to offer various amounts of a product.

Goods, Services, and Products

The terms *good*, *service*, and *product* are almost synonyms, but each does mean something slightly different. A *good* is a tangible object, such as a shoe, a car, a television, or a pizza. Goods are divided into three major categories: *consumer durables*, *consumer nondurables*, and *producer goods*. *Consumer durables* are goods that people usually buy and that can be consumed more than once. *Consumer nondurables* are goods that people usually buy and that can be consumed only once. For example, a pizza is a consumer nondurable good; a car is a consumer

---

PRODUCT *is a generic term for a good or a service.*

---

durable good. A *producer good* is a good that firms usually buy and use to produce something. For example, steel and rubber are producer goods. A *service* is an action performed by the producer for the consumer. Babysitting, waiting tables, and washing cars are all services. *Product* is a generic term for a good or a service.

CONCLUSION

This chapter introduces students to economics and its two main subfields: microeconomics and macroeconomics. The four essential concepts in microeconomics are scarcity, tradeoffs, incentives, and voluntary trade. These concepts will reappear throughout the textbook. Economists use two types of arguments: positive (objective) and normative (subjective). We will be referring to these two approaches in our analysis

in the upcoming chapters. Economists always think in terms of alternatives, weigh the costs and benefits of choices, develop models and theories to analyze economic relationships, and also may make predictions regarding the future of the economy. This chapter also covers the basic definitions of economic cost, economic agents, such as consumers and producers, markets, goods and services.

DISCUSSION QUESTIONS

1. Find other examples of how economics enters our lives.

2. How is microeconomics different from macroeconomics?

3. How are the essential concepts in microeconomics related to each other?

4. How would you explain the difference between positive and normative economics? Can you think of other examples that would show the difference between the two approaches?

5. Why are we seeing more discussion recently on income and wealth inequality?

6. Is inequality destiny?

7. What is opportunity cost? How does it relate to incentives in economics?

2 Introduction to Economic Models

I n this chapter we will be introducing the reader to economic modeling. One of the first models that described how an economy works was the *Tableau Economique* (or *Economic Table*) by Francois Quesnay in 1759. Interestingly, Quesnay was the personal physician of the French King Louis XV. Quesnay's thinking behind his economic table was based on how blood circulates through the human body. He thought that the flow of commodities in an economy is similar to blood flow in our bodies. In his thinking, the agriculture sector is to an economy what a heart is to a human body. This was, of course, before manufacturing and then service sectors became dominant in modern economies. Despite its simplicity, this circular-flow model is one of many economic models that try to emulate the world of physics, where the influences that forces exert upon objects (or individuals in economics) can be measured and analyzed.

Modeling in Economics

Economists use models to test their theories. In that way, economics is similar to other sciences. Observations give rise to theories, and then theories are tested using models and available data for the variables that are studied. Because most economic events and relationships are very complex, a model needs to be a rather strong simplification of reality in order for it to be practical. As the famous British statistician George Box once said, "all models are wrong, but some are useful." Another common feature that unites many economic models is the assumption of a self-interested, rational and therefore optimizing economic agent. After all, how many times are we told to ignore friction when making calculations in physics classes? Some assumptions, like the one of rationality or frictionless surface, may seem unrealistic to some people, but it does not necessarily invalidate the model's conclusions. Case in point: do not confuse rationality with perfection. All humans are ignorant to a degree and they have been known to make mistakes. The assumption of rationality imposes a basic constraint on individuals in economic models so that they choose better outcomes over worse ones. Models are just made simpler with the help of assumptions. For example, a theory that involves the decision making of millions of individuals could be simplified using a model of a two-person island economy.

There are, of course, other types of economies that would be alternatives to the models we feature in this textbook. Barter and gift economies are alternatives that we sometimes see even today. In a barter

---

GIFT ECONOMY IN BURNING MAN Burning Man, a weeklong event that takes place in Black Rock Desert in Northern Nevada, is a good example of a "gift economy." Burning Man is described as an event "dedicated to community, art, self-expression, and self-reliance." "Gifting" is listed as one of the ten principles of Burning Man (http://www.burningman.com/).

---

economy, no currency is used in exchanges. Rather, goods and services are traded for other goods and services in return. A gift economy is different in the sense that when a gift is given, there is no expectation of a good or service in return. These alternative economies are much less common now in modern societies.

Model 1: Major Markets and the Circular-Flow Diagram

A first model in economics, which resembles Francois Quesnay's *Tableau Economique*, can be depicted in the circular-flow diagram shown in figure 2.1. This simple model shows two types of markets—product markets and factor markets—and three types of economic agents—consumers (who also make up households), firms (who are also producers and sellers), and the government. The figure shows two types of flows: (1) the physical flows of goods, services, and the factors of production, such as labor and capital, and (2) financial flows through exchange of money.

In the circular-flow model, households or consumers demand goods and services from firms or producers in exchange for money; firms supply those goods and services to households through the product markets and receive money in return. Households and firms are also connected through the factor markets, where firms now demand labor and capital through the factor markets in exchange for wages and interest earnings received by households that supply their labor services and savings (as capital) to firms.

In the upcoming chapters, we will analyze these relationships first without the involvement of government. In reality, the government—or governments in a multitiered government structure with central (or federal), state, and local governments—plays an important role in both product and factor markets and interacts with both households and firms. That is why the government (or governments) appears at the center of our circular-flow diagram in figure 2.1. Simply put, governments collect a variety of taxes from both households and firms, who are also owned by households, and spend those tax dollars on a variety of government programs and other public services, which in turn benefit households and firms. While it is not shown on the circular-flow diagram, governments also impact both product and factor markets through the taxing and spending functions. We will examine the role of governments in markets particularly in Chapters 7 and 8.

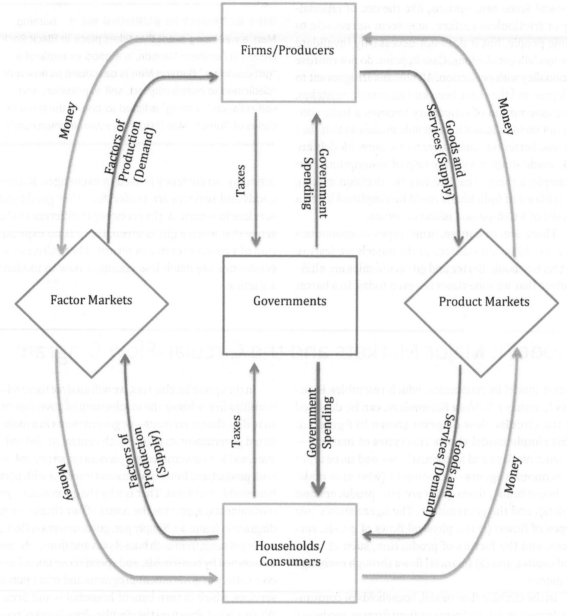

FIGURE 2.1 The Circular-Flow Diagram

Model 2: Opportunity Cost, Production Possibilities Curve, and Comparative Advantage

We have seen in chapter 1 that trade-offs are a fact of life. Because there is no free lunch, you always give up something when you engage in some activity. When a student goes to college, he or she forgoes a modest wage or salary. When a worker works an additional hour, he or she gives up an hour that can be spent

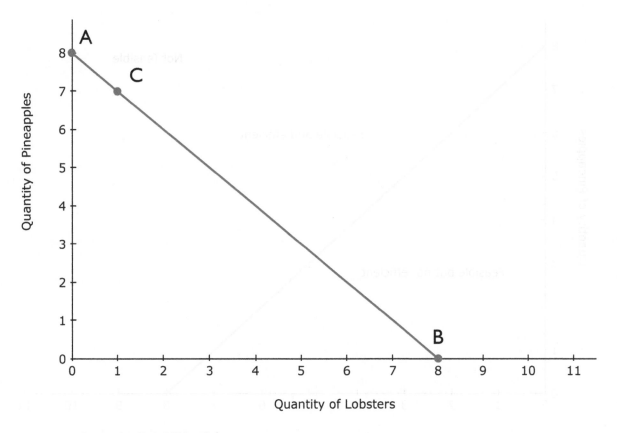

FIGURE 2.2 Production Possibilities Curve

instead with family. As we have seen in the previous chapter, these can be summarized under the concept of the opportunity cost.

The *opportunity cost* of an activity is the total value forgone by engaging in that activity as opposed to its next best alternative. An important model that uses this opportunity cost concept is the production possibilities curve (PPC) model shown in figure 2.2.[1] The figure shows the trade-off between the production of pineapples and the production of lobsters. In this figure, the PPC is drawn as a negatively sloped (or downward sloping) line that shows the negative relationship between the production of pineapples and lobsters. The opportunity cost of one more lobster is what you need to forgo in pineapple production. This figure makes a number of important points. First, it tells us about the exact magnitude of the trade-off.

Let's see how we determine this by going through some points on the PPC in figure 2.2. At point A, the economy produces eight pineapples but no lobsters. This is an extreme point, which is also referred to as an *intercept*. It is a vertical intercept, as it is on the vertical axis. At point B, the economy produces eight lobsters but no pineapples. This is the other extreme point, which is also called the horizontal intercept. At point C, the economy produces seven pineapples and one lobster. Notice that to move from point A to point C, the society gave up production of one pineapple in return for one lobster. Hence, the opportunity cost of one lobster is one pineapple, because that is what you are giving up to get that lobster. Second, the PPC also tells us about the "feasible" and "not feasible" production points. *Feasible points* are those where the economy has enough resources, such as land,

---

1   Production Possibilities Curve is also referred to as the Production Possibilities Frontier (PPF).

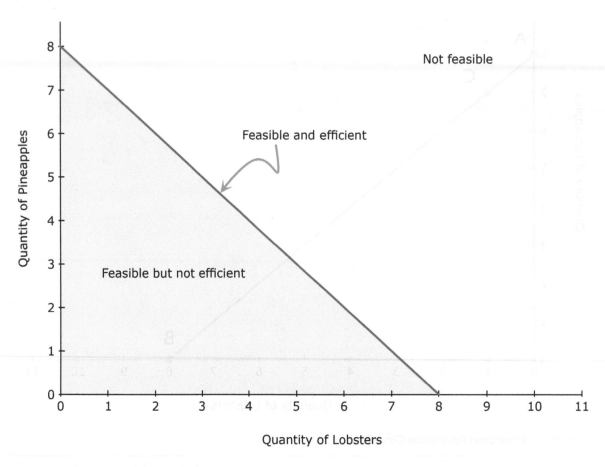

FIGURE 2.3 Production Possibilities Curve with Feasible, Not Feasible and Efficient Points

labor, and capital, to engage in such production. We can show this separately in figure 2.3. All the points below the PPC in the shaded region and on the PPC are feasible production points. Those feasible points on the PPC are also called "efficient," as they correspond to production choices that use up all available resources in the economy. For example, both points A and B are feasible, but only point B is efficient. Points outside or above the PPC are not feasible points. In other words, we don't have enough resources to produce at that level. Therefore, point C in figure 2.3 can't be a feasible point. The economy doesn't have the means to produce eight pineapples and eight lobsters at the same time.

The PPC shown in figures 2.2 and 2.3 shows a constant negative slope. A more realistic PPC, shown in figure 2.4, would indeed be a curve with a shape that is bowed out from the origin, which indicates an increasing opportunity cost. This can also be seen in the slope, because as we move from the part of the curve closer to vertical axis toward the horizontal axis (or left to right), the curve gets steeper, indicating a greater slope in absolute value. In this case, greater and greater numbers of pineapples would be sacrificed as we increase the production of boats. For example, from point A to point B, production of the first five boats would require us to give up pineapple production by two thousand units, but production of the next five boats would require us to give up pineapple production by six thousand units, as indicated by a move from point B to point C. This is because of diminishing returns to the factors used in the production of these two goods. While the first few units of a good would use the factors best suited for that specific production, more production would have to use factors much less suited, leading to a greater cost of production.

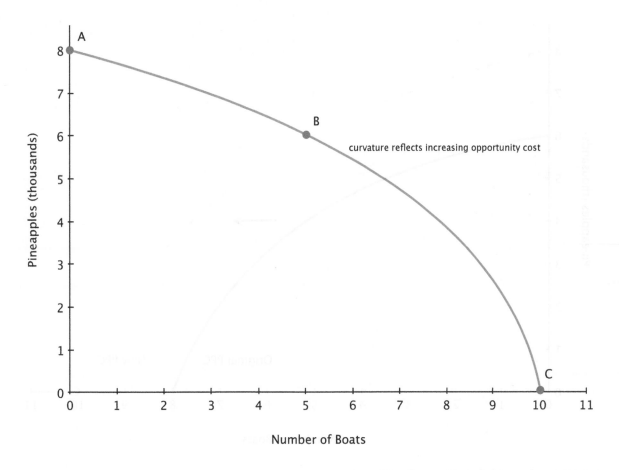

curvature reflects increasing opportunity cost

FIGURE 2.4 Production Possibilities Curve with Increasing Opportunity Cost

The PPC is usually drawn for a given time period, such as a month or a year, but it is also possible to show changes over time. An economic expansion or growth can be shown as a shift in the PPC outward, as shown in figure 2.5. This is most likely because of increases in the factors of production, such as capital and labor. For example, as population increases, which would increase the labor force in the country, we would expect the production capacity to increase as well. Technological progress is another source of economic expansion that would also shift the PPC outward.

It is also possible to show a contraction in production, which can be shown as a shift in the PPC inward. This would be because of decreases in the factors of production. When a major natural disaster hits (e.g., Hurricane Katrina, which hit New Orleans in 2005, and the earthquake and tsunami in Japan in 2011), lives are lost, and infrastructure and homes are seriously damaged or destroyed. Such disasters could diminish the productive capacity, which would lead to a contraction in the economy. Figure 2.6 shows an economic contraction as an inward shift in the PPC.

Comparative Advantage and Voluntary Trade

Another important use for the PPC analysis that we presented before is to understand comparative advantage and trade patterns. To understand comparative advantage, let's look at the PPC example with pineapples and

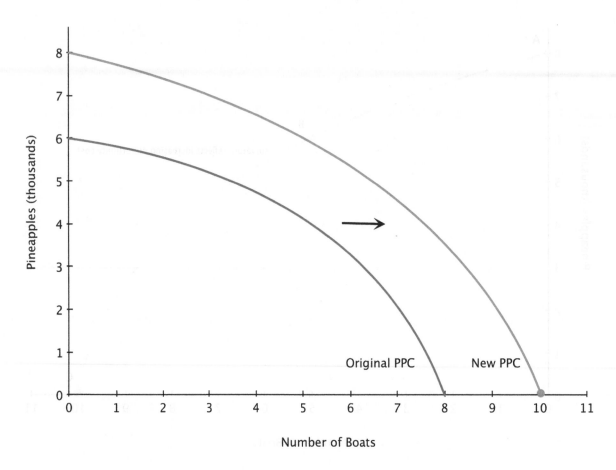

FIGURE 2.5 Economic Expansion or Growth

lobsters that we used in the previous section. This time we will introduce two PPCs for two individuals so that we can talk about trade between them. The PPC of the first individual (Phineas) is shown in figure 2.7, and the one for the second individual (Ferb) is shown in figure 2.8. With all his time and labor, Phineas can produce eighteen pineapples or nine lobsters, whereas Ferb can produce twenty pineapples or thirty lobsters. Therefore, our first observation is that Ferb is more capable than Phineas is overall. We refer to this as an "absolute advantage." Ferb has an absolute advantage over Phineas because he can produce both more pineapples and more lobsters than Phineas can. Just looking at this situation, one may be tempted to say that there is no reason for Phineas and Ferb to trade with each other. That would be wrong, however, because trade between individuals is determined by comparative advantage,

not absolute advantage. To see this point, let's first look at where they would produce and consume without trade. We can imagine that, at first, Phineas and Ferb are isolated from each other on the island. Figure 2.7 shows that Phineas would produce and consume six pineapples and six lobsters (point A) in a given week, whereas figure 2.8 shows that Ferb would produce and consume ten pineapples and fifteen lobsters (point A) in the same week. Again, Ferb produces and consumes more of the two goods than Phineas does.

We will now show that voluntary trade indeed could make both parties better off than before. We first need to find out about the trade-off between the two goods. Starting with figure 2.7, we ask ourselves, "What would it cost us to increase the production of lobsters by one unit?" Given the trade-off between the two goods, which is also indicated by the slope of the

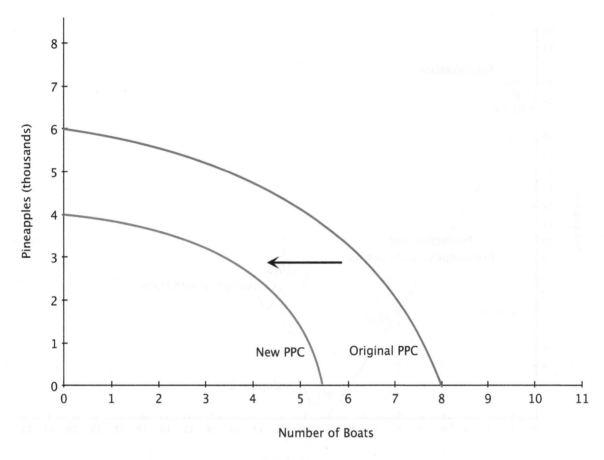

FIGURE 2.6 Economic Contraction

TABLE 2.1 Opportunity Costs for Phineas and Ferb

	Phineas	**Ferb**
Opportunity cost of lobster	2 pineapples	2/3 pineapple
Opportunity cost of pineapple	1/2 lobster	1 1/2 lobsters

PPC, the answer is two pineapples for each additional lobster. This is also the opportunity cost of a lobster. Of course, we can ask the same question from the perspective of pineapple production: "What would it cost us to increase the production of pineapples by one unit?" This time the answer can be found simply by taking the inverse of the opportunity cost calculated before. Each pineapple produced will force us to decrease lobster production by half a unit (the inverse of 2 is 1/2).

When we do the same thing for Ferb in figure 2.8, we find that the opportunity cost of a lobster is 2/3, whereas the opportunity cost of a pineapple is 3/2 (or 1 1/2). We compare these opportunity costs for the two individuals in table 2.1. We see that the opportunity cost of a lobster is lower for Ferb than it is for Phineas. At the same time, the opportunity cost of a pineapple is lower for Phineas than it is for Ferb. These numbers suggest that Ferb has a comparative advantage in

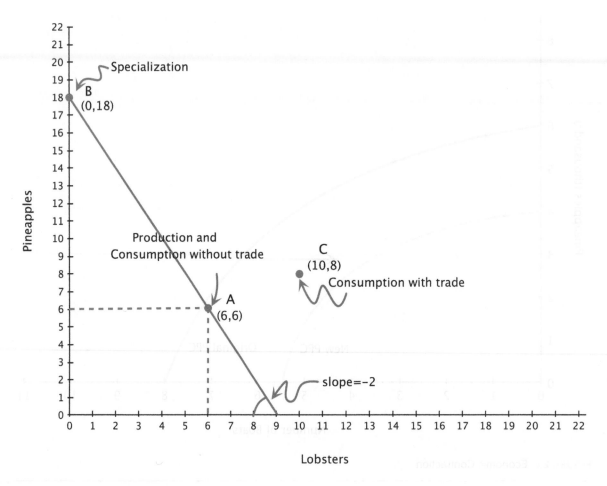

FIGURE 2.7 PPC for Phineas

lobsters, whereas Phineas has a comparative advantage in pineapples. We now take it one step further and say that each individual should specialize in the good for which he has comparative advantage and then trade with the other party. For example, because Phineas has comparative advantage in pineapples, he should produce only pineapples at point B in figure 2.7, and Ferb should in turn specialize in the production of lobsters at point B in figure 2.8. The trade pattern would then be in the following way: Phineas would give pineapples to Ferb and receive lobsters in return.

If we assume an exchange rate of one, Phineas could give ten pineapples to Ferb and then receive ten lobsters. That moves him to a new consumption point with trade at point C in figure 2.7. Notice that point C was outside his PPC and was not a feasible

point, but it became attainable with trade. Phineas is now consuming four more lobsters and two more pineapples than before trade. Ferb is also consuming outside his PPC at point C in figure 2.8. While he is consuming the same amount of pineapples as before, he is now consuming five more lobsters than before trade. This example clearly demonstrates the gains from voluntary trade between individuals. The comparative advantage concept and the analysis here apply equally to trade between countries as well. As we have said before for Phineas, some countries may be at an absolute disadvantage in some goods compared to others, but there is still room for trade between countries because they may still have comparative advantage.

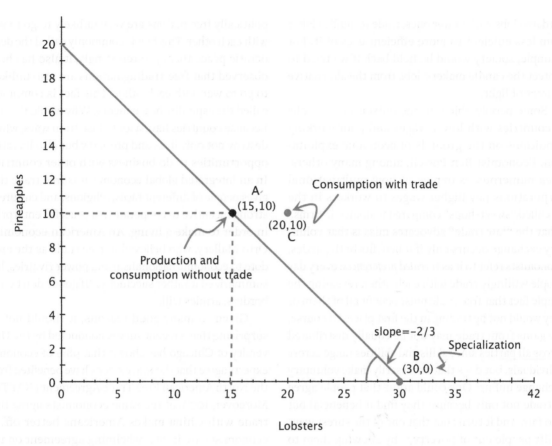

FIGURE 2.8 PPC for Ferb

The Gains from Trade and Revealed Preferences

The contribution of free trade to the economic well-being of a nation can hardly be overestimated. Since the publication of *The Wealth of Nations* in 1776 by the Scottish economist and philosopher Adam Smith, economists have confirmed repeatedly, both theoretically and empirically, his treatise that free trade makes nations more prosperous. As the Nobel prize-winning economist Paul Krugman put it: "If there were an Economist's Creed, it would surely contain the affirmations 'I understand the Principle of Comparative Advantage' and 'I advocate Free Trade'."[2] One of the reasons economists overwhelmingly support free trade is because they see it as being similar

to technological progress in its positive effect on economic development. One can outsource a task to a machine or to another person who can do it better, cheaper, faster, etc. The end result is analytically equivalent: overall prosperity increases, regardless if it comes from a job being done more efficiently by a machine or by a worker in another country. Economists' views on immigration are similar: a country can benefit just as much from goods imported from another country or produced domestically with labor brought from another country. But wouldn't free trade and immigration destroy domestic jobs? No. Just like with technological progress that replaces

---

2   Krugman, P. 1987. Is Free Trade Passé?, *The Journal of Economic Perspectives*, Vol. 1, No. 2.

outdated jobs with newer ones, trade reshuffles labor from less efficient to more efficient uses of it. For example, society would be held back if we tried to protect the candle makers' jobs from the alternative sources of light.

Some people object to the outsourcing of jobs to countries with lower wages and poor working conditions on the grounds of economic exploitation. Economist Ben Powell, among many others, cites numerous examples of how multinational corporations pay higher wages to workers in the so-called "sweatshops" compared to domestic firms.[3] What the "fair trade" advocates miss is that voluntary exchange occurs only if it benefits both parties. Economists refer to it as *revealed preferences*: every day people willingly trade with each other, revealing the simple fact that free trade must benefit all of them or they would not be trading in the first place. Of course, the gains from trade may not be equally distributed across all parties since skills and abilities range across individuals, but does that necessarily make voluntary exchange unfair? One could argue that people agree to trade not only because they find it beneficial but also fair. And it turns out that one of the surest ways to lift people out of poverty is by allowing them to trade freely. In an article titled "In Praise of Cheap Labor," liberal economist Paul Krugman argues that bad jobs at low wages are better than no jobs at all, which is what can happen to poor countries if rich countries succeed in limiting free trade. And isn't it interesting that the biggest objections to free trade come not from the workers in poor countries but from the trade unions and privileged industries in rich countries that fear foreign competition? The central lesson here is this: poor countries are poor because of low productivity. A good way to increase their productivity is by opening up their opportunities for growth through free trade.

The other often-overlooked benefit of free trade is world peace and harmony. It has been observed that politically free nations are very unlikely to go to war with each other. This fact is commonly called the democratic peace theory. Interestingly, it also has been observed that free-trading nations are also unlikely to go to war with each other. This fact is commonly called the capitalist peace theory. Why would that be? Because countries have a lot to lose from wars, which destroy not only lives and property but also lucrative opportunities to do business with other countries. In an integrated global economy, it is free trade that gives people of different races, religions, and cultures a strong incentive to cooperate in a peaceful enterprise in order to make a living. An American economist, Otto Mallery, who believed in free trade as the antidote to economic nationalism and power rivalries, has summarized it rather succinctly: "If goods don't cross borders, armies will."

Given so many good reasons, it should not be surprising that a recent survey conducted by the University of Chicago has shown that 98% of economic experts agree that the U.S. citizens have benefited from the North American Free Trade Agreement (NAFTA). Moreover, 100% of the same economists agree that trade with China makes Americans better off! If economists are in overwhelming agreement on the merits of free trade, then why do so many politicians, pundits, and voters oppose it? In his book *The Myth of the Rational Voter*, George Mason University economist Bryan Caplan argues that free trade may be hard to accept when people suffer from anti-market bias, anti-foreign bias, and pessimism bias. And politicians across the political spectrum tend to exploit these biases as evidenced in their anti-trade rhetoric and policies. Furthermore, Nobel Laureate in economics Paul Krugman offers several reasons as to why even the intellectuals may oppose free trade: it may seem intellectually fashionable to argue against it, comparative advantage is hard to understand, and people are averse to a fundamentally mathematical description of the world.

---

3 Powell, B. 2014. *Out of poverty: Sweatshops in the global economy.* Cambridge University Press.

CONCLUSION

This chapter introduces students to some basic economic models. One common assumption that threads through most economic models is the one of an optimizing individual. We start with the circular-flow diagram, which is a depiction of the physical flows of goods, services, and factors of production, and financial flows throughout the economy. This is followed by the production possibilities frontier, the second model of the economy. We have seen that this model makes very good use of tradeoffs and the opportunity cost concept. It is a simple yet very useful framework for understanding the comparative advantage and the gains from voluntary trade between individuals or countries. The general conclusion from economic theory and empirical evidence is that all countries, poor or rich, can benefit from free trade.

DISCUSSION QUESTIONS

1. Compare and contrast the barter and gift economies to the economic model shown in the circular-flow diagram.

2. Find different ways to extend the circular-flow diagram model.

3. How would the PPC change if we have more workers in the economy but no additional capital that new workers would need to produce more goods?

4. What is the difference between absolute and comparative advantage?

5. Is it possible to have a comparative advantage when a country doesn't have absolute advantage compared to potential trade partners?

6. Give examples from actual trade patterns between countries that are consistent with the comparative advantage concept.

PART 2

Demand, Supply and Price Determination in the Market

3 Consumer Decision Making and the Demand Curve

Ricard "Ricky" Rubio Vives is a professional basketball player who was born in Spain. Rubio was the youngest player ever to play in the Spanish ACB League on October 15, 2005, at age fourteen. On June 25, 2009, he was drafted with the fifth pick in the first round of the 2009 NBA Draft by the Timberwolves, making him the first player born in the 1990s to be drafted by the NBA. When drafted, Ricky did have a contract with his Spanish team, DKV Joventut, and Ricky's talents were highly coveted by both teams, so Ricky had a decision to make. Now, Ricky was unlike the majority of the consumers in the world because his budget constraint was in the millions, but he still needed to consider the differences of getting paid in American dollars instead of Euros as well as whether he would be able to buy more of the things that made him happy in Minnesota or Badalona.

In order to answer this question, we need to build a model regarding individual decision making. In this chapter we will examine how individual preferences really control the amount of happiness, or *utility*, that an individual obtains from consuming different goods and services. We will also learn that consumers face constraints when making choices and that rational consumers will attempt to maximize their happiness from consumption in the face of these constraints.

(Note: On May 31, 2011, Rubio reached an agreement with Minnesota to join the Timberwolves for the 2011–2012 NBA season.)

Consumer Theory

Utility

There is one and only one basic force that drives the economy and from the study of which all economic theory arises: the quest for happiness. It is here that the economy begins. It is from this simple quest that we shall, over the next several hundred pages, build the principles of economics. We start with the following principle.

FIRST PRINCIPLE   Individuals act in such a way as to seek out those things that they believe will yield them the most happiness.

"Individuals..." When humans gather into groups (committees, villages, towns, cities, nations), it is frequently the case that a few humans (usually those who hold a disproportionate share of the group's power) pursue what is in their own self-interest (i.e., the individuals obey the first principle) to the detriment of the group. In fact, it is also often the case that the benefit that the few obtain is less than the cost to the rest of the group. Thus, *groups* of humans do not always act in such a way as to seek out those things that they perceive as yielding them the most happiness, but individual humans do.

"...that they believe will yield..." Humans do not always pursue what is good for them. Some pursue drugs; some pursue drinks; some pursue danger; some pursue lives of sloth. An objective observer might say that such people are not pursuing happiness (assuming for a moment that happiness is an objective reality). Such people are, however, pursuing what they *believe* will bring them happiness. Their beliefs may be based on incorrect knowledge or false assumptions, but they are their beliefs nonetheless.

"...the most happiness." The first principle makes no guarantee that humans will *attain* happiness, only that they will constantly seek it. We could go so far as to say that ultimate happiness is *un*attainable. It turns out that it does not matter that humans do not attain ultimate happiness. As long as they continue to *strive* for happiness, the rest of economic theory continues to hold. What if there is *no* happiness to strive for? Suppose that there is a human in such an unfortunate state that all his potential choices end in some form of misery. The human will make the choice that yields the *least* misery: *minimizing misery is the same as maximizing happiness*. In economics, the technical term we use for happiness (or "satisfaction," or "well-being," etc.) is *utility*.

UTILITY is a measure of a person's happiness.

Discounting Future Consumption

The greatest happiness (utility) is not always what it seems. What about a student who spends four years of his life pursuing a degree instead of tending bar on a tropical island? Certainly, those who tend bar on tropical islands have a greater level of happiness than those who sit in musty classrooms all day and study all night. For the four years that the student spends in college, he definitely accrues less happiness than the person on the tropical island. However, once those four years are over, the student gets a well-paying job, buys a house and a car, puts away money for his retirement, takes vacations to tropical islands, and so on. The person tending bar continues to tend bar. Now who is the happier person? When humans seek happiness, they consider not only the present but also the future. We call this *intertemporal utility maximization*—the maximizing of the total of one's utility over time.

UTILITY MAXIMIZATION is the maximizing of one's happiness at a specific point in time.
INTERTEMPORAL UTILITY MAXIMIZATION is the maximizing of one's total discounted happiness over time.

When we consider intertemporal utility maximization, we must note that consumption of a product today is not the same thing as consumption of a product tomorrow. It is usually the case that, all other things being the same, a human would rather consume a product now than wait until later.[1] Thus, a human who exists on day 1 will not regard a beer that could be consumed on day 1 in the same way as a beer that could be consumed on day 2.[2] The human will prefer the day 1 beer to the day 2 beer—for example, if the day 1 beer gave the person twenty utils (units of happiness), the day 2 beer (as seen from the vantage point of day 1) would give something less, perhaps eighteen utils.[3] We say that the person *discounts* the utility of the future beer—that is, the person thinks less of the future beer *precisely because it exists in the future and not in the present.*

When a human decides what to consume, the human does not look to simply maximize utility but to maximize *intertemporal utility. Intertemporal utility*

DISCOUNTING is the regarding of a future product as lesser precisely because it exists in the future and not in the present.

---

is the sum of the discounted utilities received from products consumed now and in the future.

Consider again the two options facing a student: to drop out of college and tend bar on a tropical island, or to go to college, get a well-paying job, and take vacations to a tropical island. Suppose the following activities yield the following utilities: (1) tend bar on a tropical island—1,000 utils per year, (2) go to college—0 utils per year, and (3) work at a well-paying job and take vacations to a tropical island—1,500 utils per year. Suppose also that this person dies after twenty years. The total utility the person gets from tending bar is as follows:

$$1,000 \text{ utils} + 1,000 \text{ utils} + 1,000 \text{ utils} + ...$$
$$(\text{for a total of 20 years}) = 20,000 \text{ utils}$$

The utility the person gets from going to college, getting a job, and vacationing on the tropical island is as follows:

$$0 \text{ utils} + 0 \text{ utils} + 0 \text{ utils} + 0 \text{ utils} + 1,500 \text{ utils} +$$
$$1,500 \text{ utils} + ...(\text{for a total of 20 years}) = 24,000 \text{ utils}$$

---

1   A counterargument is the case in which a person derives some form of pleasure from putting off consumption—as in the case of *anticipating* receiving something. In this case, however, the person is actually receiving utility from two sources: consuming the product, and anticipating consuming the product. Given the choice of beginning anticipation of consumption now and beginning anticipation of consumption later, the human will choose to begin anticipation of consumption now. Thus, we see that the anticipation itself is a product that the human would rather consume now than later.

2   Again, we assume that all other things are the same. For example, we assume that the human is no more thirsty on day 2 than on day 1; there is no difference between the day 1 beer and the day 2 beer, and so on.

3   One might pose a counterargument that consuming in the future is sometimes better than consuming now, in that some consumption is better spread over time. For example, a person has two meals to consume. The person must consume at least one meal per day to live. If the person consumes both meals at the beginning of day 1, he dies at the beginning of day 2 from starvation. If he consumes one meal at the beginning of day 1 and one meal at the beginning of day 2, he lives until the beginning of day 3. If the person consumes both meals now, he dies sooner. If he waits to consume one meal, he dies later. Is this not proof that consuming later is sometimes better than consuming now? The fallacy in this argument is that the person is really consuming two things: (1) the meals and (2) death. Because death is a bad thing, the person will want to put it off as long as possible *precisely because of future discounting.* The further into the future the person can push death, the less the present value of the disutility of death.

The person must decide *today* which of the two options to take. According to the above calculations, the utility to be gained from going to college and taking a job exceeds the utility to be gained from dropping out of school and tending bar. However, the utility gained from the job doesn't start coming in until year 5, while the utility gained from tending bar starts coming in year 1. The first 1,500 utils the person receives after obtaining the college education is not the same as 1,500 utils today because the person must wait five years. What the person considers is not how much happiness the well-paying job will bring in the future but what that happiness is worth *today*. This is called the *present value* of the utility. *Present value* is the value of some future thing adjusted for the length of time one must wait for the thing—or the value of the future thing in today's terms.

PRESENT VALUE is the value of some future benefit adjusted for the amount of time one must wait for the benefit.

The above calculations are incorrect because they assume that the utility the person receives from something consumed in the future is the same as the utility received from consuming that same thing today. The proper calculations must include a present value adjustment, which accounts for the fact that some of what the person consumes will be consumed in the future and not today—this adjustment is the discounting. Let us suppose that the discount factor is 10 percent—that is, the utility of an activity declines by 10 percent for every year the person must wait to perform the activity. Given the discounting, the present value of the utility to be gained from tending bar at the beach is as follows:

$$1,000 \text{ utils} + \frac{1,000}{1.1}\text{ utils} + \frac{1,000}{1.1^2}\text{ utils} + \frac{1,000}{1.1^3}\text{ utils} \ldots$$

(for a total of 20 years) = 9,365 utils

The utility the person will receive in year 1 is worth one thousand utils to the person today because the person will receive that utility *now*. The utility the person will receive in year 2 is worth 10 percent less than one thousand utils because the person will not receive that utility until *one year in the future*. The utility the person will receive in year 3 is worth 10 percent less than the utility in year 2 because the person will not receive that utility until *two years in the future*. Thus, the utility received in each successive year is regarded as 10 percent less than the year before because the utility will not be received until farther into the future. Using discounting, the present value of the utility to be gained from going to college, getting a job, and taking vacations on the island is as follows:

$$0 \text{ utils} + \frac{0}{1.1}\text{ utils} + \frac{0}{1.1^2}\text{utils} + \frac{0}{1.1^3}\text{ utils} + \frac{1,500}{1.1^4}\text{utils}$$

$$+\frac{1,500}{1.5^5}\text{ utils} + \ldots \text{ (for a total of 20 years)} = 8,817 \text{ utils}$$

Thus, we see that the present value of dropping out of school and tending bar is *greater* than the present value of obtaining an education and getting a job.[4] The reason the present value calculations yield the opposite result of the straight additions performed earlier is that although the education and job yield more total utility, the experience of that utility is four years in the future, whereas the utility of tending bar can be experienced now.

It seems that humans discount future utility because of the probability of death. If there is some chance that you will die between now and the future, there is some chance that you will never get to experience a future utility.[5] If one could imagine a hypothetical world in which one would never die (and never grow old, and never encounter any debilitating disease, and never become sick or incapacitated), consuming in the future would be equivalent to

---

4   The reader should note that if this hypothetical person lives for more than thirty years, the present value of the college education and job exceeds the present value of tending bar on the tropical island.

5   Along with death, we can include any significant mishap. It is possible that some event could happen to you between now and the future, which, although bad, doesn't kill you, yet this event in some way diminishes your ability to obtain as much happiness from consuming as you had expected.

consuming now—there would be no discounting of future utility.[6]

One might propose a counterargument from child behavior. A child, when offered a choice between consumption now and consumption later, will, almost invariably, choose consumption now. One might argue that a child, having no concept of death, should be indifferent between consumption now and later—that

is, because the child has no concept of death, his discount factor is zero. The counter-counter argument is that children may have no concept of death, but they also have no concept of the future. So, a choice between consumption now and consumption later is, to a child, perceived to be a choice between consumption and no consumption at all. Thus, the child will always choose consumption now.

Marginal Utility

The second principle of economics concerns the *change* in utility caused by a change in the amount of a product one consumes. It is the case with all products that the greater the quantity one consumes, the less happiness additional units yield. It seems that this phenomenon is the result of humans deriving utility from two sources when they consume products: (1) utility from the product itself and (2) utility from the *variety* the product represents. *Variety* is a measure of degree of disparity between the different types of products consumed per unit of time. A person who consumes Pepsi and Coke can be said to experience a greater variety than someone who consumes only Pepsi. A person who consumes Pepsi and beer can be said to experience a greater variety than the person who consumes Pepsi and Coke. A person who consumes Pepsi and

clothing can be said to experience a greater variety than the person who consumes Pepsi and beer. Thus, the amount of variety one experiences is a function of the similarity of the products consumed.

VARIETY *is a measure of the degree of disparity between the different types of products consumed per unit of time.*

Whereas *utility* measures the happiness we receive from consuming products, *marginal utility* (MU) measures the *additional* happiness we receive from consuming *one more* unit of a product.

MARGINAL UTILITY is the additional utility a person obtains from consuming one more unit of a product.

Marginal utility (the mathematical definition) is calculated as follows:

$$\text{Marginal utility} = \frac{\Delta \text{Total utility}}{\Delta \text{Units consumed}}$$

For example, suppose that you have not had a beer all week. You have had three tests, you have had two semester reports due, your car broke down, and so on. On Friday, you go out and get a beer. The first beer you have gives you a large amount of utility for two

reasons: (1) it is a beer, and (2) the beer represents a tremendous increase in the variety of products you have been consuming (you haven't had any beer all week). You have a second beer. The second beer also gives you a large amount of utility, *but not as much*

---

6   One could suppose that an event might occur between now and the future that would increase one's ability to obtain happiness from consumption. This would mean that present, not future, consumption should be discounted. While one might come up with isolated examples of such a phenomenon, the existence of the phenomenon, on average, would contradict the physical law of entropy—as time passes, systems have a tendency to break down, not build up. Applying the principle of entropy to the human person implies that, as time passes, our ability to enjoy products diminishes (on average) because our bodies diminish (on average).

as the first beer gave you. The second beer gives you less utility than the first did, because although it is a beer, it represents a *lesser* increase in variety than did the first one (because you have had one beer already). Similarly, each beer you consume gives you less utility than the previous beer did. Eventually, you consume so much beer that additional beers actually represent a *decrease* in variety—each beer becomes just "more of the same." When this happens, consuming one

more actually causes your utility to *decrease*. That is, you consume so much that the marginal utility of one more beer is negative (the decrease in utility caused by the decrease in variety exceeds the increase in utility caused by the beer itself).[7] This phenomenon, caused by humans' desire for variety, gives us the second principle of economics. This is also referred to as the law of diminishing marginal utility.

SECOND PRINCIPLE: THE LAW OF DIMINISHING MARGINAL UTILITY   Each unit of a product that an individual consumes per unit of time yields less happiness than did the previous unit that the individual consumed per unit of time.

"Each unit of a product..." We use the term "product" to refer generically to objects (things that we eat, drink, wear, see, feel, taste, touch, smell, or otherwise experience) and to services (actions that people, machines, or animals perform for us).

"...consumes..." We use the term "consume" to refer generically to the "use" of an object (eating it, drinking it, wearing it, seeing it, feeling it, tasting it, touching it, smelling it, or otherwise experiencing it) and to the receiving of a service.

"...less happiness than did the previous unit..." When a human consumes the first unit of a product (the first beer of the week, the first pizza of the month, the first date with a new significant other) the human derives utility from two sources: (1) from consuming the product itself and (2) by experiencing an increase in variety. When a human consumes the second unit of a product (the second beer of the week, the second pizza of the month, the second date with a significant other), again, the human derives utility from the same two sources: the product itself and an increase in variety. However, because the human has already consumed one unit of the product, the second unit does not increase variety as much as the first did— the human is consuming a type of product that he has consumed already. Thus, the overall increase in

utility that the human derives from the second unit of the product is less than what he derived from the first unit. We call this phenomenon *decreasing marginal utility* ("marginal" means "change in"). The extreme case of diminishing marginal utility (called *negative marginal utility*) occurs when (1) the human has consumed so many units of a product that consuming another unit actually causes a *decrease* in variety, and (2) the utility that the human loses from the decrease in variety exceeds the utility that the human gains from the product itself. Marginal utility is calculated as the change in total utility divided by the change in the number of units consumed.

"...per unit of time." We speak of consumption per unit of time because humans perceive variety in terms of time. For example, the consumption of two beers in the course of thirty seconds yields a different level of utility than does the consumption of two beers in the course of thirty minutes. When one consumes two beers in thirty seconds, one receives relatively little utility because the amount of variety the person is experiencing is very low. When one consumes two beers in thirty minutes, the time between sips of beer serves to increase the person's variety measure to some degree and so also increases the utility.

---

7   I trust that most of us have experienced this at least once (perhaps recently).

The Optimal Consumption Combination

Consider how a human behaves in the presence of a choice between two or more products. The human has a fixed amount of money that he can spend on beer and pizza. The human must determine the optimal consumption combination—the combination of beer and pizza that yields the most utility for his money.

Suppose that a person has $21 to spend on either beer or pizza. Suppose also that the marginal utility of beer is five per pitcher and the marginal utility of pizza is 10 per pizza.[8] Which product should the person consume—the beer or the pizza? Some might say that the obvious answer is the pizza, because the pizza yields more additional utility than the beer does. But wait! The person must pay for what he buys, so he is not concerned with which product yields the most utility *per unit*, but which product yields the most utility *per dollar spent*.

Suppose that the price of a pitcher of beer is $2 and the price of a pizza is $5. With his $21, the person can buy either ten pitchers of beer or 4.2 pizzas. The ten pitchers of beer yield a marginal utility of five each, so the total utility the person receives from spending $21 on beer is fifty (ten pitchers at five marginal utility each). The 4.2 pizzas yield a marginal utility of ten each, so the total utility the person receives from spending $21 on pizza is forty-two (4.2 pizzas at ten marginal utility each). The result is that the person will buy the beer instead of the pizza, because although the pizza yields more marginal utility *per unit*, the beer yields more marginal *utility per dollar*.

We can calculate the marginal utility per dollar as the marginal utility of the product divided by the price of the product. Thus, the marginal utility per dollar for the beer is 5 / $2 = 2.5, and the marginal utility per dollar for the pizza is 10 / $5 = 2. The beer yields a greater marginal utility per dollar.

The fallacy of thinking that marginal utility is important instead of marginal utility per dollar is similar to a fallacy perpetrated by American car manufacturers during the oil crisis of the 1970s. When the price of gas rose dramatically almost overnight, Americans stopped buying American cars (which routinely got gas mileage of under 20 MPG) and started buying foreign cars (the German VW Rabbit reportedly got 50 MPG). It would take American car manufacturers a long time to redesign their cars to be fuel efficient, but they needed some means of keeping Americans buying American cars in the meantime. What the American manufacturers came up with were advertisements stressing the *range* that their cars got. A typical ad would show someone driving a small foreign car running out of gas in the middle of a desert. Someone driving a large American car would then zoom past, and the announcer would say that the foreign car ran out of gas because it only had a range of two hundred miles, while the American car kept going because it had a range of five hundred miles. Herein is the fallacy: the reason the American car had a five-hundred-mile range was not because it got good gas mileage, but because it had a gas tank the size of a bathtub! Quickly, American consumers realized that what was important was not how many miles a car could go, but how many miles per *gallon* a car would get. Similarly, what is important to a consumer is not how much happiness a product brings, but how much happiness *per dollar* a product brings.

Let us return to our beer-and-pizza example. Our conclusion was that the person would spend all $21 on beer because the beer gives a higher marginal utility per dollar. Recall from the second principle of economics that the more units of a product a person consumes, the lower the person's marginal utility for that product becomes. Thus, while the person's marginal utility for beer is five before he consumes any beer, as he consumes beer, his marginal utility will fall. Suppose that the person's marginal utilities for beer and pizza are as shown in the table below.[9]

---

8   To make the argument simple, we'll assume for the moment that the Second Principle no longer holds. That is, the person's marginal utility does not change as he consumes more of the products. This assumption, while unrealistic, does not change the conclusion of the argument, but does simplify the argument.

9   The marginal utilities should be interpreted as the additional utility that will be gained when each unit is consumed. For example, the marginal utility of the first beer is five, meaning that the person's utility will rise by five when he consumes the first beer. Technically, marginal utility changes with each fractional portion of the product consumed—that is, not just each beer but each successive sip of each beer yields a lesser marginal utility than the previous.

TABLE 3.1. Marginal Utility and Marginal
Utility per Dollar

Units	MU of Beer (Price = $2)	MU of Pizza (Price = $5)	MU/$ of Beer	MU/$ of Pizza
1	5	10	2.5	2
2	4	8	2	1.6
3	3	6	1.5	1.2
4	2	4	1	0.8
5	1	2	0.5	0.4
6	0	0	0	0

According to table 3.1, the first thing the person will buy is a pitcher of beer, because the first pitcher of beer yields a marginal utility per dollar that is higher than the first pizza (2.5 for beer versus two for pizza). The person buys the pitcher for $2. When the person consumes the first pitcher of beer, his marginal utility of beer falls to four, but his marginal utility of pizza is still ten because the person has not consumed any pizza. His marginal utility per dollar for beer is now two, and his marginal utility per dollar for pizza is also two—the person is indifferent between buying a pizza and buying another pitcher of beer. Let us suppose that the person buys both. His marginal utility for beer now drops to three, and his marginal utility for pizza drops to eight. He has spent a total of $9 ($2 each for two pitchers of beer and $5 for a pizza). The person's marginal utility per dollar for beer is now 1.5, and his marginal utility per dollar for pizza is 1.6. Because he gets more additional utility per dollar out of pizza, he will buy another pizza. He has now spent a total of $14. The person has now consumed two pizzas and two pitchers of beer. His marginal utility per dollar for beer is 1.5, and his marginal utility per dollar for pizza is 1.2—he will buy another pitcher of beer. This person has now spent a total of $16. His marginal utility per dollar for beer has fallen to one, and his marginal utility per dollar for pizza is 1.2, so he will buy another pizza. At this point, the person has spent his entire $21, so he stops consuming.

Notice that, at any given time, the marginal utility per dollar for the two products was nearly equal: after the first purchase, the MU per dollar for beer was two, and the MU per dollar for pizza was two; after the second and third purchases, the MU per dollar for beer was 1.5, and the MU per dollar for pizza was 1.6. Following the fourth and fifth purchases, the MU per dollar for beer was one, and the MU per dollar for pizza was 1.2. If the person could buy fractional units of beer and pizza, the marginal utility per dollar for beer and pizza would always be exactly equal. When one product yields a higher marginal utility per dollar than the other, the person will consume more of that product, and, consequently, the marginal utility (and hence the marginal utility per dollar) for that product will fall. This analysis leads us to the third principle of economics. The third principle tells us that people will always consume products in a certain combination, such that the marginal utility per dollar for each of the products the person consumes is equal.

"...combinations of products..." For the first time we consider a human consuming more than one *type* of product. "Type" can be interpreted in the broad sense of food, drink, clothing, and transportation, or in the specific sense of hamburgers, pizza, coffee, milk, socks, shirts, cars, and buses. The set of types and quantities of products the human consumes is called the *consumption combination*.

THIRD PRINCIPLE Individuals consume combinations of products such that the marginal utility per unit cost is equal for all products.

"...marginal utility per unit cost..." What is important to the human is not how much marginal utility (extra happiness) a unit of a product provides, but (because the human must pay for the product) how much marginal utility *per dollar spent on the product* the product provides. For example, a slice of pizza may yield a marginal utility of six, while a glass of beer yields a marginal utility of two. If the price of a slice of pizza is $2.00 and the price of a glass of beer is $0.50, the human would receive an additional utility of three (3 = 6 / 2) for every dollar he spends on pizza, but an additional utility of four (4 = 2 / 0.5) for every dollar he spends on beer. Notice that the third principle does not speak of marginal utility per price but marginal utility *per cost*. *Price* is the cost of the product *at the point of sale*. *Cost* is the price plus the additional expense of arriving at the point of sale.

"...is equal for all products." The human consumes many products (and many types of the same sort of product) simultaneously. As time passes, the marginal utilities of all of these products rises. As the human consumes more units of these products, the marginal utilities of these products falls. The human will balance consumption of all of these products such that the marginal utility per dollar for every product is equal.

THE AUSTRALIAN INSTITUTE OF HEALTH AND WELFARE (AIHW) released a report in 2011, which found that only one in twenty Australian men eat enough fruits and vegetables. It stated that less than half of Australian men eat enough fruit, while only 8 percent of men eat enough vegetables. Dietitian Tania Ferraretto claims that men tend to be less concerned with healthy eating, and they only need to make small changes, such as replacing a snack with a piece of fruit, to reduce the risk of chronic disease later in life. This report makes generalizations about the different *preferences* of men and women, but it is true that everyone—man or woman—has different preferences. The report claims that in general most Australian men would prefer a sausage patty for breakfast instead of a fruit cocktail, but it is true that some men in Australia would actually prefer the fruit cocktail. Some men might even be indifferent between the sausage patty and the fruit cocktail. It may not just be a result of being a man that someone chooses a sausage patty over a fruit cocktail, but perhaps sausage patties are cheaper than fruit cocktail and men tend to spend less of their income on food. We can learn a few things from AIHW's report. Most importantly, it is clear that in general men and women have different preferences when it comes to some food items. Second, given an individual's preferences, there may be various combinations of goods and services an individual consumes that produce the same level of satisfaction. This example also shows that an individual's overall satisfaction depends to some degree on prices and income.

AIHW The Health of Australia's Males report can be found at http://www.aihw.gov.au/publication-detail/?id=10737419204

Demand

The behavior of consumers is summarized by a relationship called demand. *Demand* is the relationship between the price of a product and the number of units of the product consumers are willing to buy per unit of time. The relationship between the price of a product and the number of units the consumer is willing to buy is *negative*.[10] That is, as the price of the product rises, the number of units the consumer is willing to buy decreases (or, as the price falls, the number of units the consumer is willing to buy increases). The reason that this relationship is negative can be traced back to marginal utility.

Recall that each unit of a product a human consumes yields less utility than the unit before it. Because each successive unit yields less additional utility, the value of the unit to the human is less; thus, the price the human is willing to pay falls. What if the consumer is not a human but a firm? Firms aren't interested in utility; they are interested in profit. It so happens, as we shall see later, that just as each successive unit of a product that a human consumes yields less utility, each successive unit of a product that a firm consumes yields less profit. Thus, by the same reasoning, the more units a

---

10   Economists have searched (unsuccessfully) for a product that exhibits a positively sloped demand curve. The closest examples are products whose quality cannot be judged until after they have been purchased (e.g., wines, software, movies, college educations). In these cases, consumers take the price of the product as a signal of its quality. Demand curves for these products can be interpreted as upward sloping—that is, the higher the price, the greater the perceived quality, and, hence, the greater the quantity demanded. Technically speaking, however, the demand curves are downward sloping but unobservable, because every time the price of the product changes, consumers' preferences for the product change also.

firm consumes of a product, the lesser the price the firm is willing to pay for more units.

In order to properly understand demand, one must understand what is meant by the phrase "willing to buy." Consider these three phrases: "wanting a product," "willing to buy a product," and "bought a product." The phrase "wanting a product" implies only that the consumer has a desire for the product, *not* that the consumer would actually purchase the product if given the chance. You might say that you "want a Ferrari." If, however, you cannot afford a Ferrari, you are not *willing to buy* a Ferrari. "Willing to buy" is also different from "bought." You might go to the store to buy a dozen eggs. When you get there, there are no eggs in the store. You were *willing to buy* the eggs, but you did not buy them. Thus, the phrase "willing to buy" means that the consumer will actually purchase a product *provided* that the product is available. We call the number of units of a product that the consumer is willing to buy per unit of time the *quantity demanded*.

Let's start with a simple demand schedule for an individual, shown in table 3.2. The table shows the price of a paperback textbook in the first column and the quantity demanded per month in the second column. One can imagine that we get this information fairly easily by approaching an individual and asking how many paperbacks she would be willing to buy for a given price. By asking the same question for many different prices and noting the answers, we can construct a demand schedule as shown in this table. The first thing we see is that the answers we get present a certain pattern. We see that for high prices the number of paperbacks the individual is willing to buy (or the quantity demanded) is lower than the one for the lower prices. This shows the negative relationship between the price of the good and quantity demanded of that good. This relationship can be shown graphically as well. We do this by putting the price on the vertical axis and the quantity demanded on the horizontal axis. Once we plot the numbers from table 3.2 as points and connect those points, we get a graph, shown in figure 3.1, which we refer to as a demand curve.

QUANTITY DEMANDED is the number of units of a product that a consumer is willing to buy per unit of time.

There are many factors that go into a consumer's willingness to buy a product: the amount of money the consumer has available, what other products are available and for what prices, whether or not the consumer has seen an advertisement for the product, the manner in which the product is packaged and presented, and so forth. *Demand* is the relationship between the price of a product and the number of units of the product consumers will want to buy when all these other factors are held constant. The constant factors are called *ceteris paribus assumptions for demand* ("ceteris paribus" means "all else held constant"). When we hold these extraneous factors constant, we can see clearly the relationship between the price of the product and the number of units the consumers are willing to buy (the *quantity demanded*), as shown in figure 3.1.

Obviously, things can change for an individual who demands a product. There are two types of changes or movements that we need to consider. The first is a change in the price of the good the individual demands. From a certain point on the demand curve, a price change for that good will move us to a different point on the same demand curve. This is referred to as a movement along the demand curve. This is shown in figure 3.2. An individual is initially at point A on the demand curve, where she is willing

TABLE 3.2 Demand Schedule

Demand Schedule for Paperback Textbooks	
Price of a Paperback	Quantity of Paperbacks Demanded per Month
100	1
90	2
80	3
70	4
60	5
50	6
40	7
30	8
20	9
10	10

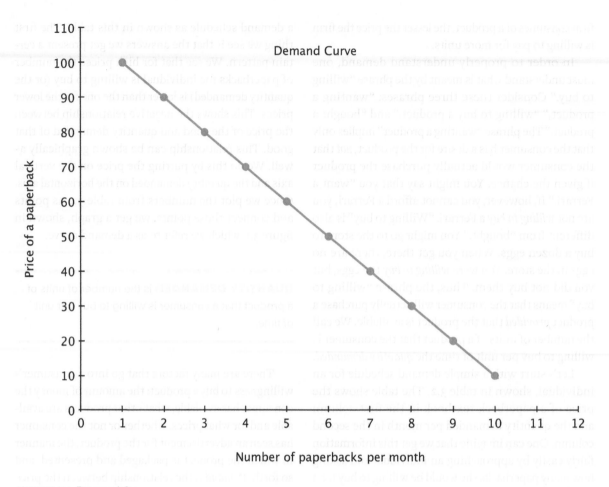

FIGURE 3.1 Demand Curve

to buy six paperbacks per month at a price of $50. If the price of a paperback drops to $40, the individual moves from point A to point B on the same demand curve, where her quantity demanded increases to seven paperbacks per month. Again, this is a movement along the demand curve.

As we defined before, the amount of a product that consumers are willing to buy is called the *quantity demanded; demand* is the relationship between the price

of a product and the quantity demanded of the product. Graphically, demand is the entire *curve*, while quantity demand is the *number* on the horizontal axis. Note that *quantity demanded* is not the same thing as *quantity purchased*. When we speak of quantity demanded, we mean the number of units the consumer would purchase at a given price *assuming that the products are available at that price and in that quantity*. Demand is concerned solely with the consumer.

MOVEMENT ALONG THE DEMAND CURVE From a certain point on the demand curve, a price change for that good will move us to a different point on the same demand curve. This is referred to as a movement along the demand curve.

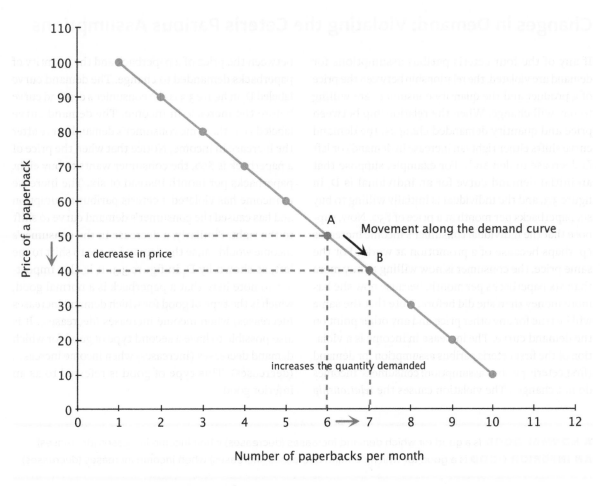

FIGURE 3.2 Movement along the Demand Curve

Questions of product availability and what the price of the product actually is are external to the question of demand.

DEMAND   Demand is the relationship between the price of a product and the number of units of the product that a consumer is willing to buy per unit of time, ceteris paribus.

Ceteris paribus assumptions for demand:

1. The consumer's available income does not change.
2. The prices of substitute and complement products do not change.
3. The consumer's preferences or tastes do not change.
4. The number of consumers does not change.

Changes in Demand: Violating the Ceteris Paribus Assumptions

If any of the four ceteris paribus assumptions for demand are violated, the relationship between the price of a product and the quantity consumers are willing to buy will change. When the relationship between price and quantity demanded changes, the demand curve shifts either right (an increase in demand) or left (a decrease in demand). For example, suppose that an initial demand curve for an individual is D_1 in figure 3.3, and the individual is initially willing to buy six paperbacks per month at a price of $50. Now, suppose that the individual consumer's income increases (perhaps because of a promotion at work). For the same price, the consumer is now willing to buy more than six paperbacks per month, because now she has more money than she did before. Note that the same will be true for any other price and any other point on the demand curve. The increase in income is a violation of the first ceteris paribus assumption for demand (first ceteris paribus assumption: consumers' incomes do not change). The violation causes the *relationship*

between the price of a paperback and the quantity of paperbacks demanded to change. The demand curve labeled D_1 in figure 3.3 is the consumer's demand curve before the increase in income. The demand curve labeled D_2 is the same consumer's demand curve after the increase in income. Notice that when the price of a paperback is $50, the consumer wants to buy eight paperbacks per month instead of six. The increase in income has violated a ceteris paribus assumption and has caused the consumer's demand curve to shift to the right. Similarly, a decrease in the consumer's income would cause the demand curve to shift to the left, as shown by D_3 in figure 3.3. It is also important to note here that a paperback is a normal good, which is the type of good for which demand increases (decreases) when income increases (decreases). It is also possible to have a second type of good for which demand decreases (increases) when income increases (decreases). This type of good is referred to as an inferior good.

A NORMAL GOOD is a good for which demand increases (decreases) when income increases (decreases).
AN INFERIOR GOOD is a good for which demand decreases (increases) when income increases (decreases)

The second ceteris paribus assumption (the prices of substitute and complementary products do not change) refers to products that have a relation to the product in question. Any two products can be related to each other in one of three ways: the two products can be complements, they can be substitutes, or they can be unrelated.

Complements are products for which, when one is consumed, the marginal utility of the other rises. Complements yield more utility when consumed together than when consumed separately.[11] The reason for this is that each product increases the consumer's perception of the variety represented by the *other* product. For example, beer and pizza are usually regarded as

complements. As one consumes pizza, one experiences flavors, smells, and textures that are, in a sense, not just different from but the opposites of those provided by beer. Likewise, when one consumes beer, one experiences flavors, smells, and textures that are the opposites of those provided by pizza. Because of this, consuming pizza actually *increases* the variety represented by beer, and consuming beer *increases* the variety represented by pizza. Thus, when one consumes beer and pizza together, the utility one receives from each is greater than the utility one would obtain when consuming them separately.

Consider the effect on the demand curve for pizza when the price of beer (a complement) changes. If the

---

11   Note that "complements" and "consumption bundle" are not the same. *Complements* are two products that when consumed together yield more utility than when consumed separately (e.g., shoes and socks, coffee and sugar). A *consumption bundle* is a set of products that a consumer consumes together and that may or may not be complements.

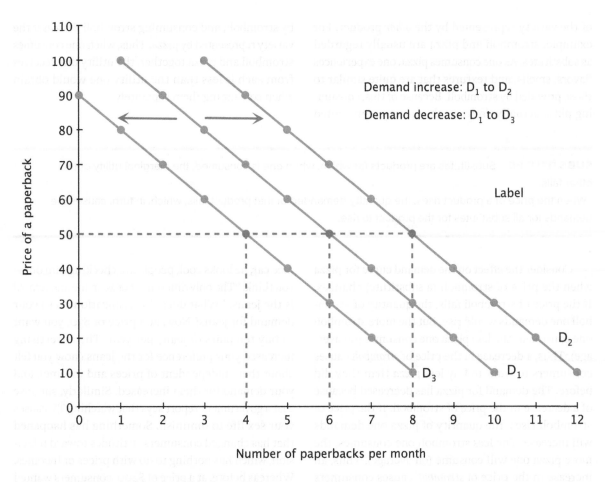

Demand increase: D_1 to D_2

Demand decrease: D_1 to D_3

Label

D_2

D_3 D_1

FIGURE 3.3 Demand Increase or Decrease

price of beer falls, the quantity of beer one demands would rise. But, the more beer one consumes, the more pizza one will also consume (on average). Thus, a decrease in the price of *beer* causes consumers to want to buy more *pizza* than they did before. The demand for pizza has increased because of a decrease in the price of

beer. If the price of beer rises, the quantity of beer one demands will fall. The less beer one consumes, the less pizza one will consume (on average). Thus, a decrease in the price of *beer* causes consumers to want to buy less *pizza* than they did before. The demand for pizza has decreased because of an increase in the price of beer.

COMPLEMENTS Complements are products for which, when one is consumed, the marginal utility of the other rises.

When the price of a product rises, the quantity demanded of that product falls, which, in turn, causes the demands for all complements to the product to fall.

Substitutes are products for which, when one is consumed, the marginal utility of the other falls. The

reason for this is that the products are so similar that each product decreases the consumer's perception of the variety represented by the *other* product. For example, stromboli and pizza are usually regarded as substitutes. As one consumes pizza, one experiences flavors, smells, and textures that are quite similar to those provided by stromboli. Because of this, consuming pizza actually *decreases* the variety represented by stromboli, and consuming stromboli *decreases* the variety represented by pizza. Thus, when one consumes stromboli and pizza together, the utility one receives from each is less than the utility one would obtain when consuming them separately.

SUBSTITUTES Substitutes are products for which, when one is consumed, the marginal utility of the other falls.

When the price of a product rises, the quantity demanded of that product falls, which, in turn, causes the demands for all substitutes for the product to rise.

Consider the effect on the demand curve for pizza when the price of stromboli (a substitute) changes. If the price of stromboli falls, the quantity of stromboli one demands would rise. But the more stromboli one consumes, the less pizza one consumes (on average). Thus, a decrease in the price of *stromboli* causes consumers to want to buy less *pizza* than they did before. The demand for pizza has decreased because of a decrease in the price of stromboli. If the price of stromboli rises, the quantity of pizza one demands will increase. The less stromboli one consumes, the more pizza one will consume (on average). Thus, an increase in the price of *stromboli* causes consumers to want to buy more *pizza* than they did before. The demand for pizza has increased because of an increase in the price of stromboli.

The phrase *consumer preferences* (the subject of the third ceteris paribus assumption) refers to how consumers "feel" about a product *independent of their incomes, the price of the product, and the prices of all other products.* Imagine that you go to a Ferrari showroom. You are looking at the Ferraris and decide that you prefer the black one with the convertible top. You have no intention (or ability) to buy any of the cars, yet you do have a preference for one of them over the others.

Advertising is an entire industry built (in large part) for the purpose of violating this ceteris paribus assumption. Suppose that when the price of jeans is $30, you want to buy four pairs per year. Suppose that you see an advertisement in which Arnold Schwarzenegger is wearing Levi's jeans. Arnold has a nice car, he looks cool, people are checking him out—you think, "The only difference between me and Arnold is the jeans!" What does this realization do to your demand for jeans? Now, at a price of $30, you want to buy ten pairs of jeans per year. The advertising increased your preference for the jeans (how you felt about them independent of prices and income), and your demand for them increased. Similarly, suppose that a government report says that watching TV causes your sex life to diminish. Something has happened that has changed consumers' attitudes toward television, which has nothing to do with prices or incomes. Whereas before, at a price of $200, consumers wanted to buy five thousand televisions per month, now, at a price of $200, consumers want to buy only one thousand televisions per month. The decrease in preference has caused the demand for televisions to decrease.

The final ceteris paribus assumption requires that the number of consumers not change. This is also important because so far we have drawn a demand curve for an individual consumer. Having more than one consumer will surely make a difference. A consumer can be someone who is currently consuming the product, someone who has consumed the product in the past, or someone who has *never* consumed the product. A consumer can even be someone who *will never* consume the product. So, what distinguishes a consumer from a nonconsumer? A consumer is one who *at some positive price* is willing to purchase more than zero units of a product. For example, suppose you don't like cauliflower. No matter how low the price of cauliflower goes, you will never buy cauliflower—even if the price goes to zero![12] Thus, you are not a consumer of cauliflower. Now consider a yacht. You may never have purchased a yacht, and you may never in your life purchase a yacht, yet you are considered to be a consumer of yachts because there is some positive price at which you would be willing to buy a yacht. Suppose that the maximum price you are willing to pay for a yacht is $2,000. If the price of yachts dropped to $2,000, you would buy one. If the price of yachts never falls to $2,000, you will never buy one. Yet whether you actually buy one or not is irrelevant—the fact is that *if* the price was low enough, you *would* buy one. Hence, you are a consumer of yachts.

Generally, we consider a change in the number of consumers to be caused by a change in population size (if the consumers are people), or by a change in the number of firms (if the consumers are firms). There are some events that could be considered to be violations of both the number of consumers and consumers' preferences. For example, if cauliflower is discovered to cure cancer, current consumers' preferences for cauliflower will increase. Then the number of consumers will increase, as people who would never eat cauliflower before at any price will now be willing to buy cauliflower.

CONSUMER PREFERENCE is the attitude of consumers toward a product independent of the consumers' incomes, the price of the product, and the prices of all other products.

Any event that violates a ceteris paribus assumption is called an *economic shock*. The following table summarizes the effects of violations of the ceteris paribus assumptions for demand.

EFFECTS OF VIOLATIONS OF CETERIS PARIBUS ASSUMPTIONS

Violation	Effect of Violation
Increase in consumers' incomes (normal good)	Demand curve shifts right (demand increases)
Decrease in consumers' incomes (normal good)	Demand curve shifts left (demand decreases)
Increase in consumers' incomes (inferior good)	Demand curve shifts left (demand decreases)
Decrease in consumers' incomes (inferior good)	Demand curve shifts right (demand increases)
Increase in the price of a complement product	Demand curve shifts left (demand decreases)
Decrease in the price of a complement product	Demand curve shifts right (demand increases)
Increase in the price of a substitute product	Demand curve shifts right (demand increases)
Decrease in the price of a substitute product	Demand curve shifts left (demand decreases)
Increase in consumers' preferences for the product	Demand curve shifts right (demand increases)
Decrease in consumers' preferences for the product	Demand curve shifts left (demand decreases)
Increase in the number of consumers	Demand curve shifts right (demand increases)
Decrease in the number of consumers	Demand curve shifts left (demand decreases)

Note that the four ceteris paribus assumptions cover most of the violations that can occur to the demand relationship, but not all. Depending on the product in question, there may be an event that causes the demand curve to shift yet does not fit neatly into one of the four ceteris paribus assumptions. In the

---

12   There will still be some negative price at which you would be willing to buy cauliflower. A negative price means that you are paid to eat the cauliflower. When determining who is and who is not a consumer, we consider only prices greater than or equal to zero. Also, don't tell me anything about buying the cauliflower when the price is very low so that you can resell it to someone else for a higher price—if you do this, the cauliflower has become (for you) an entirely different product (i.e., it is no longer a rubbery, hairy vegetable-thing; it is a source of income), and you (by the way) are no longer simply a consumer; you are also a producer.

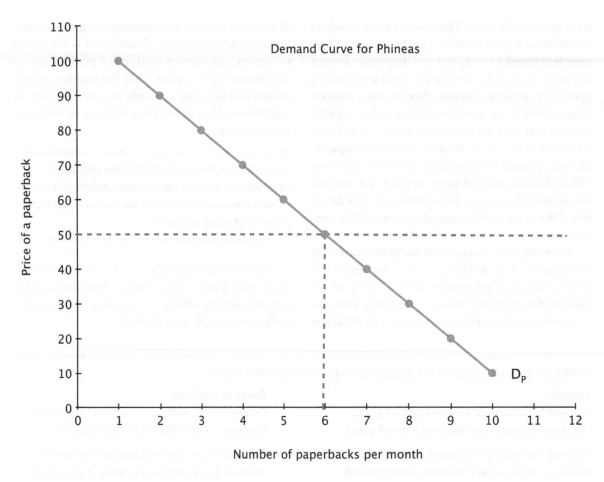

FIGURE 3.4 Derivation of a Market Demand Curve

unlikely event that you encounter such an event, the matter can be easily put to rest by considering the following: if the price of the product remains constant, yet the quantity demanded of the product changes, the demand curve has shifted.

An **economic shock** is any event that violates a ceteris paribus assumption.

Market Demand Curve

We conclude this chapter by extending the individual demand analysis to the entire market for a product. This is similar to the violation of the last ceteris paribus assumption, which was about the number of consumers. We could be analyzing demand for an individual (such as ourselves), but we also know that we are only a small part of a much bigger market. While a demand curve represents the relationship between the price of a product and an individual consumer's willingness to buy a good, a market demand curve represents the relationship between price and all consumers' willingness to buy of that good. We can show this using

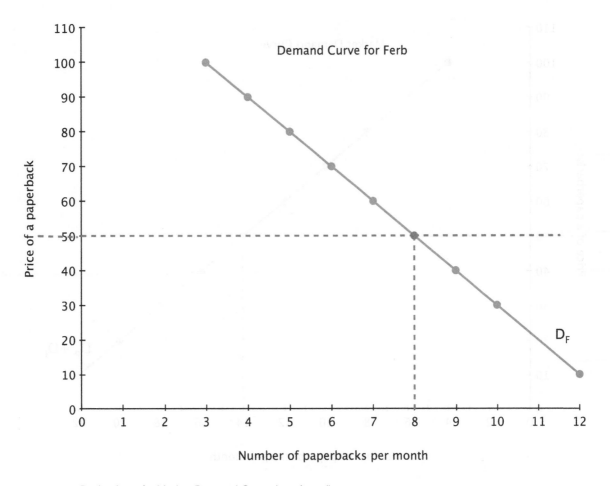

FIGURE 3.4 Derivation of a Market Demand Curve (continued)

a simple example of a market with only two consumers. Figure 3.4 shows the individual demand curves for two consumers, Phineas and Ferb, and the market demand curve. The first demand curve for Phineas is identical to the one in figure 3.1. The second demand curve is for Ferb (his brother). While the two demand curves look similar, you should realize that Ferb has a higher quantity demanded than Phineas at any given price. For example, at a price of $50, Phineas is willing to buy six paperbacks, while Ferb is willing to buy eight paperbacks at that price. The market demand is found by summing the individual demands at each price. Graphically, this is referred to as *horizontal summation*. In figure 3.4, we first find the sum of the quantity demanded (on the horizontal axis) for the two

individuals for each price and then plot those sums as points in a separate graph on the righthand side. Once we connect those points, we get a new demand curve, which is the market demand curve. While this is drawn as a separate curve, our analysis for individual demand, including the violation of ceteris paribus assumptions, also holds for the market demand curve.

THE MARKET demand curve for a product is the horizontal sum of all individual demand curves for that product.

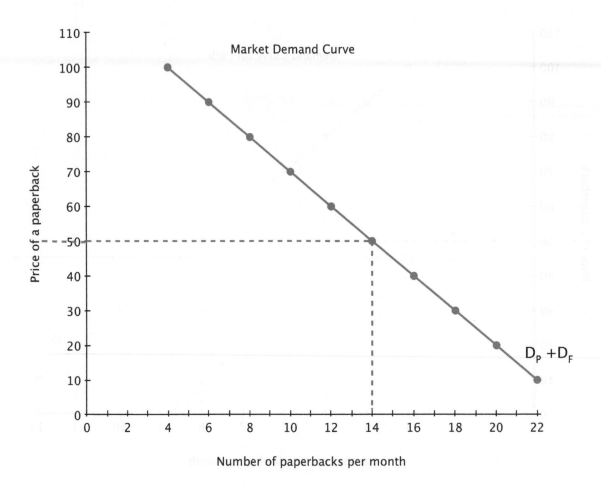

FIGURE 3.4 Derivation of a Market Demand Curve (continued)

CONCLUSION

This chapter is about consumers' decision making, which is ultimately shown as a relationship between the price of a good and the quantity demanded of that good, holding all other factors constant. This is also summarized in a demand curve. Consumer choice theory is based on the assumption that consumers are rational and act in a way to maximize their happiness (or utility) given their resource (or budget) constraint. Behavioral economics, a relatively new field in economics, has challenged this rationality assumption in lab experiments with human subjects playing games or answering hypothetical questions. The methods and conclusions of behavioral economics are discussed in more detail in Chapter 15.

DISCUSSION QUESTIONS

1. Why is it important to discount all future benefits to calculate intertemporal utility?

2. Can you give examples of consumption goods that you think are subject to diminishing marginal utility?

3. What is the difference between demand and quantity demanded, and also between individual demand and market demand?

4. What is an economic shock? Give examples of economics shocks that would shift a demand curve.

5. Find examples of normal goods, inferior goods, substitutes and complements.

6. How does the field of behavioral economics approach rationality and consumers' decision-making?

Producer Decision Making and the Supply Curve

Just outside of Munich in Dingolfing lies BMW's largest production facility. It employs approximately twenty-one thousand people, and it produces more than 1,300 cars per day. The plant in Dingolfing opened its doors and began producing more than thirty years ago and has churned out more than six million cars to date. All 5 Series and 7 Series models that are on the roads today were produced in Dingolfing. Over the years BMW has grown to be one of the world's most popular luxury cars. The high demand for these automobiles has led the plant to create a very flexible layout to meet the needs of its highly diversified production process. This allows the employees to assemble up to four different models on a single line. The Dingolfing plant is also well known for its efficiency in processing aluminum, which is critical for manufacturing the BMW's entirely aluminum bodies. Like most producers, the Dingolfing plant utilizes *labor inputs*, the twenty-one thousand employees, *factor inputs*, the aluminum and other car parts, and *capital inputs*, the machinery used on the lines to assemble the highly desired luxury cars. Over the years the Dingolfing plant has changed its production process in order to improve the quality of its automobiles, to increase the speed at which they are assembled, and to decrease the overall cost of the process. For example, the plant has undoubtedly increased the ration of capital inputs to labor inputs. In this chapter, we will examine the nature of a firm and how it makes decisions about its inputs in order to produce most efficiently.

Producer Theory

Firms

Firms come in two varieties: *publicly-owned* and *privately-owned*. A *privately-owned firm* is a firm that is owned by people (or owned by other firms, which are, in turn, owned by people). A *publicly-owned firm* is a firm that is owned by a government entity.[1] Privately-owned firms come in two basic varieties: *proprietorships/partnerships* and *corporations*. A *proprietorship/partnership* is a firm that is, in the eyes of the law, indistinguishable from its owners. Under the law, a proprietorship/partnership is the same as its owners.[2] A *corporation*, on the other hand, is a distinct legal entity separate from its owners. This question of the distinction between the owner and the firm manifests itself in two places: (1) taxation and (2) liability.

When a corporation earns profit, the profit is taxed. The owner can then take this profit for himself, but the owner must pay income tax on what he takes. Because there is a legal distinction between the firm and the owner, each must pay tax on the money that each receives. When a proprietorship or partnership earns profit, the profit is taxed. The owner can then take this profit for himself without paying any further tax. Because there is no legal distinction between the firm and the owner, under the law only one entity has received money, and therefore only one entity pays tax.

We already know that the goal of a human is to maximize utility. A firm, however, is an inanimate object—can a firm have a goal, and what would be the goal of a firm? All privately-owned firms (i.e., those not operated by a government entity) are owned by people. The profits the firms make go to the owners. Because the goal of people is to maximize their utilities, and because utility (generally) increases as one consumes more things, and because the more money one has, the more things one can consume, the people who own firms see to it that the goal of their firms is to maximize profit.[3] The goal of all privately-owned firms is to maximize profit. Privately-owned firms have this goal because they are owned by people whose goals are to maximize utility. This can be seen as the first corollary to the first principle of economics from chapter 3.

A PROPRIETORSHIP/PARTNERSHIP is a firm that is legally identical to its owners.

A CORPORATION is a firm that is legally independent of its owners.

Only privately-owned firms are guaranteed to seek out the greatest profit, because privately-owned firms are guided by owners who reap the profits that the firms earn. Firms that are also managed by the owners may seem to be earning less profit than possible (as shown on the accounting statements) but only because some of the profit has been reaped by the owners in their capacity as managers in the form of perks (i.e., travel, cars, memberships, entertainment) provided at the firm's expense. While these perks decrease the accounting profits of the firm, they are in reality profits reaped by the owner but done so in such a way as to avoid taxation.

---

1   In finance, a *public corporation* is a corporation whose stock is traded on a stock exchange; a *private corporation* is a corporation whose stock is not traded on an exchange.

2   A *proprietorship* has one owner, while a *partnership* has more than one owner.

3   Some privately-owned firms are "nonprofit" firms. The goal of these firms is not to maximize profit but to provide some benefit to society. For example, most colleges are nonprofit firms. The primary goal of these colleges is not to turn a profit but to educate students.

CORPORATION VERSUS PROPRIETORSHIP/PARTNERSHIP The question of taxation would seem to favor partnerships and proprietorships over corporations. Consider now, however, the question of liability. Because there is no legal distinction between the proprietorship/partnership and the owner, the owner is fully liable for the actions of the firm. If the firm takes on debt and fails to repay it, the owner must pay the debt out of his personal assets. If the firm injures someone, both it and the owner can be sued. Because there is a legal distinction between the corporation and the owner, the owner has limited liability. If the firm fails to repay its debt, the creditors cannot seize the owner's personal assets. If the firm injures someone, the owner cannot be sued for the injury.[1] Limited liability means that the owner's liability with respect to the firm is limited to his original investment in the firm. That is, if the firm goes bankrupt, the maximum amount of money the owner stands to lose is the amount that he invested in the firm.

While more than 90 percent of business in the United States is conducted by corporations, more than 90 percent of the businesses in the United States are proprietorships or partnerships. This implies that individual proprietorships and partnerships are very small relative to individual corporations. The reason for this is that owners of small firms stand to lose more from the double taxation of corporate status than they do from incurring full liability, while owners of large firms stand to lose more from incurring full liability than they do from double taxation.

Because firms are managed by humans, they are subject to the same judgmental errors and uncertainties as are humans. Thus, in the same way that humans may pursue things that are not good for them in an objective sense because they falsely believe that these things *are* good, firms sometimes pursue things that are not (objectively) profitable because they falsely believe them to be profitable.

Present Value

In the same way that an individual pursues the greatest discounted present value of utility, so too do firms pursue the greatest discounted value of profit. A firm will always discount future profits by a factor equal to the rate of return that the firm could have achieved. For example, consider a software company that has a choice of producing a new game or a new business application. The game will bring large profits but for a short period of time. The business application will bring small profits but over a greater time period. If the firm produces the game, it will earn $20,000 profit in year 1, $17,000 profit in year 2, $12,000 in year 3, and no profit thereafter. If the firm produces the business application, it will earn $5,000 profit every year for fifteen years and no profit thereafter. Which piece of software will the firm produce? The total profit from the game is $20,000 + $17,000 + $12,000 = $49,000. The total profit from the business application is ($5,000)(15) = $75,000. It appears to be more profitable for the firm to produce the business application. But, wait, we have not accounted for the fact that the profit the firm earns on the game comes in the first three years, while the profit the firm earns on the business application comes over ten years. We must compute the present value of the profits of each piece of software.

PROFIT MAXIMIZATION Privately-owned firms act in such a way as to seek out those things that they believe will yield the greatest profit for their owners.

THE FIRST PRINCIPLE OF ECONOMICS: Individual humans act in such a way as to seek out those things that they believe will yield them the most happiness.

Suppose that the interest rate is 10 percent. The present value of the profit from the game is as follows:

$$\frac{\$20,000}{1.1} + \frac{\$17,000}{1.1^2} + \frac{\$12,000}{1.1^3} = \$42,247$$

The present value of the profit from the business application is as follows:

$$\frac{\$5,000}{1.1} + \frac{\$5,000}{1.1^2} + \frac{\$5,000}{1.1^3} + \cdots + \frac{\$5,000}{1.1^{15}} = \$38,030$$

Thus, we see that the firm that seeks to maximize profit will choose to produce the game instead of the business application.

What about publicly-owned firms? Recall that a publicly-owned firm is one that is owned by the government. We said that the goal of a privately-owned firm is to maximize profit because the firm is owned by people whose goal is to maximize utility. In the case of a publicly-owned firm, the people who control the company do not get to keep the profit the firm earns. What happens when these utility-maximizing people control a company but do not get to keep the company's profit? These utility-maximizing people will continue to behave in a manner that maximizes their utilities. This behavior, however, will be manifest not in turning a profit, but in attaining job security, high salary, perks, and power. The best way to do this in a publicly-owned firm is to make the firm as large as possible. The bigger the firm is, the more people are needed to work; the more people are needed to work, the more management is needed—job security for the managers. The bigger the firm, the more responsibilities management has; the more responsibilities management has, the more pay and perks management can demand. The bigger the firm is, the more influential the firm is in the marketplace; the more influential the firm is, the more influential the firm's management is; the more influential the firm's management is in the marketplace, the more power those managers have. The size of a firm is most easily measured by the amount of sales the firm has—the firm's total revenue. Thus, when utility-maximizing people control publicly-owned firms (firms whose profits they do not get to keep), these people cause the firms to maximize their total revenue. Note that maximizing total revenue is *not* the same as maximizing profit. It is usually the case that publicly-owned firms become larger and larger, yet their profits decline, because although their total revenue rises, their total costs rise even faster. While public corporations in more capitalist economies will tend to maximize revenue, public corporations in socialist economies (in which revenue has less meaning than it does in capitalist economies) will be managed in such a way as to yield greater utility (i.e., security, salary, perks, power, access to products, etc.) for its management.

Suppose that someone offers you a job in Tibet that pays 1,000 Tibetan dollars per day. Would you accept the job? The answer is—you don't know. You don't know because you do not know the exchange rate between a Tibetan dollar and a US dollar. If the exchange rate were one to one, the job would definitely be worth taking. If the exchange rate were 1,000 Tibetan dollars to one US dollar, the job would definitely not be worth taking. In short, one cannot compare foreign dollars to US dollars without first converting the foreign dollars to US dollars.[4]

The same conversion problem exists when one attempts to compare US dollars today with US dollars of the future or the past. Suppose that someone offers you a choice between (a) $1,000 to be paid to you today and (b) $1,000 to be paid to you one year from today. Most everyone would take the $1,000 today. This proves that a dollar today is not the same as a dollar tomorrow. Why? Is it because of inflation? Let us assume that we are guaranteed that there will be no inflation at all, ever. Again, someone offers you a choice between (a) $1,000 to be paid to you today and (b) $1,000 to be paid to you one year from today. Again, most everyone would take the $1,000 today. This proves that *even in the absence of inflation* a dollar today is not the same as a dollar tomorrow. Why?

Recall our discussion of utility. We said that given a choice between consuming a product now and consuming the same product later (all other things being the same), a person would rather consume now. The reason,

---

4   This assumes, of course, that products in Tibet cost the same (after adjusting for the exchange rate) as products in the United States do.

we argued, had to do with the uncertainty associated with consuming in the future—events may transpire (i.e., accidents, death, etc.) that would cause us not to be able to consume in the future or that would greatly diminish the happiness we gain from consuming.

If (all other things being the same) we get more utility from consuming a product now than we do from consuming the same product in the future, it follows that we would rather have $1 now than $1 in the future, because when one has $1 now, one can purchase products now. When one has to wait for the future to get one's dollar, one can consume only in the future.

People would rather have their dollars now than later because a dollar now is better than a dollar later. A dollar now is better than a dollar later because consuming now is better than consuming later. Consuming now is better than consuming later because later we might be dead.

INTEREST is an amount of money that a borrower must pay a lender to entice the lender to forgo spending money now and loan the money instead.

If a dollar now is better than a dollar later, to entice someone to give up a dollar now, we must offer the person something in return. This something is called *interest*. *Interest* is an amount of money that a borrower pays a lender to entice the lender to forgo purchasing products with the money until some future time.

Suppose that a new CD player costs $300. If you would rather have a new CD player now than wait for a year to have a new CD player, you would rather have $300 now (which you would use to buy the CD player) than have $300 one year from now. If I want to borrow your $300 for one year, I will have to give you something in return that will make up for the loss in utility you incur from having to wait a year to buy a new CD player. Suppose that the loss in utility you would incur from waiting one year to buy a new CD player is the same as the utility that you would gain from having $20—then, the minimum amount of interest you would charge me for one year for the $300 loan is $20.

Thus, borrowers must pay lenders interest to entice the lenders to loan their money, because lenders would rather have their dollars now than later. Lenders would rather have their dollars now than later because a dollar now is better than a dollar later. A dollar now is better than a dollar later because consuming now is better than consuming later. Consuming now is better than consuming later because later we might be dead.

Our discussion assumes zero inflation. If there is inflation, a dollar today is better than a dollar tomorrow for two separate reasons: (1) everything we discussed above (i.e., a person would rather have a dollar and consume with it now than a dollar tomorrow and consume with it tomorrow), and (2) dollars tomorrow will buy less than dollars today will (i.e., because of inflation). If there is deflation, a dollar tomorrow might be better than a dollar today—not because our above discussion is no longer valid but because *despite the fact that a person would rather have a dollar now and consume with it now than a dollar tomorrow and consume with it tomorrow*, the dollar tomorrow will buy more than the dollar today will. The fact that the dollar will buy more tomorrow than today *might* outweigh the desire to consume today rather than tomorrow.

So, we have determined that a dollar today is not the same thing as a dollar tomorrow, in the same way that a US dollar is not the same thing as a Canadian dollar. When we see something for sale in Canada, we can convert the price in Canadian dollars into a price in US dollars for comparison. We can make the same sort of conversion across time so that we can compare tomorrow's dollars and today's dollars. The conversion is called *present value*. *Present value* tells us the value of a dollar received in the future in terms of dollars today. For example, suppose that you could put $100 in the bank for one year at 6 percent interest. At the end of the year, you would get back $106. Thus, $106 one year in the future is the *same* as $100 today. Or, in other words, the present value of $106 one year in the future is $100. We say that the *discount rate* (or the amount of value, subjectively speaking, that money loses over time) is 6 percent per year.[5]

---

5   It is possible that you would not be willing to part with $100 for one year in exchange for $106 at the end of the year. If this is the case, your subjective discount rate is higher than 6 percent. Interest rates, however, are a function of the *average* discount rates of all borrowers and lenders.

The present value calculation, then, is the reverse of an interest calculation:

$$\text{Interest Calculation} \Rightarrow \$100 \; in \; 2014 = \$100(1+0.06)$$
$$= \$106 \; in \; 2015$$
$$\text{Present Value Calculation} \Rightarrow \frac{\$106 \; in \; 2015}{1+0.06}$$
$$= \$100 \; in \; 2014$$

Suppose that you could put $100 in the bank for two years at 6 percent interest per year. At the end of the two years, you would get back $112.36. Thus, $112.36 two years in the future is the *same* as $100 today—the present value of $112.36 two years in the future is $100. The interest and present value calculations are as follows:

$$\text{Interest Calculation} \Rightarrow \$100 \; in \; 2014 = \$100(1+0.06)^2$$
$$= \$112.36 \; in \; 2016$$
$$\text{Present Value Calculation} \Rightarrow \frac{\$112.36 \; in \; 2016}{(1+0.06)^2}$$
$$= \$100 \; in \; 2014$$

Factors

What companies produce is generically referred to as *output*. What companies use to produce output are generically referred to as *factors*. Factors can be divided into two groups: short-run factors and long-run factors (see figure 4.1). *Short-run factors* are those factors whose quantities can be altered relatively quickly. *Long-run factors* are factors whose quantities cannot be altered quickly. In the real world, the long run seems to be (on average) any period of time longer than six months. The short run would then be (on average) any period of time less than this. We call the costs of short-run factors *variable costs* and the costs of long-run factors *fixed costs*.

SHORT-RUN FACTORS are factors whose quantities can be altered in the short run (e.g., labor and materials).
LONG-RUN FACTORS are factors whose quantities can be altered only in the long run (e.g., capital and technology).

The two major types of short-run factors are labor and materials. Long-run factors are those factors whose quantities can be altered only after a substantial period of time. The two major types of long-run factors are capital and technology. *Capital* (in economics) is a generic term for those physical things that a producer uses to produce a product but that do not *become* the product. Examples of capital are buildings, land, and machinery. When a producer produces a car, it uses (among other things) steel, rubber, plastic, labor, robots, a factory, and land (on which the factory sits). The steel, rubber, plastic, and labor (not the worker, just the worker's labor) become the car. The robots, the factory, and the land do not. Thus, the robots, factory, and land are considered to be capital.

People usually think of computers or high-tech machines as technology. Computers and machines are not technology (in the economic sense); they are capital. Technology is an intangible. Like happiness, it cannot be measured, although one can easily point to those who have it and those who don't. Technology can be thought of as the overall sophistication of the production process—how adept the management team is, how skilled the workers are, how well tasks are broken down, and and how well assembly lines are arranged. The more technology a producer has, the more output the producer can produce using a given number of factors.

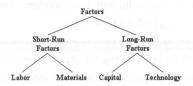

Factors

Short-Run Factors   Long-Run Factors

Labor   Materials   Capital   Technology

FIGURE 4.1 Factors of Production

VARIABLE COSTS are the costs of short-run factors.
FIXED COSTS are the costs of long-run factors.

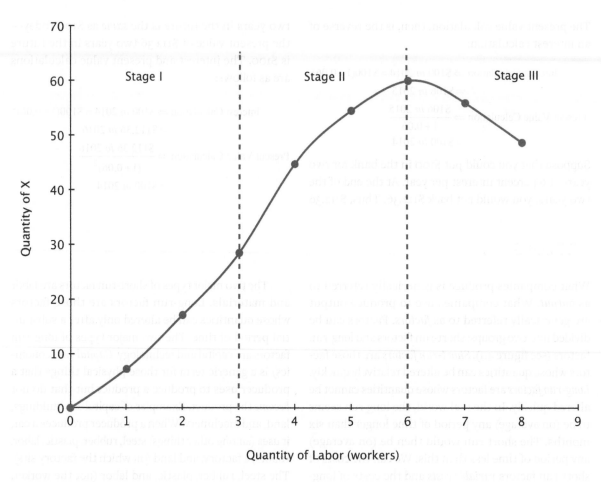

FIGURE 4.2 Total Product Curve

The Product Curves

If you graph the output function for a firm with units of the short-run factor on the horizontal axis and output on the vertical axis, you get a graph like the one shown in figure 4.2. This figure shows the amount of output X (or *total product*) the firm can produce *per unit of time* when it uses various amounts of the short-run factor. For example, suppose that the short-run factor is labor.

We divide the graph into three areas (called "stages of production"). In stage I, as the company increases its labor, output of X increases at an increasing rate. That is, output not only rises, but rises more and more rapidly. The reason that output increases at an

increasing rate in stage I is because the company has relatively few workers. Every worker added not only provides two more hands to produce, but *also* presents the opportunity to *specialize* the workers. *Specialization* occurs when the production process is broken down into separate tasks and individual workers concentrate on performing just a single task.

SPECIALIZATION is the breaking down of a task into individual steps, which are then assigned to different workers.

Consider two software companies. In company A, six workers each perform all the tasks: each worker designs and writes a program, debugs the program, writes the manual, designs the packaging, packages the manual and disk, and mails the product. Every time a worker switches from one task to another, he must put away the tools associated with the first task and bring out the tools associated with the second task. In company B, each of the six workers specializes in a single task: one worker designs and writes the program, one worker debugs the program, one worker writes the manual, and so on. Because time and effort is expended when a worker stops performing one task and begins to perform another, the six workers in company B can produce more output than the six workers in company A can because they are not switching from one task to another—each performs only one task. As long as opportunities for further specialization exist, each worker hired will cause output to rise by more than the previous worker hired did. Thus, in stage I, output increases at an increasing rate.

In stage II, hiring more of the short-run factor increases output but at a slower and slower rate, because all possibilities for specialization have been exhausted (i.e., the production process has been broken down into the greatest number of tasks possible). One would expect that if all possibilities for specialization have been exhausted, adding more units of the short-run factor would cause output to rise proportionally (i.e., each worker hired would produce the same amount of output as the previous worker hired). The reason for the output increasing at a decreasing rate in stage II has to do with two things: (1) no further specialization is possible, and (2) the short-run factor is beginning to exceed the capabilities of the long-run factor.

For example, as you move from left to right along the graph, the number of workers (short-run factor) the company has is increasing, but the amount of *capital* (long-run factor) the company has remains constant. As more and more workers are added, they have access to less and less capital. Imagine a lumber company that has one hundred chainsaws (capital) and one hundred workers. When this company hires one more worker, that worker must wait around until someone else goes on break in order to get a chainsaw. With one hundred chainsaws, the worker may not have to wait very long before one becomes available. However, the more workers the company adds, the more time the additional workers must spend waiting around for a chainsaw. Thus, in stage II, each worker hired increases output but by less than the previous worker.

In stage III, the limits of the long-run capital are completely exhausted, and adding more units of the short-run factor actually causes output to fall. Continuing the example of the workers and the chainsaws, if there are too many workers waiting around for chainsaws, these workers get in the way of the workers who do have chainsaws and disrupt their work. Imagine a software company that has a factory (the long-run factor) the size of your classroom. Now imagine how much output that company would produce if it hired ten thousand workers and tried to squeeze them all into the factory. There would be so many workers that they would get in each other's way and none would accomplish anything—output would be zero.

We can extend the analysis of the effects of short-run factors on output by defining two more measures: *marginal product* and *average product*. *Marginal product* is the *extra* output generated from employing one additional unit of the short-run factor. For example, to say that the marginal product of labor is five means that if the firm hires one more worker, the firm's output will increase by five units. In stage I, because of specialization, each worker hired produces more output than the previous worker hired—another way of saying this is to say that the marginal product of labor is rising. In stage II, because there are no further opportunities for specialization, and because the firm is approaching the limits of its capital, each worker hired produces less output than the previous worker hired—another way of saying this is to say that the marginal product of labor is falling. In stage III, because the firm has exhausted the limits of its capital, each worker hired actually detracts from the firm's output—another way of saying this is to say that the marginal product of labor is negative. Figure 4.3 shows a typical marginal product curve for a firm. Notice that in stage I, the marginal product curve is rising. Marginal product reaches a peak at the border of stages I and II. In stage II, marginal product is falling. Marginal product equals zero at the border of stages II and III. In stage III,

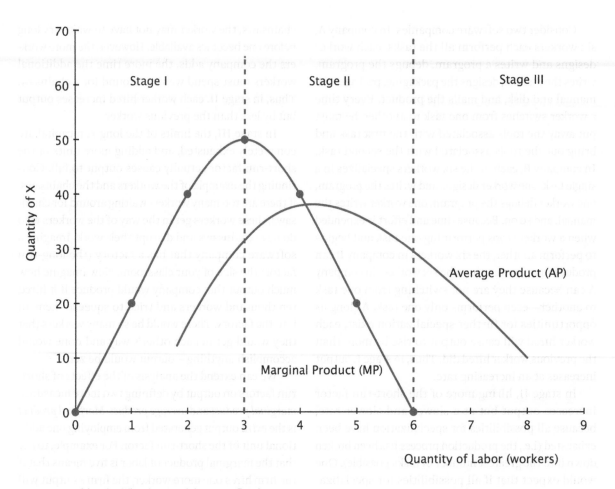

FIGURE 4.3 Marginal Product and Average Product

marginal product is negative. Marginal product is calculated as the change in total product divided by the change in the units of the short-run factor (each triangle in the following equation is the Greek letter delta, meaning "change in").

$$\text{Marginal Product} = \frac{\Delta \text{ Total Product}}{\Delta \text{ Units of Short-Run Factor}}$$

For example, suppose that when the firm uses ten units of labor, it produces fifty units of output, and when the firm uses twelve units of labor, it produces sixty-four units of output. As the firm increases its labor from ten to twelve, the change in the firm's total product is fourteen (14 = 64 – 50), and the change in the firm's

units of labor is two (2 = 12 – 10). The firm's marginal product as it moves from ten to twelve units of labor is seven (7 = 14 / 2). That is, on average, as the firm increases its labor from ten to twelve, it gains seven output for each unit of labor it adds.

MARGINAL PRODUCT is the additional output produced when a firm employs one more unit of a factor.

$$\text{Marginal Product} = \frac{\Delta \text{ Total Product}}{\Delta \text{ Units of Short-Run Factor}}$$

Our analysis of marginal product is summarized in the fourth principle of economics, which states that when a firm employs few units of a factor, each additional unit the firm employs produces more than the previous unit (increasing marginal product),

and when the firm employs many units of a factor, each additional unit the firm employs produces less than the previous unit (decreasing marginal product). This is also referred to as the *law of diminishing marginal productivity*.

FOURTH PRINCIPLE: THE LAW OF DIMINISHING MARGINAL PRODUCTIVITY When a producer employs few units of a factor, each additional unit the producer employs yields more output than the previous unit. When a producer employs many units of a factor, each additional unit the producer employs yields less output than the previous unit.

Figure 4.3 also shows a measure called average product. *Average product* is the amount of output each unit of the short-run factor is producing, *on average*. For example, if the firm employs ten workers and produces fifty units of output, its average product is five (5 = 50 / 10). Average product is calculated as follows:

$$\text{Average Product} = \frac{\text{Total Product}}{\text{Units of Short-Run Factor}}$$

Average product and marginal product are similar, yet the difference is important. While marginal product measures the *extra output* generated by *one more* unit of the short-run factor, average product measures the *average output* generated by *all* the units of the short-run factor together. There is the same relationship between marginal and average product as there is between a test grade and a course grade. A test grade is a measure of the impact of *one* test. A course grade is the average impact of *all* tests. If your course grade is currently 80 percent and you receive 100 percent on your next test, your course grade rises. If your course grade is currently 80 percent and you receive 70 percent on your next test, your course grade

falls. There is the same relationship between marginal product and average product. When the extra output generated by one more unit of labor is greater than the average output of all the workers who are currently working, the average output for the workers rises. When the extra output generated by one more unit of labor is lower than the average output of all the workers who are currently working, the average output for the workers falls. This can be seen in figure 4.3. Whenever marginal product is greater than average product, average product is rising. Whenever marginal product is less than average product, average product is falling. Hence, the marginal product curve always intersects the average product curve at the average product curve's maximum point. Further, this intersection will always occur in stage II.

AVERAGE PRODUCT *is the output per unit of short-run factor employed.*

$$\text{Average Product} = \frac{\text{Total Product}}{\text{Units of Short-Run Factor}}$$

Optimal Factor Combination

Recall from our discussion of utility maximization in chapter 3 that a person will always consume a certain combination of products, which maximizes his utility. The proper combination of products the person should consume depends on how much additional utility the

person gets from each product and the price of each product. Specifically, the third principle of economics states that people will consume products in a certain combination, such that the marginal utility per dollar is equal for all the products. This principle, in effect, says that a person will consume more of whatever product gives him the most additional happiness per dollar spent.

AVERAGE PRODUCT is the output per unit of short-run factor employed.

There is a similar principle at work in a firm that must decide how much of various factors to employ in the production process. Suppose, for example, that a clothing manufacturer uses two short-run factors: labor and sewing machines.[6] It is not necessarily true that the firm will want to employ one worker for every sewing machine. If the firm wants to work two shifts per day, it may employ two workers for every one sewing machine. If it wants extra sewing machines available so that a worker is never idle should his sewing machine break down, it may employ more than one sewing machine per worker. Suppose that the firm's marginal product of labor is ten and its marginal product of sewing machines is two. This means that if the firm were to hire one more worker, its production would rise by ten units per day; if the firm were to purchase one more sewing machine, its production would rise by two units per day. Which should the firm employ, one more worker or one more sewing machine? It seems that it would be better for the firm to employ one more worker, because the worker produces eight more units per day than the machine does. However, consider the cost of the worker and the machine. If the worker costs the firm $50 per day and the machine costs the firm $4 per day, the machine is definitely the better buy. Why? Because the worker produces ten additional units per day at a cost of $50 per day—that means that the firm gets 0.2 extra units per day for every dollar it spends on the extra worker (0.2 output per day per dollar = 10 output per worker / $50 per worker per day). The machine produces two additional units per day at a cost of $4 per day—that means that the firm gets 0.5 extra units per day for every dollar it spends on the extra machine (0.5 output per day

per dollar = 2 output per machine / $4 per machine per day). Although the additional worker produces more output than the additional machine does, the output *per dollar spent* on the machine is *higher* than the output *per dollar spent* on the worker. Thus, the firm is better off employing an additional machine rather than an additional worker.

What happens when the firm employs one additional machine? We know that for small quantities of a factor, each additional unit of the factor produces more output than the previous unit (increasing marginal product—stage I on the total product curve). As long as the firm is in stage I, it will always continue to employ more units of the factor, because each unit produces more than the previous unit but costs the same as the previous unit.[7] Thus, as long as the firm finds it profitable to employ one unit of the factor, it is guaranteed that the firm will find it even more profitable to employ more units—provided that the firm is in stage I.

Suppose that the firm is in stage II. What happens when it employs one additional machine? We know that the marginal product of the next machine will be lower—the second additional machine will produce less additional output than did the first additional machine. Thus, if the firm employs one additional machine, the marginal product of a second additional machine is less than for the first additional machine, for example, one instead of two. What should the firm do now: Employ an additional worker or employ a second additional machine? The marginal product of the additional worker is still ten. This means that the marginal product per dollar spent on an additional worker is 0.2. The marginal product per dollar spent on an additional machine, however, has fallen to 0.25 (0.25 output per day per dollar = 1 output per machine per day / $4 per machine). It is better for the firm to employ a second additional machine than an additional worker—the second machine will produce 0.25 output per day for every dollar spent on the machine, whereas the worker will produce only 0.2 output per day for every dollar spent on the worker. So, the firm employs a second additional machine,

---

6   The sewing machines are capital because they contribute to the production of the product without becoming the product. We treat them here as short-run factors because more sewing machines can be obtained relatively quickly. Thus, we see that while capital (in general) can be considered to be a long-run factor, there are specific examples of capital that are short-run factors.

7   We assume, for clarity of argument, that the firm can sell all the output it produces at a constant price per unit.

and, according to the fourth principle, the marginal product of the third additional machine is 0.6. What should the firm do now: Employ a third additional machine, or employ an additional worker? The marginal product per dollar for the third additional machine is 0.15 (0.15 = 0.5 / $4). The marginal product per dollar for the additional worker is still 0.2. Now the firm is better off employing the additional worker. If the firm employs an additional worker, it receives 0.2 extra units of output per day for every dollar it spends; but if the firm employs a third additional machine, it receives only 0.15 extra units of output for every dollar it spends. In short, if the firm is going to employ more units of a factor, it will always employ more units of the factor that has the highest marginal product per dollar.

We can see from this that the best combination of factors is the combination for which the marginal products per dollar are *equal* for all factors. When the marginal products per dollar are equal for all factors, the firm is employing neither too much nor too little of any factor relative to the others. This gives us the fifth principle of economics.

FIFTH PRINCIPLE Producers employ combinations of factors, such that the extra output produced per unit cost is equal for all factors.

The fifth principle is stated below in its mathematical form, where A and B are factors the firm uses in producing its product.

The fifth principle (in its mathematical form):

$$\frac{\text{Marginal Product of } A}{\text{Price of } A} = \frac{\text{Marginal Product of } B}{\text{Price of } B} = \dots$$

To better understand the fifth principle, consider a case in which it is violated. A restaurant employs two types

of workers: waiters and cooks. There is, of course, an optimal combination of waiters and cooks. Too many waiters, and orders come in faster than what the cooks can handle, and some waiters sit around idle waiting for the cooks to complete their orders. Too many cooks, and the food is completed too quickly, and some of the cooks sit around idle waiting for more orders to come in, and some of the food gets cold because there are no available waiters to take it to the patrons. Suppose that the marginal product of waiters is ten and the marginal product of cooks is twelve. That is, employing one more waiter means that the firm can serve ten more customers per day; employing one more cook means that the firm can serve twelve more customers per day. Suppose as well that the price of a waiter is $40 per day and the price of a cook is $60 per day. The marginal product per dollar for an additional waiter is 0.25 (0.25 = 10 / $40). The marginal product per dollar for an additional cook is 0.2 (0.2 = 12 / $60). Because the marginal product per dollar for an additional waiter is greater than the marginal product per dollar for an additional cook, we know that the firm is employing not enough waiters and too many cooks.

Watch this! Suppose that the firm fires one of its cooks and hires 1.2 waiters (one full-time waiter and one part-time waiter). What happens? Firing the cook causes output to fall by twelve (the marginal product of the cook) and saves the firm $60 (the cost of the cook). Hiring the additional 1.2 waiters causes output to increase by twelve (the marginal product of one waiter times 1.2 waiters) and costs the firm $48 ($40 per waiter times 1.2 waiters). What has happened to the firm? The firm's output is unchanged, and the firm has *saved* $12. The conclusion is that the firm was employing the wrong combination of cooks and waiters because a different combination produces the same amount of output at a lower cost.

Thus, when a firm employs the correct combination of factors, it produces its chosen output at the lowest possible cost.

The Cost Curves

Now that we have discussed the optimal factor combination, let us assume that the firms we discuss *always*

achieve the optimal factor combination. The optimal factor combination only tells us in what ratios to use

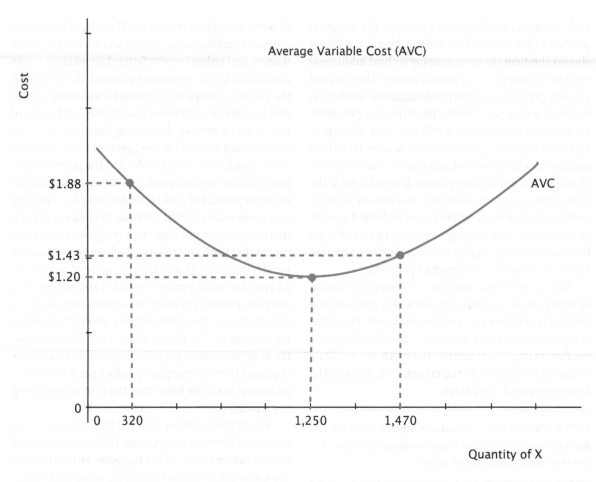

FIGURE 4.4 Average Variable Cost

our various factors. There is a further question: how much output to produce.

Given that the firm has found the optimal combination of labor and materials, we can construct a variety of relationships that provide useful information about the firm's costs of production. Assuming that the firm is using the optimal combination of factors, the firm's average variable cost is computed by dividing the firm's variable cost (the short-run factors) by the number of units of output the firm produces.

$$\text{Average Variable Cost} = \frac{\text{Variable Cost}}{\text{Total Product}}$$

By plotting the firm's average variable cost at various output quantities against those output quantities, we obtain the *average variable cost curve*. The *average variable cost curve* is the relationship between the firm's average variable cost and the amount of output it produces.

Figure 4.4 shows a typical average variable cost curve. According to the diagram, when the firm produces 320 units of output, its average variable cost is $1.88 per unit. That is, the firm spends $1.88 per unit of output on short-run factors. When the firm produces 1,250 units of output, its average variable cost falls to $1.20 per unit. That is, the cost of its short-run factors is $1.20 per unit of output produced. As the firm increases its output to 1,470 units, its average variable cost rises to $1.43 per unit. As the firm increases the production of its output from 0 units up to 1,250 units, its average variable cost decreases. As the firm increases the production of its output beyond 1,250 units, its average variable cost rises.

Why does the firm's average variable cost change as it alters the amount of output it produces? The answer lies in the fact that in order to alter the amount of output it produces, the firm must alter the amount of short-run factors it is employing. When the firm alters the amount of short-run factors it is employing, the marginal product and average product of those short-run factors changes.

Consider the following example, in which a firm's only short-run factor is labor. Table 4.1 shows how much output various amounts of labor will produce. Notice that the table gives a realistic depiction of a firm: the firm has three stages of production (stage I, where marginal product is rising is from zero labor to forty labor; stage II, where marginal product is falling is from forty labor to seventy labor; stage III begins between seventy and eighty labor).

TABLE 4.1 Total Product, Marginal Product, and Average Product

Labor	Total Product	Marginal Product	Average Product
0	0	—	—
20	320	16	16
30	630	31	21
40	960	33	24
50	1,250	29	25
60	1,440	19	24
70	1,470	3	21
80	1,440	−19	19

Suppose that this firm pays $30 per day for each of its workers. We can now compute the variable cost the firm incurs from hiring various amounts of labor. This is shown in table 4.2. Variable cost, the cost of the short-run factors, in this example is the quantity of labor times $30.

TABLE 4.2 Variable Cost

Labor	Variable Cost
0	$0 = (0)($30)
20	$600 = (20)($30)
30	$900 = (30)($30)
40	$1,200 = (40)($30)
50	$1,500 = (50)($30)
60	$1,800 = (60)($30)
70	$2,100 = (70)($30)

We can now compute the average variable cost (AVC = variable cost / total product) and compare it to the average product. This is shown in table 4.3.

As the firm increases its labor from zero to fifty, the firm's average product rises (because each additional worker the firm hires produces more output than the average of the existing workers). To say that the average output per worker rises is the same as saying that the average cost per unit of output is falling. Thus, there is an inverse relationship between average product and average variable cost: as average product rises, average variable cost falls; as average product falls, average variable cost rises. This inverse relationship between average product and average variable cost

TABLE 4.3 Average Variable Cost and Average Product

Labor	Total Product	Variable Cost	AVC	Average Product
0	0	$0	—	—
20	320	$600	$1.88 = $600/320	16 = 320/20
30	630	$900	$1.43 = $900/630	21 = 630/30
40	960	$1,200	$1.25 = $1,200/960	24 = 960/40
50	1,250	$1,500	$1.20 = $1,500/1,250	25 = 1,250/50
60	1,440	$1,800	$1.25 = $1,800/1,440	24 = 1,440/60
70	1,470	$2,100	$1.43 = $2,100/1,470	21 = 1,470/70

can be shown mathematically as follows (where P_L is the price of labor):

$$\text{AVC} = \frac{\text{Variable Cost}}{\text{Total Product}} = \frac{(P_1)(\text{Labor})}{\text{Total Product}}$$

$$= (P_L)\left(\frac{1}{\text{Average Product}}\right)$$

We can now see the relationship between the graph of average product in figure 4.3 and the graph of average variable cost in figure 4.4: the various amounts of short-run *factors* that trace out the average product curve *produce* the various amounts of *output* that trace out the average variable cost curve; also, the amount of short-run *factor* that maximizes average product *produces* the amount of *output* that minimizes average variable cost.

$$\text{Average Fixed Cost} = \frac{\text{Fixed Cost}}{\text{Total Product}}$$

Recall that there are two sources of cost associated with running a firm: (1) the cost of short-run factors (i.e., labor and materials), called "variable cost," and (2) the cost of long-run factors (i.e., machinery, buildings, and land), called "fixed cost." Because the quantities of short-run factors the firm employs can be changed relatively quickly (i.e., in the short run), we call these costs "variable." Because the quantities of long-run factors the firm employs can be changed only over a longer period of time (i.e., the long run), we call these costs "fixed" (i.e., these costs are fixed in the short run). We have already

seen average variable cost and observed that as the firm increases the amount of output it produces, the average variable cost falls, reaches a minimum, and then rises again. We can, similarly, examine the firm's *average fixed cost*. *Average fixed cost*, shown in figure 4.5, is defined as follows:

While the firm's *variable* costs increase as the firm produces more output, the firm's *fixed* costs remain unchanged. Thus, the firm's *average* fixed costs fall as the firm produces more and more output. Going back to the example we used for average variable cost, suppose that, in addition to labor, the firm has a factory that, each day, incurs $600 worth of depreciation. This is shown in table 4.4. Each day, the firm incurs a cost of $600 whether it produces a lot of output or a little. Even if the firm produces nothing, it still owns a factory, and that factory continues to depreciate at the rate of $600 worth of depreciation per day.

Notice that because the fixed cost remains constant, as the amount of output the firm produces rises, the firm's average fixed cost gets smaller and smaller. What is happening is that the fixed cost of depreciation is being spread over a greater and greater number of units of output, so that the fixed cost *per unit of output* asymptotically approaches zero.

Variable cost is the cost of the firm's short-run factors; *fixed cost* is the cost of the firm's long-run factors; *total cost* is the sum of the variable and fixed costs and represents the total cost to the firm of producing its output. Continuing our example, we can compute the firm's total cost by adding its variable and fixed costs. This is also shown in table 4.5.

TABLE 4.4 Fixed Cost and Average Fixed Cost

Labor	Total Product	Fixed Cost	Average Fixed Cost
0	0	$600	—
20	320	$600	$1.88 = $600/320
30	630	$600	$0.95 = $600/630
40	960	$600	$0.63 = $600/960
50	1,250	$600	$0.48 = $600/1,250
60	1,440	$600	$0.42 = $600/1,440
70	1,470	$600	$0.41 = $600/1,470

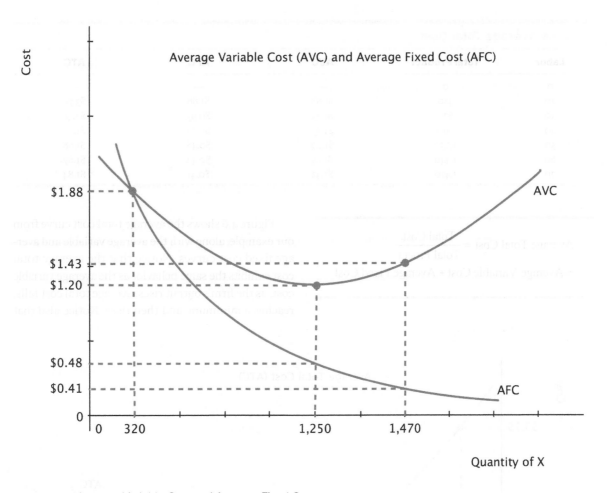

FIGURE 4.5 Average Variable Cost and Average Fixed Cost

$$\text{Total Cost} = \text{Variable Cost} + \text{Fixed Cost}$$

We can also compute the firm's average total cost (ATC) by dividing its total cost by the units of output produced. Thus,

TABLE 4.5 Total Cost

Labor	Total Product	Variable Cost	Fixed Cost	Total Cost
0	0	$0	$600	$600 = $0 + $600
20	320	$600	$600	$1,200 = $600 + $600
30	630	$900	$600	$1,500 = $900 + $600
40	960	$1,200	$600	$1,800 = $1,200 + $600
50	1,250	$1,500	$600	$2,100 = $1,500 + $600
60	1,440	$1,800	$600	$2,400 = $1,800 + $600
70	1,470	$2,100	$600	$2,700 = $2,100 + $600

TABLE 4.6 Average Total Cost

Labor	Total Product	AVC	AFC	ATC
0	0	—	—	—
20	320	$1.88	$1.88	$3.76
30	630	$1.43	$0.95	$2.38
40	960	$1.25	$0.63	$1.88
50	1,250	$1.20	$0.48	$1.68
60	1,440	$1.25	$0.42	$1.67
70	1,470	$1.43	$0.41	$1.84

$$\text{Average Total Cost} = \frac{\text{Total Cost}}{\text{Total Procut}}$$
$$= \text{Average Variable Cost} + \text{Average Fixed Cost}$$

Figure 4.6 shows the average total cost curve from our example, along with the average variable and average fixed cost curves. Notice that the average total cost exhibits the same behavior as the average variable cost: as the firm's output rises, average total cost falls, reaches a minimum, and then rises. Notice also that

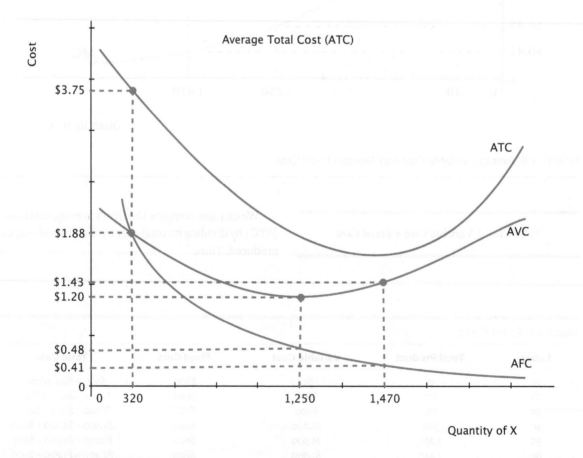

FIGURE 4.6 Average Total Cost

the greater the output the firm produces, the less the difference between the average variable cost and the average total cost. The reason is that the difference between the two (ATC minus AVC) is the average fixed cost, and as the firm's output rises, the average fixed cost approaches zero. Thus, as the output rises, average total cost and average variable cost become closer.

THE EFFICIENT OUTPUT QUANTITY is the quantity of output that minimizes the firm's average total cost.

While the average total cost curve has a minimum, like the average variable cost curve, the average total cost curve's minimum is positioned to the right of the average variable cost's. According to figure 4.6, the firm's *average variable cost* (the cost of labor and materials per unit of output) is minimized when the firm produces 1,250 units of output, but the firm's *average total cost* (the cost of labor, materials, *and* depreciated capital per unit of output) is minimized when the firm produces 1,440 units of output. We give the minimum point on the average total cost curve a special name: the *efficient output quantity*. We say that a firm is *efficient* when it produces at this level. For example, the efficient output quantity for the firm in figure 4.6 is 1,440 units of output. If the firm produces any more or any less output than 1,440, its average total cost will rise. For the firm to produce its product at the lowest possible average total cost, the firm must produce exactly 1,440 units of output.

Breakeven and Shutdown Prices

When a firm attempts to sell its product, it faces three possible scenarios: (1) the market price of its product is greater than the firm's average total cost, (2) the market price of its product is less than the firm's average total cost but greater than the firm's average variable cost, or (3) the market price of its product is less than the firm's average variable cost. In the first scenario, the firm is making an economic profit. In the second and third scenarios, the firm is incurring an economic loss.

In scenario 1, the firm is making an economic profit (i.e., the price the firm gets for a unit of output exceeds the cost per unit of producing the output). We call the minimum attainable average total cost the breakeven price. As long as the price of the firm's output stays above the breakeven price, the firm will make an economic profit.

In scenario 2, the price of the firm's output is less than the breakeven price, but greater than the average variable cost. Because the price is greater than the breakeven price, the firm is incurring an economic loss.

In the long run, the firm should either (1) do something to lower its minimum attainable average total cost (such as investing in more capital or more technology), or (2) leave the industry and move to one in which the market price is greater than what the firm's breakeven price would be in the new industry. Meanwhile, in the short run, should the firm continue to produce output or not? Because the price of the firm's output is greater than its average variable cost, when the firm produces and sells a unit of output, it earns enough money to *completely* pay for its variable cost (i.e., the labor and materials) and still have some money left over that will *partially* pay for its fixed cost (i.e., capital depreciation). If the firm does not produce and sell output, it will not earn any money and therefore will not be able to pay for *any* of its capital depreciation. We call the minimum attainable average variable cost the shutdown price. In the short run, as long as the price of the firm's output stays below the breakeven price but above the shutdown price, the firm should continue to produce output while waiting to implement its long-run decision.

THE BREAKEVEN PRICE is the price at which the firm makes zero economic profit when it produces at its profit-maximizing output quantity.

THE SHUTDOWN PRICE is the price at which the firm incurs the same economic loss from producing zero output as from producing at the profit-maximizing output quantity.

In scenario 3, the price of the firm's output is less than its shutdown price. This means that not only is the firm losing money; if it produces and sells output, it will not earn enough money to cover even the cost of labor and materials. The firm's long-run decision should be to either (1) obtain more capital or technology or (2) leave the industry. In the short run, the firm should not produce any output while waiting to implement its long-run decision.

The last of the cost curves, *marginal cost*, has the same relationship to total cost as marginal product does to total product. Whereas marginal product is the extra *output* generated from using one more unit of the short-run factor, marginal cost is the extra *cost* generated from producing one more unit of output. Marginal cost is calculated as follows:

MARGINAL COST *is the extra cost generated from producing one more unit of output.*

$$\text{Marginal Cost} = \frac{\Delta \text{ Total Cost}}{\Delta \text{ Total Procuct}}$$

In the same way that average variable cost and average product are related, marginal cost and marginal product are similarly related. Taking the definitions of each, we have

$$\text{Marginal Product} = \frac{\Delta \text{ Total Product}}{\Delta \text{ Short-Run Factor}}$$

$$\Rightarrow \Delta \text{ Total Product} = (\text{Marginal Procuct})$$
$$(\Delta \text{ Short-Run Factor})$$

$$\text{Marginal Cost} = \frac{\Delta \text{ Total Cost}}{\Delta \text{ Total Procuct}}$$

$$= \frac{\Delta \text{ Total Cost}}{(\text{Marginal Procuct})(\Delta \text{ Short-Run Factor})}$$

$$= \frac{P_{\text{Short-Run Factor}}}{\text{Marginal Procuct}}$$

Thus we can see that marginal cost (MC) is, essentially, the inverse of marginal product (MP). Continuing our example, we can compute marginal cost.

Figure 4.7 shows a typical marginal cost curve. Notice that the marginal cost curve always intersects the average variable and average total cost curves at their minimum points. Marginal cost declines briefly and then increases. The downward-sloping portion of the marginal cost curve corresponds to the increasing portion of the marginal product curve. When the marginal product curve is increasing (i.e., the firm is in stage I), every unit of the short-run factor the firm employs produces more output than the previous unit. This is the same thing as saying that every unit of output the firm produces costs less than the previous unit—decreasing marginal cost.

MARGINAL COST is the extra cost generated from producing one more unit of output.

TABLE 4.7 Marginal Cost and Marginal Product

Labor	Total Product	Total Cost	MC	MP
0	0	$600	—	—
20	320	$1,200	$1.88	16
30	630	$1,500	$0.97	31
40	960	$1,800	$0.91	33
50	1,250	$2,100	$1.03	29
60	1,440	$2,400	$1.58	19
70	1,470	$2,700	$10.00	3

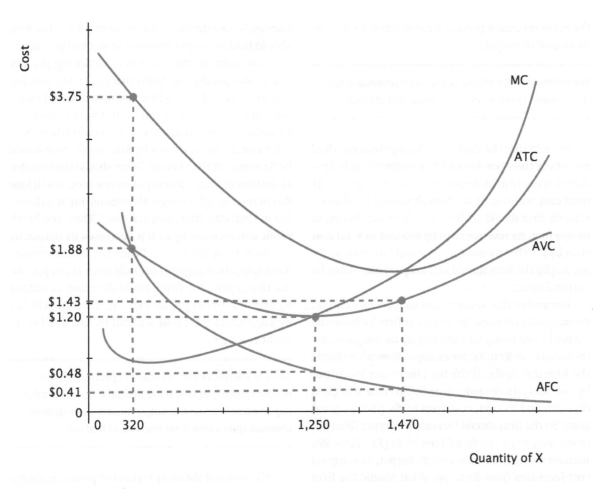

FIGURE 4.7 Marginal Cost

Optimal Output Quantity

We have discussed the fifth principle, which tells us the optimal factor combination—what ratio of factors the firm should employ when it produces output. The fifth principle, however, does not tell us how much output the firm should produce. The fifth principle would tell us something like this: *the firm should employ 1.1 chainsaws for every one worker.* The fifth principle does not tell us, however, whether we should employ 11 chainsaws and 10 workers, or 110 chainsaws and 100 workers, or 1,100 chainsaws and 1,000 workers. Merely knowing the optimal ratio of factors does not tell us how many units of the factors to employ.

Suppose for a moment that the firm can sell as many trees as it cuts at a constant price of $10 per foot. Suppose also that the firm is currently producing three hundred feet of cut trees per day and that its marginal cost is $7 per foot (we also assume that the firm is employing the optimal combination of factors—1.1 chainsaws for every one worker). Here is the question: Should the firm increase its output, decrease its output, or leave its output unchanged? Remember that the firm can sell as many feet of cut trees as it likes at $10 per foot. Ten dollars is the price of the firm's product, but we can also describe it as the firm's *marginal revenue. Marginal revenue* is the extra revenue a producer earns when it sells one more unit of output.

MARGINAL REVENUE is the extra revenue a producer earns when it sells one more unit of output.

We said that the firm is producing three hundred feet of cut trees per day and its marginal cost is $7—that is, if the firm increases its output by one foot, its total cost will rise by $7. Now, it should be obvious what the firm should do. If the firm increases its output by one foot, its revenue rises by $10 and its total cost rises by $7. That means that its profit has risen by $3. So, maybe the firm should just keep on increasing its output forever. Not so fast!

Remember that when a firm increases its output, its marginal cost *rises*.[8] So when our firm increases its output by one foot (from 300 to 301), its marginal cost increases from $7 to $8, for example. Now what should the firm do? Again, if the firm increases its output by one foot, its revenue rises by $10 (the marginal revenue) and its total cost rises by $8 (the marginal cost). So the firm should increase its output from 301 to 302 feet, and its profit will rise by $2 ($2 = $10 – $8). Because the firm has increased its output, its marginal cost increases from $8 to $9. What should the firm do? If the firm increases its output by one foot, its revenue rises by $10 (the marginal revenue) and its total cost rises by $9 (the marginal cost). So the firm should increase its output from 302 to 303 feet, and its profit will rise by $1. Because the firm has increased its output, its marginal cost rises again, this time to $10. Now what should the firm do? If it increases its output by one foot, its revenue rises by $10 and its total cost rises by $10, so the firm gains no more profit. The firm should hold its output constant at 303 feet per day.

Now, suppose that the firm is producing 305 feet of cut trees per day. The firm's marginal revenue is $10 and its marginal cost is $12. The firm definitely does not want to increase its output. If it were to increase its output by one foot, its revenue would rise by $10, but its total cost would rise by $12, and the firm would be $2 worse off than before. What should the firm do? If the firm *decreases* its output by one foot, it will lose $10 in revenue (the marginal revenue), but it will *save* $12 in total cost (the marginal cost). Thus, the firm's profit will increase by $2 if it decreases its output by one foot, from 305 to 304. When the firm decreases its output, the marginal cost falls from $12 to $11. We see that, again, the firm should decrease its output by one foot (from 304 to 303)—its revenue will fall by $10, but its total cost will fall by $11, making its profit rise by $1.

SIXTH PRINCIPLE Producers produce at the output quantity at which the marginal cost of producing an additional unit of output equals the marginal revenue generated from the sale of that unit.

The moral of the story is this: the producer always maximizes its profit when it produces the output quantity at which marginal revenue and marginal cost are equal—and this is the sixth principle of economics.

Thus, the fifth and sixth principles tell the producer exactly how many units of factor to employ: *we must employ 1.1 chainsaws for every one worker, and we must employ enough chainsaws and workers to enable us to cut down 303 feet of trees per day.*

Supply

The behavior of consumers is summarized by the relationship called demand. The behavior of producers is summarized by the relationship called supply. *Supply* is the relationship between the price of a product and the number of units of the product producers are willing to offer for sale.

The number of units a producer is willing to offer for sale is not necessarily the same thing as the number of units the producer actually sells. It is possible that when

---

8 Assuming, of course, that the firm is in stage II, which, if it isn't, it very quickly will be.

the price of a product is high, producers are willing to sell many units, yet consumers are willing to buy only a few units. Therefore, only a few units will actually be sold.

To understand supply, we must consider how many units of a product the producer would be willing to offer, *provided* that it could sell as many units as it wanted at a particular price. Consider labor. You are a producer of labor. If you could sell as many hours of your time as you wanted per week at a price of $5 per hour, how many hours would you be willing to sell? You need time to study, time to be with friends, time to eat, time to sleep, and time to go to class. Suppose that after you do all of these things, you have ten hours per week left over. At a price of $5 per hour, you are willing to sell your ten hours of time per week as labor to an employer. Now, suppose that the employer offers you $20 per hour. At a price of $20 per hour, you are willing to sleep less, to miss lunch, and to spend less time with friends. By cutting back on the time you spend doing these things, you manage to squeeze out another fifteen hours of time per week that you sell to your employer as labor. At a price of $20 per hour, you are willing to offer a total of twenty-five hours of your time per week. Now, suppose that the employer offers you $100 per hour. At a price of $100 per hour, you are willing to drop out of school entirely. This frees up another thirty hours of time per week. At a price of $100 per hour, you are willing to offer a total of fifty-five hours of your time per week.

As the price of the product (labor) rises, you (the producer) are willing to offer more units of the product for sale. The number of units the producer offers for sale per unit of time is called the *quantity supplied*.

QUANTITY SUPPLIED is the number of units of a product that a producer is willing to offer for sale per unit of time.

Let's start again with a simple supply schedule for a producer. Table 4.8 shows the price of a paperback novel in the first column and the quantity supplied per month in the second column. Similar to what we said for demand schedule for an individual consumer, we can get this information fairly easily by approaching an individual producer and asking how many paperbacks they

TABLE 4.8 Supply Schedule

Supply Schedule for Paperbacks

Price of a Paperback	Quantity of Paperbacks Supplied per Month
110	10
100	9
90	8
80	7
70	6
60	5
50	4
40	3
30	2
20	1

would be willing to supply for a given price. By asking the same question for many different prices and noting the answers, we can construct a supply schedule, as shown in table 4.8. The first thing we see is that the answers that we get present a certain pattern. We see that for high prices the number of paperbacks the producer is willing to sell (or the quantity supplied) is higher than the one for the lower prices. This shows a positive relationship between the price of the good and quantity supplied for that good. This relationship can be shown graphically as well. We do this by putting the price on the vertical axis and the quantity supplied on the horizontal axis. Once we plot the numbers from table 4.8 as points and connect those points, we get the graph shown in figure 4.8, which we refer to as a supply curve.

There are many factors that go into a producer's willingness to offer a product: the cost of the materials used to manufacture the product, the level of expertise needed to manufacture the product, and so on. *Supply* is the relationship between the price of a product and the number of units of the product producers are willing to offer for sale when all of these other factors are held constant. The constant factors are called *ceteris paribus assumptions for supply*.

Just as we said for demand, things can change for a producer that sells a product. There are two types of changes or movements that we need to consider. The first is a change in the price of the good the producer supplies. From a certain point on the supply curve, a price change for that good will move us to a different

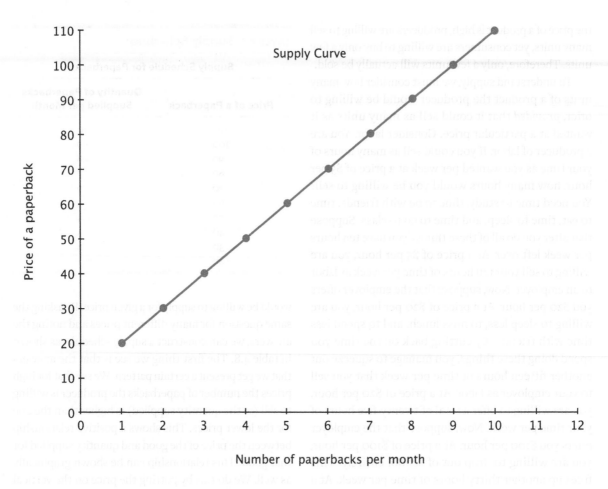

FIGURE 4.8 Supply Curve

point on the same supply curve. This is referred to as a movement along the supply curve. This is shown in figure 4.9. An individual is initially at point A on the supply curve, where she is willing to sell four paperbacks per month at a price of $50. If the price of a paperback increases to $60, the producer moves from point A to point B on the same supply curve, where her quantity supplied increases to five paperbacks per month. Again, this is a movement along the supply curve.

MOVEMENT ALONG THE SUPPLY CURVE

From a certain point on the supply curve, a price change for that good will move us to a different point on the same supply curve. This is referred to as a movement along the supply curve.

As we already defined, the amount of a product that producers are willing to offer for sale is called the *quantity supplied*; *supply* is the relationship between the price of a product and the quantity supplied of the product. Graphically, supply is the entire *curve*, while quantity supplied is a *number* on the horizontal axis. Just as demand is concerned solely with the consumer, supply is concerned solely with the producer. When we ask how many units consumers are willing to buy at a given price, we mean *assuming that the units are available*. When we ask how many units producers are willing to offer at a given price, we mean *assuming that the units will be purchased*.

Think back to our description of the marginal cost curve. We said that marginal cost is the extra cost generated from producing one more unit of output.

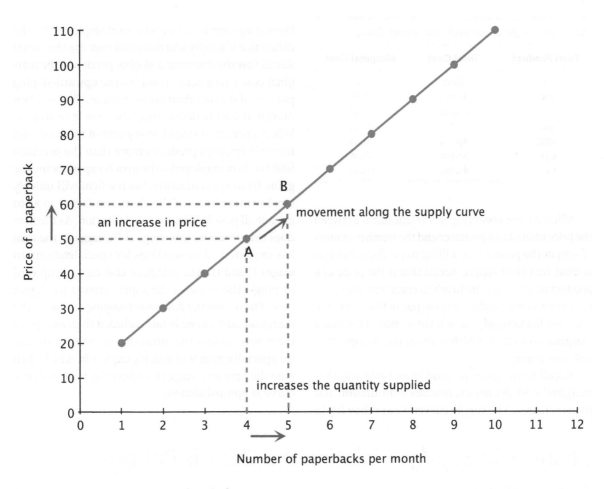

FIGURE 4.9 Movement along the Supply Curve

Consider a firm that has the marginal cost curve shown in table 4.9.

According to table 4.9, when the producer increases its output from 960 units to 1,250 units, its marginal cost (on average) is $0.98 ($0.98 = [$1.03 + $0.91] / 2). This means that for every unit the producer's output increases, the producer's total cost rises by $0.98 (on average). What is the minimum price per unit we would have to offer the producer in order to entice it to increase its output from 960 units to 1,250 units? The answer: $0.98. If the producer were to increase its output from 1,250 units to 1,440 units, its total cost would rise (on average) by $1.31 per unit of output ($1.31 = [$1.58 + $1.03] / 2). What is the minimum price per unit we would have to offer the producer in order

to entice it to increase its output from 1,250 units to 1,440 units? The answer: $1.31 per unit.

SUPPLY is the relationship between the price of a product and the number of units of the product producers are willing to offer for sale per unit time, ceteris paribus.

Ceteris paribus assumptions for supply:

1. The prices of factors or cost of inputs do not change.

2. The amounts of capital and technology the producer has does not change.

3. The number of producers does not change.

TABLE 4.9 Total Cost and Marginal Cost

Total Product	Total Cost	Marginal Cost
0	$600	—
320	$1,200	$1.88
630	$1,500	$0.97
960	$1,800	$0.91
1,250	$2,100	$1.03
1,440	$2,400	$1.58
1,470	$2,700	$10.00

What we are observing is a relationship between the price offered to a producer and the number of units of output the producer is willing to produce. But this is what we called supply. Recall that if the price of a product is less than the firm's average variable cost, the firm will not produce any output in the short run. Thus, the firm's supply curve is the section of the firm's marginal cost curve, which is above the average variable cost curve.

Recall from figure 4.7 (and from table 4.9) that marginal cost decreases, reaches a minimum, and then increases. The supply curves we are showing in these diagrams are always upward sloping. Why the difference if supply and marginal cost are the same? Recall that the downward-sloping portion of the marginal cost curve corresponds to the upward-sloping portion of the marginal product curve. That is, when marginal cost is decreasing, the firm is in stage I. When a firm is in stage I, every unit of the short-run factor it employs produces more than the previous unit the firm employed—the firm is experiencing the gains from specialization. Such a firm will quickly employ more units of the short-run factor so as to exploit all possibilities for specialization. As the firm does this, it moves into stage II (in stage II, the firm has exploited all possibilities for specialization). In stages II and III, the marginal cost curve is upward sloping—the same as the supply curves we depict here. The reason the downward-sloping section of the marginal cost curve is not included in drawings of the supply curve is that firms that see an opportunity for specialization will quickly exploit it, which then puts the firm into stage II—where the marginal cost curve is upward sloping.

Changes in Supply: Violating the Ceteris Paribus Assumptions

If any of the three ceteris paribus assumptions for supply are violated, the relationship between the price of a product and the quantity producers are willing to offer for sale will change. When the relationship between price and quantity supplied changes, the supply curve shifts either left (a decrease in supply) or right (an increase in supply). For example, suppose that initial supply curve for a producer is S_1 in figure 4.10, and the producer is initially willing to sell five paperbacks per month at a price of $50. Now, suppose that the cost of paper increases, which increases the cost of production for this producer, because paper is an important input for paperback production. For a given price the producer is now willing to sell fewer than five paperbacks per month because of lower profit expectation from each paperback. Note that the same will be true for any other price and any other point on the supply curve. The increase in price of a factor or cost of an input is a violation of the first ceteris paribus assumption for supply. The violation causes the *relationship* between the price of a paperback and the quantity of paperbacks supplied to change. The supply curve labeled S_1 in figure 4.10 is the producer's supply curve before the increase in cost of paper. The supply curve labeled S_2 is the same producer's supply curve after the increase in that cost. Notice that when the price of a paperback is $50, the producers wants to sell only three paperbacks per month instead of four. The increase in cost has violated a ceteris paribus assumption and has caused the producer's supply curve to shift to the left. Similarly, a decrease in the cost of paper would cause the supply curve to shift to the right, as shown by S_3 in figure 4.10.

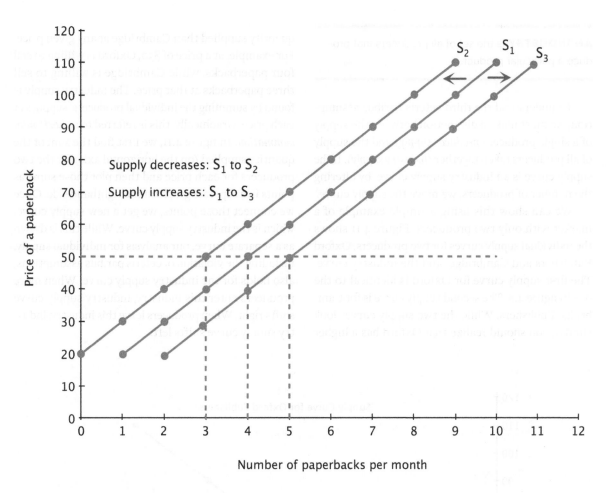

FIGURE 4.10 Supply Increase or Decrease

THE PRODUCER'S supply curve is the section of its marginal cost curve, which is above the average variable cost curve.

The second ceteris paribus assumption requires that the amount of capital and technology the producer has does not change. Recall that capital is land, buildings, and machinery; technology is an abstract measure of how efficient the producer is at converting factors into product. If the amount of technology the producer has increases, the producer will be able to produce a given amount of output at a lower cost. If the producer can produce the output at a lower cost, the minimum price the producer is willing to accept for a quantity of the good will decrease. The result is that the supply curve will shift to the right. A similar thing happens when the producer increases the amount of capital it has—if the producer increases its capital, it can produce a given amount of output at a lower cost, and, hence, the minimum price the producer is willing to receive for the product will fall. It is possible, however, for a producer to have too much capital (although, in practice, "too much" is usually such a large amount that most producers need not worry about it). If a producer has too much capital, adding more capital actually causes the producer's cost of production to rise. For our purposes, let us assume (unless we specifically say otherwise) that increasing capital causes the producer's cost of production to fall.

AN INDUSTRY is the set of all producers that produce a particular product.

To understand the third ceteris paribus assumption, we must make a distinction between the supply of a single producer (*producer supply*) and the supply of all producers taken together (*industry supply*). If the supply curve is an industry supply curve, by altering the number of producers, we move the supply curve.

We can show this using a simple example of a market with only two producers. Figure 4.11 shows the individual supply curves for two producers, Oxford Publishers and Cambridge, and the industry curve. The first supply curve for Oxford is identical to the one in figure 4.8. The second supply curve is for Cambridge Publishers. While the two supply curves look similar, you should realize that Oxford has a higher quantity supplied than Cambridge at any given price. For example, at a price of $50, Oxford is willing to sell four paperbacks, while Cambridge is willing to sell three paperbacks at that price. The industry supply is found by summing the individual producers' supplies at each price. Graphically, this is referred to as *horizontal summation*. In figure 4.11, we first find the sum of the quantity supplied (on the horizontal axis) for the two producers for each price and then plot those sums as points in a separate graph on the righthand side. Once we connect those points, we get a new supply curve, which is the industry supply curve. While this is drawn as a separate curve, our analysis for individual supply, including the violation of ceteris paribus assumptions, also holds for the industry supply curve. When more producers enter this industry, industry supply curve shifts right. When producers leave this industry, industry supply curve shifts left.

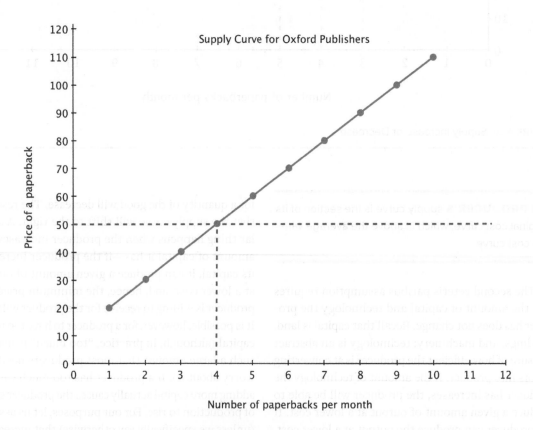

FIGURE 4.11 Derivation of Industry Supply Curve

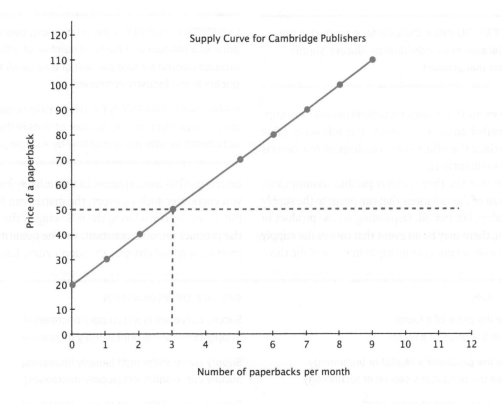

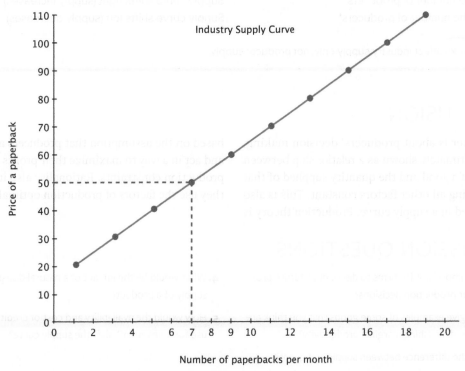

FIGURE 4.11 Derivation of Industry Supply Curve (continued)

INDUSTRY SUPPLY CURVE for a product is the horizontal sum of all individual producers' supply curves for that product.

INDUSTRY SUPPLY is the relationship between the price of a product and the total number of units of the product offered for sale per unit of time by all the producers in the industry combined.

PRODUCER SUPPLY is the relationship between the price of a product and the number of units of the product offered for sale per unit of time by a single producer.

Any event that violates a ceteris paribus assumption is called an *economic shock*. The following table summarizes the effects of violations of the ceteris paribus assumptions.

Note that the three ceteris paribus assumptions cover most of the violations that can occur to the supply relationship, but not all. Depending on the product in question, there may be an event that causes the supply curve to shift yet does not neatly fit into one of the three

ceteris paribus assumptions. In the unlikely event that you encounter such an event, the matter can be easily put to rest by considering the following: if the price of the product remains constant, yet the quantity of the product supplied changes, the supply curve has shifted.

VIOLATION	EFFECT OF VIOLATION
Increase the price of a factor	Supply curve shifts left (supply decreases)
Decrease the price of a factor	Supply curve shifts right (supply increases)
Increase the producer's capital or technology	Supply curve shifts right (supply increases)
Decrease the producer's capital or technology	Supply curve shifts left (supply decreases)
Increase the number of producers*	Supply curve shifts right (supply increases)
Decrease the number of producers*	Supply curve shifts left (supply decreases)

*These shocks affect industry supply only, not producer supply.

CONCLUSION

This chapter is about producers' decision making, which is ultimately shown as a relationship between the price of a good and the quantity supplied of that good, holding all other factors constant. This is also summarized in a supply curve. Production theory is based on the assumption that producers are rational and act in a way to maximize their profits given their production constraints. Rationality also implies that they use the factors of production optimally.

DISCUSSION QUESTIONS

1. Why is it important for firms to discount all future profits in their production decisions?

2. Can you give examples of some goods that you think are subject to diminishing marginal productivity?

3. What is the difference between supply and quantity supplied, and also between a producer's supply and industry supply?

4. What would be the impact of a natural disaster on the supply of a product?

5. How would the availability and cost of credit (that firms use for investment) shift the supply curve?

Mathematical Model Deriving Marginal Product and Average Product

Verbal Description: A firm uses labor and capital to produce a product. Find an expression for the firm's marginal product and average product.

Definitions: Let Q be the quantity of output the firm produces. Let L be the quantity of labor the firm employs, and let K be the quantity of capital the firm employs.

Assumptions: Let the firm's production function be $Q = L^2 K^3$.

Procedure: The marginal product of a factor is the derivative of the output function with respect to that factor. The average product of a factor is the ratio of the output function to the factor.

Solution: The marginal product of labor is given as follows:

$$\partial Q / \partial L = 2LK^3$$

The marginal product of capital is given as follows:

$$\partial Q / \partial K = 3L^2 K^2$$

The average product of labor is given as follows:

$$Q/L = LK^3$$

The average product of capital is given as follows:

$$Q/K = L^2 K^2$$

Problem: Plot these functions (with labor and capital on the horizontal axes) and note that the firm appears to be exactly between stages I and II (with respect to labor) *regardless* of how much labor it employs (i.e., marginal product increases as labor increases, but it neither increases at an increasing rate [as it would in stage I] nor increases at a decreasing rate [as it would in stage II]). Note also that the firm is also always in stage I with respect to capital, no matter how much capital it employs.

Derive the marginal products and average products for labor and capital and comment on which stage the firm is in with respect to each factor for the following production functions (where a is a positive constant):

1. $Q = \sqrt{LK}$

2. $Q = LK - aL^2 K^2$

3. $Q = L^2 K^2 - aL^3 K^3$

Mathematical Model Deriving the Optimal Factor Combination

Verbal Description: A firm uses labor and capital to produce a product. Find the optimal combination of labor and capital for the firm to employ.

Definitions: Let Q be the quantity of output the firm produces. Let L be the quantity of labor the firm employs, and let K be the quantity of capital the firm employs. Let the prices of labor and capital be P_L and P_K, respectively.

Assumptions: Let the firm's production function be $Q = L^2 K^3$.

Procedure: Derive an expression for the ratio of the marginal product of each factor to its price. Set these ratios equal. Solve for the ratio K/L.

Solution: The marginal product of labor is given as follows:

$$\partial Q / \partial L = 2LK^3$$

The marginal product of capital is given as follows:

$$\partial Q / \partial K = 3L^2 K^2$$

Setting the ratios of these to their prices equal to each other yields the following:

$$\frac{2LK^3}{P_L} = \frac{3L^2 K^2}{P_K}$$

Solving for K/L yields the following:

$$\frac{K}{L} = \frac{3P_L}{2P_K}$$

Thus, we see that the firm should employ $3P_L/2P_K$ units of capital for every one unit of labor.

Problem: Derive the optimal combinations of capital and labor for each of the production functions below:

1. $Q = \sqrt{LK}$

2. $Q = L^2 K^2$

3. $Q = L^2 K$

Mathematical Model Deriving the Cost Curves

Verbal Description: A firm uses labor and capital to produce a product. Derive and plot the firm's average variable cost, average fixed cost, average total cost, and marginal cost curves.

Definitions: Let Q be the quantity of output the firm produces. Let L be the quantity of labor, and let K be the quantity of capital the firm employs. Let the prices of labor and capital be P_L and P_K, respectively. Let the depreciation rate of capital be δ.

Assumptions: Let the firm's production function be $Q = LK - L^{3/2}K^{3/2}$. Let the price of labor (P_L) be $10, the price of capital (P_K) be $100, and the depreciation rate (δ) be 0.1. The firm has one thousand units of capital in the short run (i.e., $K = 1,000$).

Procedure: 1. We know that the optimal combination of labor and capital is as follows:

$$\frac{K}{L} = \frac{P_K}{P_L}$$

Solving this expression for K, we have

$$K = \left(\frac{P_L}{P_K}\right)L$$

2. Substituting the optimal factor combination into the production function, we have the expression for output, given that the firm employs the optimal combination of labor and capital:

$$K = \left(\frac{P_L}{P_K}\right)L^2 - \left(\frac{P_L}{P_K}\right)^{3/2}L^3$$

3. We know that the average variable cost is given by

$$AVC = \frac{VC}{Outout} = \frac{(P_L)(L)}{\dfrac{P_L}{P_K}L^2 - \left(\dfrac{P_L}{P_K}\right)^{3/2}L^3}$$

While we cannot write the AVC function in terms of L, we can select arbitrary values for L, compute both the AVC and the output, and plot the AVC against the output. For example, suppose that $P_L = 10 and $P_K = 100. Setting $L = 1$, we have AVC = 0.14 and $Q = 0.03$. This gives us one point on the AVC curve ($Q = 0.03$, AVC = 0.14).

Mathematical Model (continued)

4. The firm's average fixed cost is equal to its fixed cost (FC) divided by its quantity of output:

$$AFC = \frac{FC}{Output}$$

The firm's fixed cost (FC) is equal to the value of the capital it will lose to depreciation. A depreciation rate of d means that the firm will lose (on average) d units of capital for every one unit of capital the firm has. Thus, the total number of units of capital the firm will lose to depreciation is dK. The value of this loss is found by multiplying the number of depreciated units by the price of capital. Thus,

$$FC = \delta K P_K$$

The average fixed cost curve can be plotted by selecting arbitrary values for L, computing Q and AFC, and plotting AFC against Q.

5. The firm's average total cost is found by adding the firm's average variable cost and average fixed cost at each value of Q.

$$ATC = AVC + AFC$$

6. We know that the marginal cost is

$$MC = \frac{P_L}{MP_L}$$

The firm's marginal product is

$$MP_L = \frac{\partial Q}{\partial L}$$

The firm's marginal cost curve can be determined by finding the equation for marginal product of labor, selecting arbitrary values for L, finding Q and MC, and plotting MC against Q.

Demand and Supply in the Product Market

5

British football hooligans were all in a "tizzy" last winter when they convened at their local watering hole in Brigg and found out that the price of beer had increased. It would now cost them 10 percent more (now nearly 3 pounds) to enjoy a pint while cheering madly for their dearest team. Lucy Fensome, the landlady of the Brigg pub, believes that, unlike the football fanatics, most of her regulars will understand the price increase. But what causes the price of such a coveted commodity to increase? It is the result of an increase in the price of a major ingredient of beer: barley. The price of barley in Britain rose by 90 percent in 2010. So, what caused the price of barley to increase? John Woods, a North Lincolnshire farmer, has continued to grow barley even after many farmers have switched over to crops that are considered more profitable, such as wheat. Mr. Woods is now reaping the benefits and says, "I think because barley became unfashionable, people stopped growing it. So it is a simple supply and demand equation.'" We will learn about market equilibrium and how shifts of supply and demand alter price in this chapter. We will also learn about the different things that shift supply and demand, such as changes in the price of inputs and changes in preferences.

---

1   http://news.bbc.co.uk/local/humberside/hi/people_and_places/newsid_9378000/9378678.stm

Markets

Market and Equilibrium

Demand summarizes the behavior of consumers. Supply summarizes the behavior of producers. When we put consumers and producers together, they begin to interact. The interaction between consumers and producers concerning a particular product is called a *market*. The market for chairs is the sum of all the interactions of producers of chairs and consumers of chairs. The market for computers is the sum of all the interactions of producers of computers and consumers of computers.

When producers and consumers come together to form a market, the market immediately begins to move toward equilibrium. *Equilibrium* is a state in which the number of units of product consumers are willing to buy per unit of time is exactly equal to the number of units of product producers are willing to offer for sale per unit of time.

EQUILIBRIUM is a state in which the quantity demanded of a product is equal to the quantity supplied.

Consider the market for paperback textbooks shown in figure 5.1. This market is in equilibrium when the price is $60, because at that price both quantity demanded and quantity supplied are equal at five units.

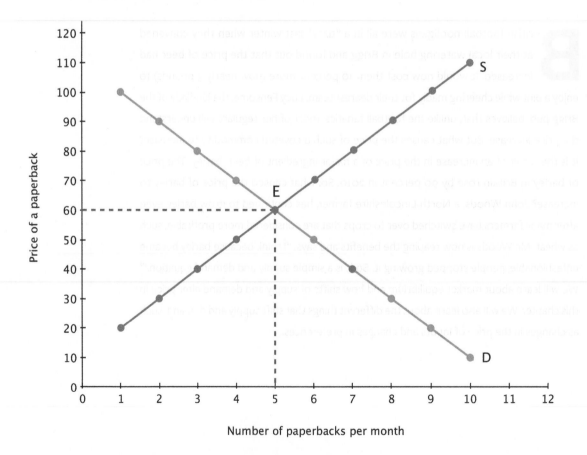

FIGURE 5.1 Market Equilibrium

When the price of a paperback is $80, consumers are willing to buy three units per month and producers are willing to offer for sale seven units per month. The result is that when the producers and consumers come together, only three units will actually be *sold*. The remaining five units will sit on the store shelf as unsold inventory. This extra four units per day is called a *surplus*. This is shown in figure 5.2. A *surplus* is a condition in which the quantity demanded of a product is less than the quantity supplied.

The unsold product represents a cost to the producers—the product is taking up shelf space needed for units just coming out of the factory. The units just coming out of the factory are taking up space needed by product just being produced. The whole manufacturing process has become backed up, and the firm finds itself paying for labor and materials to produce product that

consumers aren't buying. So, what happens? Producers compete against each other, trying to entice consumers to buy their excess product, not their competitors'. The way the producers compete is by offering lower prices for their products. The surplus causes the price of the product to fall. As the price of the product falls, the quantity demanded by the consumers rises. Also, as the price of the product falls, the quantity supplied by the producers falls.

Figure 5.2 shows the market as it approaches equilibrium. The surplus has caused the price of the product to fall from $80 to $70. As the price fell, the quantity demanded rose from three units to four units. Also, as the price fell, the quantity supplied fell from seven units to six units. The result is that the market is still in surplus, but the surplus is now only two units. Because of the surplus, the price will continue to fall.

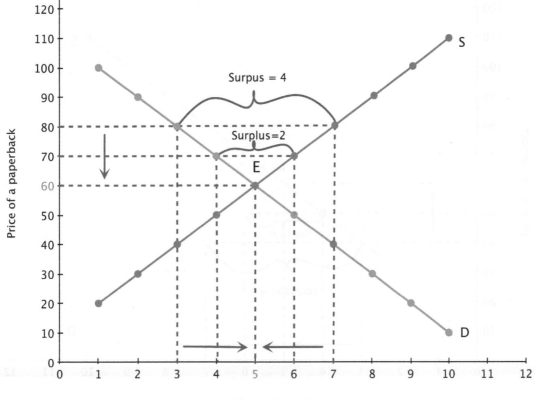

FIGURE 5.2 Surplus in the Market and Move to Equilibrium

Eventually, the price will fall to $60. When the price reaches $60, the quantity demanded of the product is five units per month, and the quantity supplied of the product is also five units per month. Because the surplus is gone, producers do not need to compete with each other by lowering their prices, because they can sell exactly as much as they want to produce. Therefore, the price of the product stops falling.

A **surplus** is a state in which the quantity demanded of a product is less than the quantity supplied.

Consider the case in figure 5.3. When the price of the product is $40, consumers are willing to buy seven units of the product, but at that price producers are willing to offer only three units. When we bring the producers and the consumers together, only three units will be *sold* every day. The difference of four units is called a shortage. A *shortage* is a state in which the quantity demanded of a product is greater than the quantity supplied. Let us suppose that anyone who would buy this product would buy only one unit per month. When the price of the product is $40, consumers (as a group) are willing to buy a total of seven units—this means that when the price of the product is $40, there are more consumers looking to buy the product than there are products for. How do we know which of the consumers will get the product? The answer is that the consumers will compete with each other for the limited product. The way a consumer competes with other consumers is by offering a higher price to

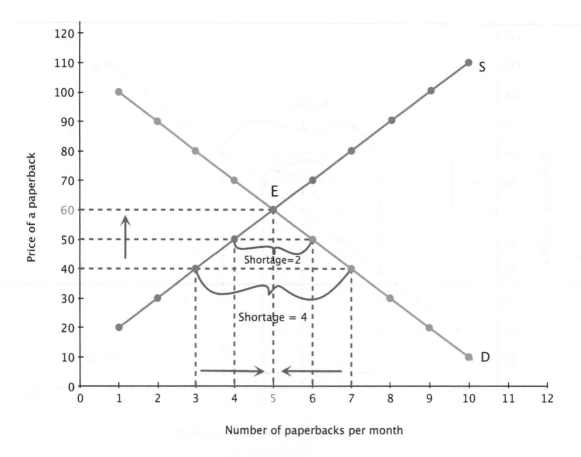

FIGURE 5.3 Shortage in the Market and Move to Equilibrium

the producer than the other consumers are offering[2]. The result is that the price of the product will rise. As the price of the product rises, the quantity demanded will fall and the quantity supplied will rise.

A SHORTAGE is a state in which the quantity demanded of a product is greater than the quantity supplied.

Figure 5.3 also shows the effect of the shortage on the market for our product. The shortage causes the price of the product to rise. As the price rises to $50, consumers are willing to buy fewer units, so the quantity demanded falls from seven units to six units.

Also, as the price rises to $50, producers are willing to offer more units, so the quantity supplied rises from three units to four units. When the price of the product reaches $50, the market is still in shortage, so the price continues to rise.

In fact, the price will continue to rise until it reaches $60. When the price is $60 (as shown in figure 5.3), consumers are willing to buy five units of the product, and producers are willing to offer five units for sale. At a price of $60, the quantity demanded equals the quantity supplied. There is no shortage, which means there is no competition among the consumers that would drive the price upward. There is no surplus, which means there is no competition among the producers that would cause the price to fall.[3]

MARIJUANA LEGALIZATION IN COLORADO AND EXCESS DEMAND Colorado is the first state to have legalized marijuana sales, which became effective on January 1, 2014. Sales are limited to adults age twenty-one and older who can purchase up to one ounce from licensed stores. At the same time, Colorado residents can grow marijuana on their own for their personal use—again, up to a certain limit, which is six plants with only three flowering at a given time. The state government didn't impose any other price restrictions and left this "new" market to demand-and-supply forces.

With the start of sales on January 1, 2014, there was an influx of resident and nonresident consumers to licensed marijuana retailers throughout the state, which led to shortages or excess demand. Given the lack of artificial price restrictions, eventually marijuana prices rose soon after official sales started. This is what we expect given our knowledge of shortages and move to market equilibrium.

All markets constantly try to move toward equilibrium. How quickly or slowly a market achieves equilibrium depends on a number of factors: how much time it takes to produce the product, the cost of holding unsold product in inventory, how easily the consumer can judge the quality of the product, the difference between the current price of the product and the equilibrium price, and so on. Some markets, such as the housing market, require months to achieve equilibrium because of the costs involved in searching for a suitable house and then moving. Some markets,

such as the stock market, can achieve equilibrium in a matter of seconds because of the low (almost zero) cost of conducting stock transactions.

IN A FREE MARKET, a surplus causes price to fall; a shortage causes price to rise.

---

2   In advanced economies, the consumers do not usually haggle with the producer or against other consumers. Rather, the consumer looks at the price the producer asks and either accepts (i.e., buys) or rejects (i.e., does not buy). In such economies, consumers still compete with each other; the competition is, however, more subtle. The producers will ask higher and higher prices, and some consumers will accept the higher prices while others will reject. The result is the same as if the consumers had bid the prices against each other.

3   Another interpretation is that the upward pressure on price exerted by producers seeking ever higher prices is balanced with the downward pressure on price exerted by consumers seeking ever lower prices.

Shocks and the Return to Equilibrium

A *shock* is any violation of a ceteris paribus assumption. If you begin with a market that is in equilibrium and then introduce a shock, either the demand or the supply curve will shift, resulting in a disequilibrium.

Consider the following example. Let's say the equilibrium price of aspirin is $4 per bottle. In equilibrium, there are ten thousand bottles of aspirin sold across the country every day. The market for aspirin is shown in figure 5.4.

A scientific report is published, which says that people who take an aspirin every day have a significantly lower incidence of heart attacks than do people who do not take an aspirin every day. This report alters how people feel about aspirin *independent of the price of*

aspirin, the prices of any other goods, and their incomes. This report has violated the ceteris paribus assumption for demand "fixed preferences."

By increasing people's preferences for aspirin, the demand curve for aspirin shifts to the right. Figure 5.5 shows the movement in the demand curve from D_1 to D_2 caused by the violation of the ceteris paribus assumption. When the price of aspirin was $4, consumers were willing to buy ten thousand bottles of aspirin per day. Now, when the price of aspirin is $4, consumers are willing to buy fourteen thousand bottles of aspirin per day. The change in preferences, however, does not affect the supply curve. Before the report was released, producers were willing to offer

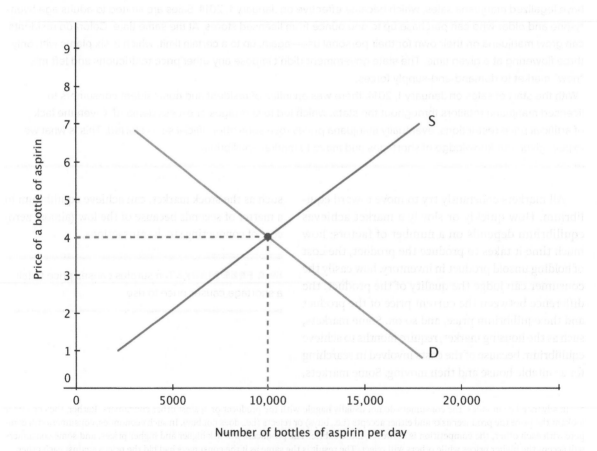

FIGURE 5.4 Market Equilibrium and Shocks

ten thousand bottles for sale per day at a price of $4. After the report was released, producers are still willing to offer only ten thousand bottles for sale per day *at a price of $4*. The result is a shortage. The price of aspirin is $4: consumers are willing to buy fourteen thousand bottles, and producers are willing to offer only ten thousand bottles. The shortage causes the price of aspirin to rise. The shift in demand and the resulting shortage is shown in figure 5.5.

The shortage of aspirin causes the price of aspirin to rise. As the price rises, the number of units consumers are willing to buy (the quantity demanded) falls, and the number of units producers are willing to offer (the quantity supplied) rises. The quantity demanded continues to fall, and the quantity supplied continues to rise until the two become equal. When the quantity demanded and quantity supplied are equal, there is no

further shortage and the price stops rising. The market has achieved a new equilibrium. Figure 5.5 also shows the market for aspirin moving to its new equilibrium. When the price of aspirin is $4, there is a shortage of four thousand bottles per day. The shortage causes the price of aspirin to rise. As the price rises, the quantity demanded falls and the quantity supplied rises. Quantity demanded and quantity supplied become equal at twelve thousand bottles per day. At this point, the price of aspirin has reached $5 per bottle. Because the shortage is gone, the price stops rising. At the new equilibrium, the price of aspirin is $5 per bottle, and twelve thousand bottles are sold every day.

Let's now consider the case of a supply shift using our previous example of paperback textbooks. Currently, the price of a paperback is $60. The equilibrium for the market is a price of $60 and a quantity sold

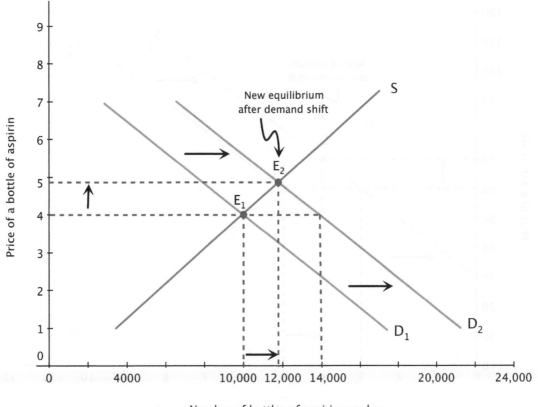

FIGURE 5.5 Market Equilibrium and Demand Shift

of five paperbacks. Figure 5.6 shows the market at its starting equilibrium.

Because paper is an input in the production of paperback textbooks, an increase in the price of paper violates the ceteris paribus assumption for supply that requires that the prices of factors or inputs not change. The violation causes the supply curve to shift to the left. When the curve shifts to the left, at a price of $60, the quantity supplied of paperbacks is three and the quantity demanded is five. The shock has caused a shortage in the market for paperbacks. The shortage will cause the price to rise until the quantity demanded and quantity supplied are again equal.

Figure 5.6 shows the effect of the increase in paper on the market for paperbacks. The market moves from the old equilibrium of five paperbacks per month and a price of $60 to the new equilibrium of four paperbacks

and a price of $70. The result of the increase in the price of paper, then, is that fewer paperbacks will be sold, and they will cost more per unit.

It is also quite possible that both demand and supply shift at the same time. While the price of paper increases, we also see a rise in the income of consumers of paperback textbooks. We then have two shocks occurring simultaneously: a shock to supply (an increase in the price of an input) and a shock to demand (an increase in consumers' incomes). When two shocks occur simultaneously and we don't know which shock has the greater impact, we must consider two cases: the case in which the impact on supply is larger than the impact on demand, and the case in which the impact on demand is larger than the impact on supply.

Figure 5.7 shows the case in which the impact of the shock on supply is larger than the impact of the shock

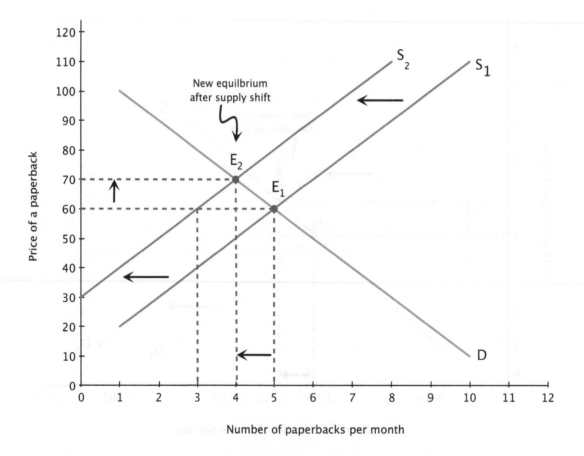

FIGURE 5.6 Market Equilibrium and Supply Shift

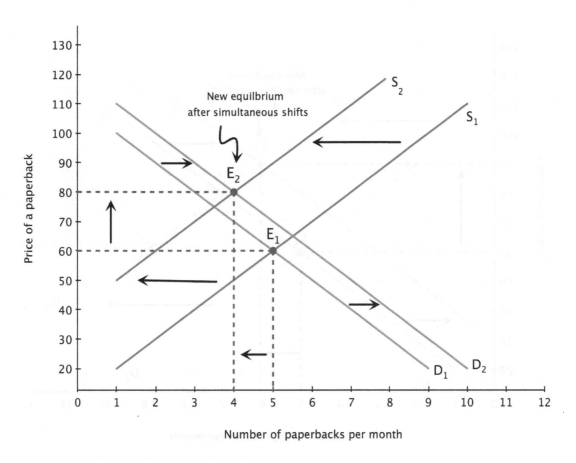

FIGURE 5.7 Simultaneous Shifts with Stronger Supply Shift

on demand. Because the impact of the shock is larger on supply, the supply curve shifts by a greater amount than does the demand curve. The result of the two shocks is that the market for paperbacks moves from the old equilibrium of five paperbacks sold at a price of $60 to the new equilibrium of four paperbacks sold at a price of $80. Does this mean that the two shocks always result in an increase in the price of paperbacks and a decrease in the quantity sold? Not necessarily:

consider figure 5.8. In that figure, the impact of the shock on demand is greater than the impact of the shock on supply. Notice that, like in figure 5.7, the demand curve is shifting to the right and the supply curve is shifting to the left. The paperback market in figure 5.8 moves from the old equilibrium of five paperbacks sold per month at a price of $60 to the new equilibrium of six paperbacks sold per month at a price of $90.

The Effects of Price Controls

Price controls are legal limits imposed on the prices of products. Price controls come in two forms: price ceilings and price floors. A *price ceiling* is a legally imposed upper limit on the price of a product. A *price*

floor is a legally imposed lower limit on the price of a product.

Consider the market for housing in San Francisco in 1906 (this is a true story; the quantities and prices

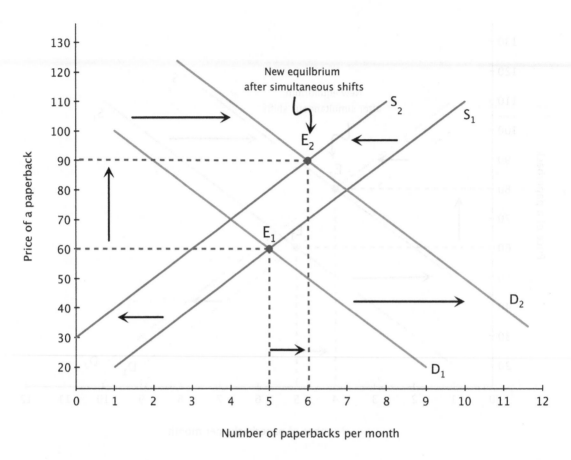

FIGURE 5.8 Simultaneous Shift with Stronger Demand Shift

are fictitious). There was a devastating earthquake in 1906 that leveled much of the city. Much of what survived the earthquake was subsequently consumed in the fires that resulted from the quake. Figure 5.9 shows the market for housing in San Francisco prior to the earthquake. Prior to the earthquake, the price of housing was $5,000 per year, and there were twenty thousand housing units sold per year.[4]

A PRICE CEILING is a legally imposed upper limit on the price of a product.
A PRICE FLOOR is a legally imposed lower limit on the price of a product.

The earthquake destroyed a substantial number of housing units. Destroying a building that someone rents out for apartments decreases the number of producers of housing. Thus, the earthquake violated the ceteris paribus assumption of supply that requires that the number of producers not change. This shock caused the supply curve for housing to shift to the left, as shown in figure 5.10.

The shift in supply caused a shortage of housing to develop at the $5,000 price. At $5,000, the quantity demanded of housing was twenty thousand units, and the quantity supplied was ten thousand units. This left a ten-thousand-unit shortage. Normally, this shortage would cause the price of housing to rise. However, the

4   You can think of the "price of housing" as being either the rental price for an apartment or the mortgage payment for a house. The figures here are expressed in per-year terms. A "housing unit" is a house or apartment.

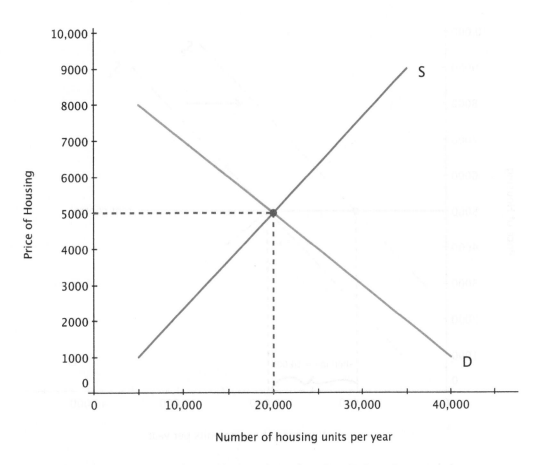

FIGURE 5.9 Equilibrium in the Housing Market in San Francisco

city council, fearing that rising housing costs would only compound the people's misery, imposed a price ceiling on housing at the $5,000 price. Thus, by law, no one was allowed to charge more than $5,000 per year for a housing unit.

The problem is that at $5,000 per unit, producers are willing to offer only ten thousand housing units per year. As long as the price is prevented from rising, producers have no incentive to offer more housing. This shortage of housing remained for several years. Finally, the city council realized that there were many people willing to pay more than $5,000 per year for

housing and that the producers of housing would not produce more housing unless then received more than $5,000 per unit. In short, the city council realized that the price ceiling was the cause of the persistent housing shortage. The city removed the price ceiling, and very quickly the price of housing rose to its new equilibrium of $6,000. As the price of housing rose, the shortage disappeared.

Another interesting thing happened. Now that the price of housing was $6,000, people who owned apartment buildings and who built houses were earning more profit than people in other businesses.[5] Some

5   You can prove this by pointing out the fact that before the earthquake, the people who offered housing were earning just as much profit (adjusted for risk) as people who owned other businesses. If this were not the case, producers would have moved into or out of the housing industry depending on whether it offered more or less profit than other industries, and we would have been left with a new equilibrium price of housing that provided the producers of housing with exactly the same amount of profit (adjusted for risk) as producers in other industries.

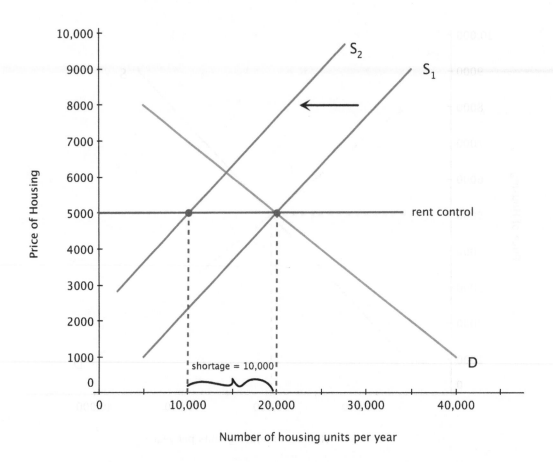

FIGURE 5.10 Supply Shock and Price Ceiling (Rent Control) in the Aftermath of the San Francisco Earthquake

of these people in other businesses closed down their other businesses and went into the housing business as producers of housing. As more and more producers moved into the market for housing, the ceteris paribus assumption for supply requiring that the number of producers remain fixed was again violated—this time in the other direction. The supply curve shifted back to its original position. The market then moved to its original equilibrium of twenty thousand housing units sold per year at a price of $5,000 per unit.

Contrast this example with the same city, San Francisco, and the earthquake of 1989. In 1989 another devastating earthquake hit San Francisco, with much the same effect as the earthquake of 1906. The number of producers of housing dropped as housing units were destroyed and the supply curve for housing shifted left. This time, however, the city council allowed the price

of housing to rise. As the price of housing rose, producers who were in the housing industry made much profit. Other producers, seeing the profit, entered the housing industry. The result: within six months the housing market had returned to its original equilibrium. In 1906, it took years for the market to return to equilibrium because the price ceiling prevented the price of housing from rising, which prevented housing producers from earning large profits, which prevented producers of other products from entering the housing market and offering housing.

A *price floor* is a legally imposed lower limit on price. The most prevalent example of a price floor is the minimum wage. One interpretation of the minimum wage is that it prevents employers from paying employees less than a certain amount. The other (equally valid) interpretation of the minimum wage is that it prevents employees from selling their labor for less than a certain amount—even if they are willing to sell their labor for less.

Consider the market for labor. Keep in mind that in the market for labor, the traditional roles of producer and consumer are reversed. The producers (those offering the product) are the people (i.e., the employees). The consumers (those desiring the product) are the firms (i.e., the employers). This means that the supply curve (and its ceteris paribus assumptions) refers to the people, while the demand curve (and its ceteris paribus assumptions) refers to the firms.

It seemed that toward the end of Reagan's presidency, the market for labor was in equilibrium. There was a minimum wage of $3.35 per hour, but most employers were paying more than that. Let us suppose that the lowest wage that employers were paying was

$3.75. The market did not want to pay workers less than $3.35; in fact, the market wanted to pay more. The result is that the minimum wage (practically speaking) did not exist. Figure 5.11 shows the market for labor that would normally be considered "minimum wage" labor (although the workers are earning more than the minimum wage). According to the figure, the equilibrium wage was $3.75 per hour, and there were 9.6 million labor hours sold each month (at forty hours per week per person, this translates into sixty thousand workers being employed every month).

If sixty thousand workers have jobs in any given month, how much unemployment is there? Does the amount of unemployment depend on the number of people in society? Suppose that there are eighty thousand people in this society. If sixty thousand of them are employed, how much unemployment is there? The

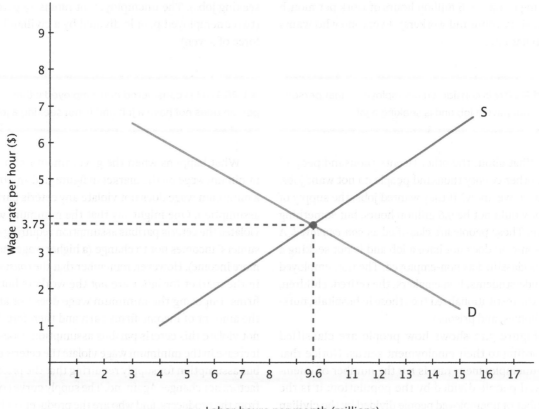

FIGURE 5.11 Price Floor (Minimum Wage)

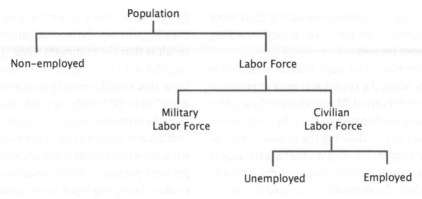

FIGURE 5.12 Employed, Unemployed, Non-employed

answer is none. A person is considered *unemployed* if that person does not have a job and is seeking a job. According to figure 5.11, when the wage rate is $3.75, employers desire 9.6 million hours of work per month (i.e., sixty thousand jobs), and employees are willing to offer 9.6 million hours of work per month (i.e., sixty thousand workers). Everyone who wants a job has one.

A PERSON is considered unemployed if that person does not have a job and is seeking a job.

What about the other twenty thousand people? The other twenty thousand people do not want jobs. How do we know? If they wanted jobs, the supply of labor would not be 9.6 million hours, but something more. These people are classified as *non-employed*. A person who does not have a job and is not seeking a job is classified as non-employed. The non-employed include students, homemakers, the retired, children, and the institutionalized (i.e., those in hospitals, nursing homes, and prisons).

Figure 5.12 shows how people are classified according to their employment status. Notice that the unemployment rate is *not* the number of unemployed people divided by the population; it is the number of unemployed people divided by the civilian labor force. The unemployment calculation does not take into account people who are non-employed. For example, suppose that the population consists of ten

people, three of whom are non-employed (such as students or the retired), five of whom are employed, and two of whom are unemployed (they do not have jobs, but are seeking jobs). The civilian labor force is seven (the five who have jobs, plus the two who are seeking jobs). The unemployment rate is 29 percent (two unemployed people divided by a civilian labor force of seven).

A PERSON is considered non-employed if that person does not have a job and is not seeking a job.

What happens when the government imposes a minimum wage on the market in figure 5.13? Imposing a minimum wage does not violate any ceteris paribus assumption. One might say that the minimum wage violates the ceteris paribus assumption requiring consumers' incomes not to change (a higher wage means more income). However, remember that the *consumers* in the market for labor are *not* the workers but the firms. Imposing the minimum wage does not affect the amount of income firms earn and therefore does not violate this ceteris paribus assumption. Does the increase in the minimum wage violate the ceteris paribus assumption for supply requiring that the prices of factors not change? Again, no. The supply curve comes from the producers, and who are the producers of labor in the market for labor? The workers. In order for the minimum wage to violate this ceteris paribus assumption, it would somehow have to increase the prices of

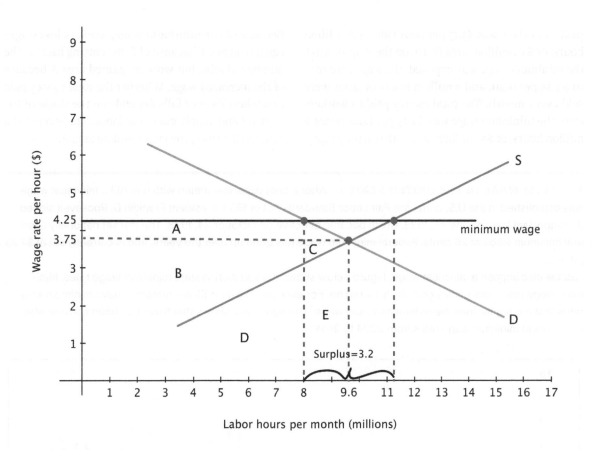

FIGURE 5.13 Price Floor (Minimum Wage)

factors that went into the production of people.[6] The bottom line is that the minimum wage does not violate any ceteris paribus assumptions in the market for labor, so neither the demand curve for labor nor the supply curve of labor will shift.

Congress increased the minimum wage to $4.25 per hour in 1991. This price floor was above the then-equilibrium price of $3.75. The result of the increase in the minimum wage was (1) to increase the number of workers who were willing to work (i.e., some of the non-employed joined the work force) and (2) to decrease the number of workers firms desired (i.e., some of the employed became unemployed).

Figure 5.13 shows the effect of imposing a minimum wage, which is above the equilibrium wage rate. When the minimum wage is imposed, the wage rate immediately (by law) increases from $3.75 per hour to $4.25 per hour. Because the wage is higher, workers are willing to offer more hours of their time to employers, and employers are less willing to purchase labor. The result is that the number of people seeking jobs rises from sixty thousand to seventy thousand per month (i.e., from 9.6 million hours to 11.2 million hours of labor per month). The number of jobs available, however, declines from sixty thousand jobs to fifty thousand jobs per month (i.e., from 9.6 million hours to 8 million hours per month). The result is a surplus of 3.2 million hours of labor, or twenty thousand workers.

Notice the areas labeled A through E in figure 5.13. When the wage rate was $3.75, there were 9.6 million hours of labor sold every month. The total money

6   We all know what goes into the production of people. Fortunately, the government has yet to regulate any of that.

paid to workers was $3.75 per hour times 9.6 million hours, or $36 million (area BCDE on the graph). After the minimum wage was imposed, the wage rate rose to $4.25 per hour, and 8 million hours of labor were sold every month. The total money paid to workers after the minimum wage was $4.25 per hour times 8 million hours, or $34 million (area ABD on the graph).

Because of the minimum wage, workers lost wages equal to area CE because of firms cutting back on the number of jobs, but workers gained area A because of the increased wage. Whether the total money paid to workers rises or falls depends on the shape of the demand and supply curves of labor. The steeper the demand for labor, the larger will be area A.

MINIMUM WAGE IN THE UNITED STATES   After a brief experimentation with it in 1933, minimum wage was established in the U.S. under the Fair Labor Standards Act of 1938. President Franklin D. Roosevelt signed this important law on June 25, 1938, which became effective on October 24, 1938. The law set nationally a federal minimum wage at 25 cents. Federal minimum wage has gone up over the years, and is currently set at $7.25 per hour.

 States also impose a minimum wage. Figure below shows the variation in state minimum wage rates. Minimum wage rates vary quite significantly by region. For example, Western States generally have minimum wage rates that are higher than the federal minimum wage. The figure also shows that there has been considerable increases in minimum wage rates from 2004 to 2014.

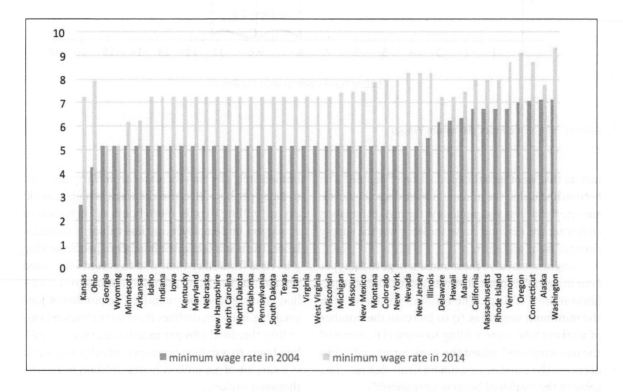

Source: Bureau of Labor Statistics, Monthly Labor Review, January issues; Department of Labor, Employee Standards Administration, http://www.dol.gov/esa/minwage/america.htm

CONCLUSION

In this chapter we brought together what we learned in Chapters 3 and 4, and examined both demand and supply in a market. We have seen that consumers and producers would interact within a market, and the market would move towards an equilibrium where the quantity demanded is equal to the quantity supplied. We have also examined how a market equilibrium would change when there are demand and supply shifts. Markets may not always reach an equilibrium particularly when there are artificial price controls. In the case of a price ceiling, we end up with a shortage in that market. Rent control is a good example of a price ceiling. In the case of a price floor, we end up with a surplus in that market. Minimum wage is a good example of a price floor.

DISCUSSION QUESTIONS

1. Explain how markets would move towards an equilibrium. Why would markets stay at that equilibrium point?

2. Can you explain recent price changes for certain food products (e.g. corn, soybean, milk) using our demand-supply framework? Show how market equilibrium would change.

3. Why do we get ambiguous results on either price or quantity changes when there are simultaneous shifts of demand and supply curves?

4. What is a price floor? What is a price ceiling? Explain and give examples other than the ones used in this chapter.

5. Would a minimum wage really lead to unemployment? How does the U.S. compare to other countries in terms of minimum wage rates? How does the minimum wage help with inequality in the U.S.? What is the empirical evidence on the economic consequences of minimum wage?

PART 3

Markets in Action

6

Role of Prices, Surplus, and Elasticity

Over the past decade, Afghanistan has seen tremendous success in controlling opium poppy seed cultivation. Unfortunately, recently this progress has come to a standstill. Prices and the demand for the drug continue to soar. Afghanistan's Western allies provide little assistance in the war on opium, as they are more concerned with fighting terrorism. Since it is difficult to convince farmers not to cultivate the poppy seed, it is likely that the country's attempts to curtail the drug will continue to falter. Opium prices increased from $29 per pound in 2009 to $77 per pound in 2010. Yet, people still consume about $58 billion worth of opiate-based narcotics because of the drugs' highly addictive nature.[1] This may seem odd because we have already showed that there is a negative relationship between the quantity demanded of a product and its price. One would expect that this 265 percent price increase would induce a severe decrease in the quantity of opium consumed. In this chapter, we will learn that the demand's responsiveness depends on its *elasticity*. We will also learn about the role of prices and the way to quantify the net benefits from exchange to consumers and producers in a market economy.

The Role of Prices in a Market Economy

Like traffic signals that encourage an orderly and efficient flow of transportation, the price mechanism guides society's scarce resources toward their most-valued uses. In other words, prices signal to people what to produce, how to produce, and for whom to produce—as if every individual is being led, in Adam Smith's words, "by an

---

1 *Pamela Constable,* "As opium prices soar and allies focus on Taliban, Afghan drug war stumbles," *Washington Post Foreign Service,* January 14, 2011, http://www.washingtonpost.com/wp-dyn/content/article/2011/01/13/AR2011011306738. html?hpid=topnews.

invisible hand to promote an end, which was no part of his intention."[2] The price mechanism ensures an efficient allocation of resources in a competitive free market. In most instances and under certain conditions, society's interest is served best when it allows for a free determination of prices by competitive markets.[3]

How can we show that this is indeed the case? We need a way to show quantitatively the benefits and costs to both consumers and producers from their actions in a market economy. We now turn to consumer and producer surplus analysis.

Consumer, Producer, and Total Surplus

Suppose you are thinking about buying a car from a friend. You look the car over and decide on the maximum price you would be willing to pay. You don't tell your friend (of course), but you decide that the maximum you are willing to pay for the car is $3,000. Your friend, on the other hand, doesn't tell you, but knows that the minimum price he would be willing to accept for the car is $2,000. Suppose that you offer your friend $2,700 for the car. You have paid $300 less than the maximum you were willing to pay—we say that you have a *consumer surplus* of $300. Your friend has received $700 more than the minimum he was willing to accept—we say that he has a *producer surplus* of $700. *Consumer surplus* is an extra amount of money that consumers were willing to pay for a quantity of a product *but they did not have to pay. Producer surplus* is an extra amount of money that producers receive for a quantity of a product *in excess of the minimum required to entice them offer the product.*[4]

Producer surplus is not equal to profit, but it is proportional to profit. If producer surplus rises by $1, producer profit rises by $1; if producer surplus falls by $1, producer profit falls by $1. Thus, the *change* in producer surplus is the same as the *change* in producer profit.[5]

CONSUMER SURPLUS is an extra amount of money that consumers were willing, but did not have to pay for a quantity of a product.

PRODUCER SURPLUS is an extra amount of money that producers did not have to receive to entice them to offer a quantity of a product.

PRODUCER SURPLUS is a dollar measure that is proportional to producers' profits.

Producer Surplus = Total Revenue – Variable Cost

Consider the happiness a person obtains from consuming a product. We call this happiness *utility*. When a person goes out and buys, for example, a beer, he receives utility (happiness) when he consumes the beer and loses utility when he pays for the beer. We can call the amount of utility the person is left with (what is gained from consuming the beer minus what is lost from paying for it) *net utility*.

---

2 Adam Smith, *The Theory of Moral Sentiments*, Indianapolis: Liberty Fund, 1984, 184–185. http://files.libertyfund.org/files/192/ 0141-01_Bk.pdf

3 We will examine when markets fail to achieve efficiency in chapter 8.

4 Be careful not to confuse the idea of consumer surplus and producer surplus with just the word surplus, which implies overproduction. A *surplus* is a state in which quantity demanded is less than quantity supplied. A consumer (or producer) surplus is an entirely different animal. It is quite unfortunate, but the technical terms used in economics sometimes are either similar to other technical terms or similar to words used in common language, yet they represent an entirely different concept.

5 It turns out that producer surplus is the same as profit plus fixed cost. Thus, a firm that has a producer surplus of (for example) $1,000 may or may not be making a profit. If the firm's fixed cost is $200, the firm is making $800 economic profit ($1,000 = $800 + $200). If the firm's fixed cost is $1,500, the firm is making a $500 economic loss ($1,000 = –$500 + $1,500). What is certain is that an *increase* in producer surplus is the same as an *increase* in profit because fixed cost does not change in the short run.

NET UTILITY is the utility derived from consuming a product minus the utility lost from paying for it.

Consumer surplus is the dollar value of a consumer's net utility (i.e., how much the net utility is worth to the consumer as measured in dollars). While there is no way to measure utility or to compare one person's utility to another's, it is very easy to measure a person's consumer surplus. Suppose that I have a pizza, which you want. I offer to sell you the pizza for $100, and you tell me to get lost. I offer to sell you the pizza for $30, and you ignore me. I offer to sell you the pizza for $10, and you are indifferent between buying the pizza and not. Because you are indifferent between having the pizza and keeping your $10, we know that the utility you expect to get from the pizza exactly equals the utility you expect to get from the $10. Thus, the dollar value of the utility you would obtain from the pizza is $10. Now, suppose that I offer to sell you this pizza for $6. If you buy the pizza, your consumer surplus will be $4 (you get $10 worth of utility from the pizza and lose $6 worth of utility when you pay for it). What if you don't buy the pizza? If you don't buy the pizza, your consumer surplus is zero (you get $0 worth of utility from having no pizza and lose no utility because you pay nothing).[6]

Imagine that you go out for beer and pizza. When you leave the restaurant, how happy are you? Two things have happened to you: (1) you have consumed beer and pizza, and (2) you have paid for the beer and pizza. The happiness that you walk away with is the net of these two factors: the happiness gained from consuming the beer and pizza *minus* the happiness lost

---

CONSUMER SURPLUS is a dollar measure of consumers' net utilities.

---

paying for the beer and pizza. The measure of your happiness as you leave the restaurant is consumer surplus. Have you ever gone to a restaurant, perhaps spent a lot of time, and then received a bill that was much larger than you expected? Perhaps you left the restaurant thinking that you would have been just as happy to stay home and not have incurred that huge bill. In this case, your consumer surplus was zero—the amount of utility you gained from the beer and pizza was equal to the amount of utility you lost from paying the bill.[7]

We can measure the amount of consumer and producer surplus generated in a market by looking at the demand and supply curves. Graphically, consumer surplus is the area above the price, below the demand curve, and to the left of the quantity purchased.

Consider a person who purchases four pairs of jeans at $25 each (for simplicity's sake, let us assume that all four pairs of jeans are identical). We have already shown that the marginal utility of the first pair of jeans is high, the marginal utility of the second

---

GRAPHICALLY, consumer surplus is the area above price, below the demand curve, and to the left of the quantity purchased.

---

pair is a bit lower, the marginal utility of the third pair is lower still, and so on. Each pair of jeans yields a lesser *additional* utility. Suppose that this person has no jeans at all. The person would receive a lot of utility from the first pair of jeans, and therefore would be willing

---

6 We assume here that you do not get utility from having money in your pocket—if you don't buy something with the money, you don't get any utility. In reality, people do get utility from having (and not spending) money, but this utility really comes from the knowledge that they will be able to spend the money in the future—thus, the utility that people get from saving money is really utility from consuming products in the future and not utility from the money at all. But wait! What about people who don't intend to spend their money, but just keep it in case of an emergency, which may never happen? These people are actually purchasing a product called *insurance*—the knowledge that, no matt er the circumstances, they will not be without a house, car, health care, and so on. But wait! What about people who don't save for an emergency, but just want to have something to give to their heirs when they die? These people are also buying insurance, but they are buying it for their heirs instead of themselves. Th e bott om line is that people do not get utility from money, only from the things that money buys (or will buy, or might buy).

7 We said that you receive no utility from money. So, why do you lose utility when you pay the restaurant bill? The utility you are losing is actually an *opportunity cost*. It is the utility that the money could have generated for you if you had spent it elsewhere.

to pay a high price for the first pair of jeans. Suppose that the maximum price the person would have paid for the first pair of jeans is $40. The second pair of jeans yields less additional utility than the first pair, so the person will not be willing to pay as much for the second pair of jeans. Let us suppose that the maximum the person would be willing to pay for the second pair of jeans is $35. Similarly, the maximum price the person would be willing to pay for the third pair of jeans is $30, and the maximum price the person would be willing to pay for the fourth pair of jeans is $25. How much consumer surplus does the person receive? The person receives $15 in consumer surplus for the first pair of jeans ($40 worth of utility minus $25 price), $10 in consumer surplus for the second pair ($35 minus $25), $5 in consumer surplus for the third pair ($30 minus $25), and $0 in consumer surplus for the fourth pair ($25 minus $25). Notice that the person will not buy more than four pairs of jeans because the consumer surplus of the fifth pair would be negative—the value

of the utility the person would receive from the fifth pair of jeans would be less than the price of the jeans.

Figure 6.1 shows the consumer surplus the person receives. According to figure 6.1, the maximum price the person is willing to pay for the first pair of jeans is $40. In the figure, $40 is the area of rectangle ABCG ($40 [the height] times one pair of jeans [the width]). The person paid $25 for the first pair of jeans (area G), so the person's consumer surplus for the first pair of jeans is $40 minus $25, or area ABC. The maximum price the person is willing to pay for the second pair of jeans is $35, or area DEH. The person paid $25 (area A). The consumer surplus the person receives from the second pair of jeans is area DE (DEH minus area H). Similarly, area F is the consumer surplus the person receives from the third pair of jeans, and the person receives no consumer surplus from the fourth pair of jeans. The person's total consumer surplus for the four pairs of jeans is area ABCDEF.

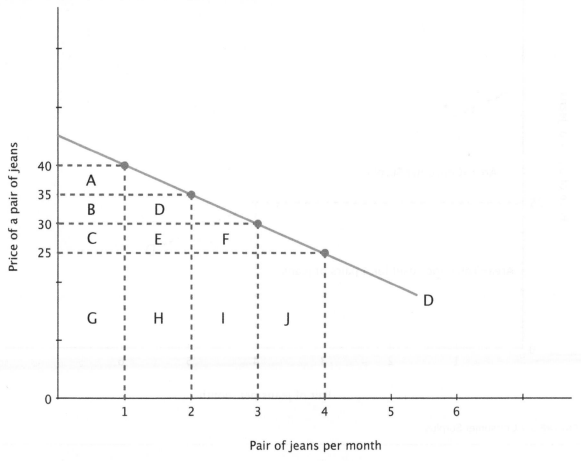

FIGURE 6.1 Demand Curve, Willingness to Pay, and Consumer Surplus

Our analysis here is slightly erroneous—in reality, the little triangles above areas A, D, and J are also part of the consumer surplus. These do not show up in our analysis because we described the jeans as indivisible units. If the person could buy the jeans one thread at a time, the person would pay a high price for the first thread, a lower price for the next thread, and so forth. Thus, even though the jeans cannot be purchased in fractional units, *if they could be purchased in fractional units*, the person would be willing to pay a higher price for the first fractional unit, a lower price for the second, and so on. The person's true consumer surplus is shown in figure 6.2. The rectangle below the

$25 price is the total price the person paid for the four pairs of jeans. The triangular area above this is the consumer surplus—the dollar value of the net utility the person obtained from the four pairs of jeans.

Consider now the case of producer surplus. According to the supply curve in figure 6.3, the minimum price required to entice the producer to offer one pair of jeans per year is $10.[8] To entice the producer to offer a second pair of jeans, we must offer the producer a minimum of $15. The minimum price the producer requires for the second pair of jeans ($15) is greater than for the first pair ($10) because of increasing marginal cost—each unit the producer produces costs the producer

8 The numbers in this example become a bit ridiculous because we are considering a case in which there is one consumer and one producer. Normally, the number of consumers is larger than the number of producers. For example, if there are ten thousand consumers and each one is willing to purchase two pairs of jeans per year, the total demand for jeans is twenty thousand units per year.

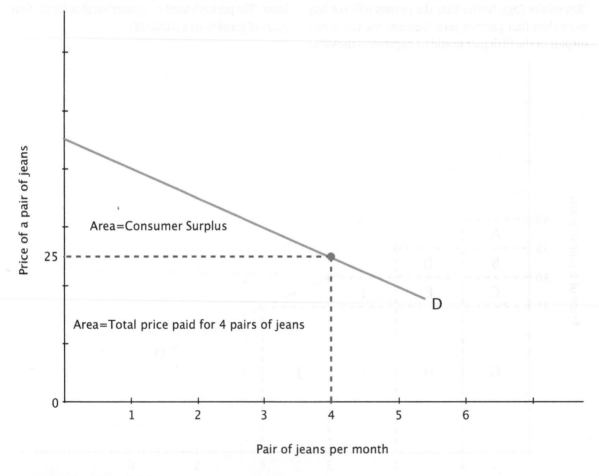

FIGURE 6.2 Consumer Surplus

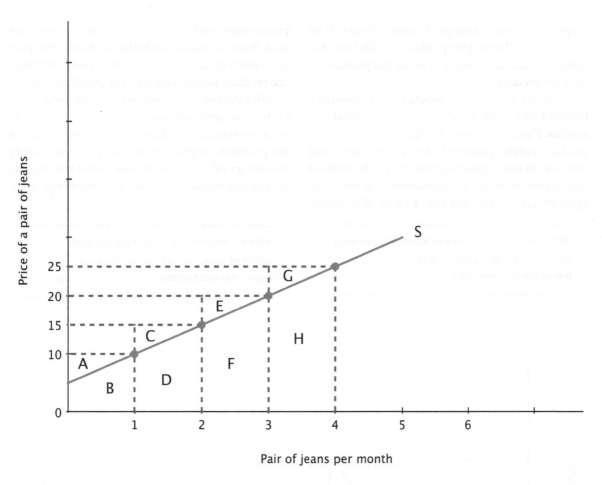

FIGURE 6.3 Supply Curve and Producer Surplus

more than the previous unit. To entice the producer to offer a third pair of jeans, we must offer a minimum of $20, and so on. Suppose that we pay the producer the absolute minimum price he is willing to accept for each pair of jeans: $10 for the first pair, $15 for the second pair, and so forth. The amount of money the producer would receive, then, is area AB for the first pair, area CD for the second pair, and areas EF and GH for the third and fourth pairs. However, this is not how we normally pay for products—normally we pay the same price for each unit we purchase (i.e., $25 for the first pair, $25 for the second pair, etc.). If we pay the producer $25 for the first pair of jeans, the producer receives a surplus of $15 ($25 price minus $10 minimum price required to offer the product). If we pay the producer $25 for the second pair of jeans, the producer receives a surplus

of $10 ($25 price minus $15 minimum price required to offer the product). In reality, the triangles A, C, E, and G are also part of the producer surplus, because even though the producer cannot sell a fractional quantity of a pair of jeans, if he *could*, he would be willing to sell the first fractional quantity at a price of less than $10. Thus, the actual consumer surplus is the area below $25 and above supply. Graphically, producer surplus is the area below price, above supply, and to the left of the quantity sold.

Figure 6.4 shows the true producer surplus for the producer that sells four jeans per year at $25 each. The total revenue the firm receives for the jeans is the upper and lower triangles. The lower triangle is the minimum amount of money the producer required in order to be enticed to offer the product. The producer surplus is the upper triangle. Producer surplus is an extra amount of money the producer received over the minimum amount required to entice the producer to offer the product.

Now, let us bring the producer and consumer together and observe the consumer and producer surplus. Figure 6.5 shows the consumer surplus and producer surplus generated when the consumer and producer of jeans come together. Given the demand and supply of jeans, the consumer and producer agree on a price of $25 per unit. As with all economic

transactions, both the consumer and producer walk away from the transaction better off than before. How much better off are they? This is exactly what consumer and producer surplus measure. The consumer is better off after the transaction than before by the amount of the consumer surplus. The producer is better off after the transaction than before by the amount of the producer surplus. In fact, we can now identify how better off *society* is because of the transaction. We call this measure *total surplus*. *Total surplus* is the

---

GRAPHICALLY, producer surplus is the area below price, above the supply curve, and to the left of the quantity sold.

TOTAL SURPLUS is the total net benefit to all members of society from an economic transaction.

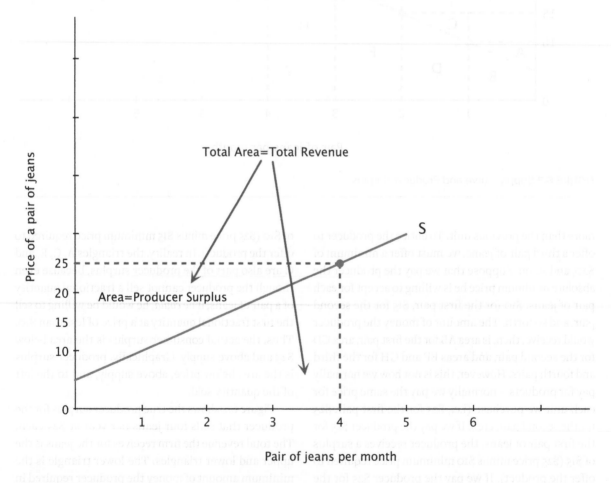

FIGURE 6.4 Producer Surplus

total net benefit to all members of society from an economic transaction.

Let us suppose that the consumer received $120 worth of happiness from the four pairs of jeans (that is, the consumer received the same amount of utility from *consuming* the four jeans as he would have from being given $120 cash). The four jeans cost $100, so the consumer has a consumer surplus of $20 (the consumer received the same amount of utility from *buying and consuming* the four jeans as he would have

from being given $20). Suppose that the variable cost of producing the four jeans was $70. The producer has received a producer surplus of $30 ($100 price minus $70 variable cost). The net benefit to the consumer from the transaction is $20. The net benefit to the producer is $30. The net benefit to society is $50. The important lesson here is that total surplus and, by extension, society's benefit from exchange are at their maximum only when the market is in equilibrium.

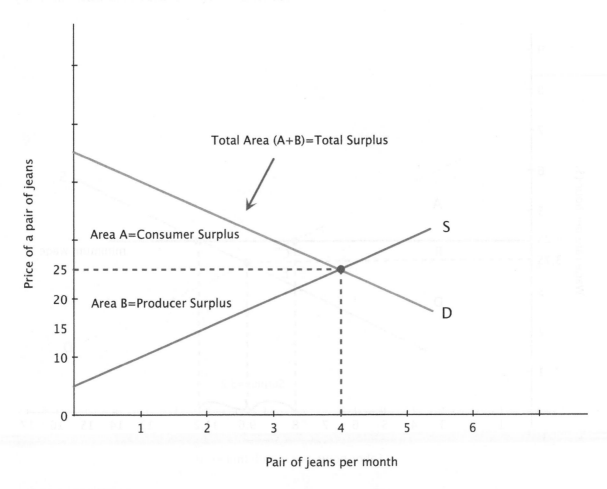

FIGURE 6.5 Total Surplus

The Impact of a Price Control on the Surpluses

We can use consumer and producer surplus measures to observe the effect of price controls—like an increase in the minimum wage. Let us return to our previous example, in which the equilibrium wage rate is $3.75 and the government imposes a minimum wage of $4.25. As we see in figure 6.6, at the equilibrium wage rate of $3.75, there are 9.6 million jobs available (the quantity of labor demanded), and there are 9.6 million people seeking jobs (the quantity of labor supplied). When the government imposes the minimum wage of $4.25, the number of jobs available falls to 8 million, and the number of people seeking jobs rises to 11.2

million. Thus, the minimum wage creates a surplus of labor (i.e., unemployment).

At the free market price of $3.75, the consumer surplus (the net benefit to firms that hire workers) is area ABC, and the producer surplus (the net benefit to people who sell their labor) is area DE. When the government imposes the minimum wage of $4.25, the consumer surplus decreases to area A and the producer surplus rises to area B. Areas C and E are deadweight losses—an amount of profit and utility the market could have generated, but didn't. Notice three things: (1) firms are worse off (consumer surplus has fallen from ABC to A), (2) workers may be better off or may

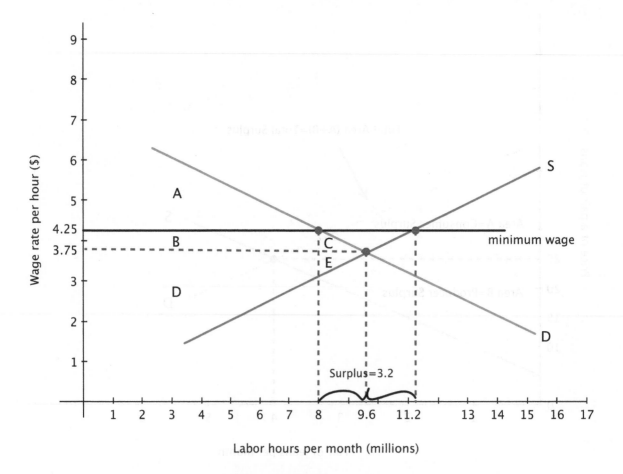

FIGURE 6.6 Minimum Wage and Change in Total Surplus

be worse off (producer surplus has gone from DE to BD)—workers are better off only if area B is larger than area E (which depends on the slopes of the demand and supply curves), and (3) society as a whole is worse off under the minimum wage (society surplus before the minimum wage is area ABCDE, and after the minimum wage is area ABD).

Let us examine the relative sizes of areas B and E. As the demand curve for labor becomes steeper, as shown in figure 6.7, area B becomes larger and area E becomes smaller. As the supply curve becomes steeper, as shown in figure 6.8, area B becomes smaller and area E becomes larger.

The question that we are attempting to answer is whether the minimum wage (1) hurts firms more than it helps workers or (2) hurts both firms and workers. The answer lies in areas B and E in the previous figures. If area B is larger than area E, workers have been helped. If area B is smaller than area E, both firms and workers have been hurt.

This is also a great segue to our next important topic of elasticity, which gives us a quantitative measure of the responsiveness of demand and supply, and is directly related to how steep or flat these curves are.

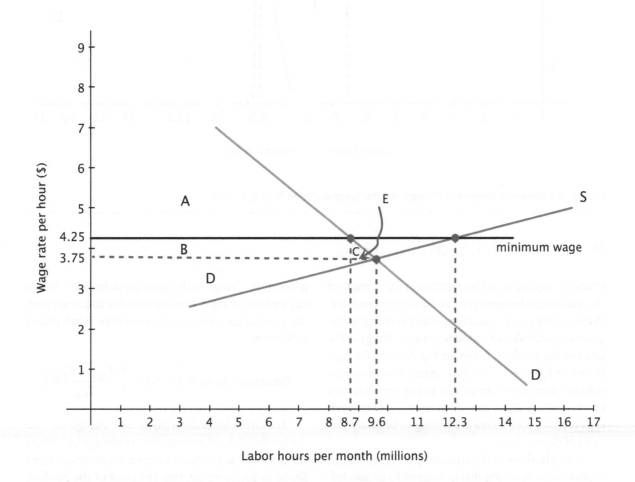

FIGURE 6.7 Minimum Wage and Change in Total Surplus (Flat Supply Curve)

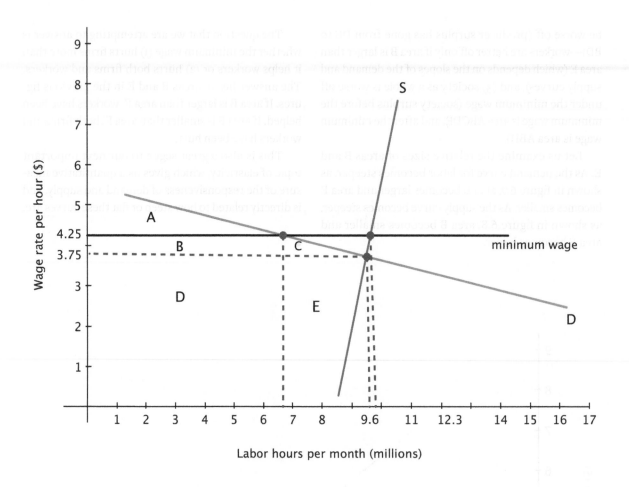

FIGURE 6.8 Minimum Wage and Change in Total Surplus (Steep Supply Curve)

Price Elasticity of Demand

Price elasticity of demand is a measure of the strength of the relationship between price and quantity demanded. Price elasticity of demand measures the *change* in the quantity demanded of a product given a change in the price of the product. Consider the demand for eggs shown in figure 6.9. When the price of a dozen eggs is $2.00, consumers are willing to buy one thousand units of this product. But when the price of a dozen eggs is $2.10, consumers are willing to buy only 980 units of the product.

Price elasticity of demand compares this change in price to the resulting change in quantity demanded. Specifically, price elasticity of demand is the ratio of the percentage change in the price of the product to the percentage change in the quantity demanded. When any variable changes from its old value to a new value, the percentage change in that variable is calculated as follows:

$$\text{Percentage Change in } X = \%\Delta X = \left(\frac{X_{\text{New}} - X_{\text{Old}}}{X_{\text{Old}}} \right)$$

The Greek letter delta (Δ) means "change in," and the symbol $\%\Delta$ means "percentage change in." When the price of the product in Figure 6.9 increases from $2.00 to $2.10, we say that the price of the product increased by 5 percent. We calculate this as follows:

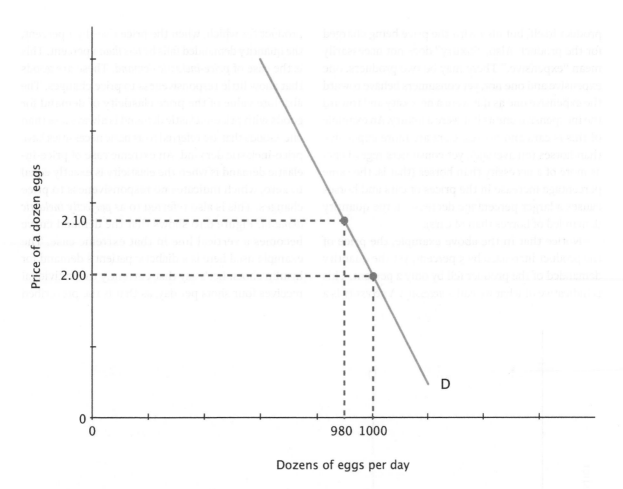

FIGURE 6.9 Demand and Price Elasticity of Demand (Inelastic Demand)

Percentage Change in Price $= \%\Delta P = \dfrac{\$2.10 - \$2.00}{\$2.00}$

$$= 0.05$$

As the price of the product rises from $2.00 to $2.10, the quantity demanded falls from 1,000 to 980. This is a 2 percent *decrease* in the quantity demanded. We can calculate this percentage change as follows:

Percentage Change in Quantity Demanded $= \%\Delta Q_D$

$$= \dfrac{980 - 1000}{1000}$$

$$= -0.02$$

Using the percentage change in price and the percentage change in quantity demanded, we can compute the price elasticity of demand as follows:

Price Elasticity of Demand $= \dfrac{\%\Delta Q_D}{\%\Delta P} = \dfrac{\dfrac{980 - 1000}{1000}}{\dfrac{\$2.10 - \$2.00}{\$2.00}}$

$$= \dfrac{-0.02}{0.05} = -0.4$$

Price Elasticity of Demand $= \dfrac{\%\Delta \textbf{Quantity Demanded}}{\%\Delta \textbf{Price}}$

Note that consumers may behave toward a product as if it were a luxury when the price is high, but may behave toward the same product as if it were a necessity when the price is low. The question of luxury versus necessity does not have to do solely with the product itself, but also with the price being charged for the product. Also, "luxury" does not necessarily mean "expensive." There may be two products, one expensive and one not, yet consumers behave toward the expensive one as if it were a necessity and toward the inexpensive one as if it were a luxury. An example of this is cars and horses. Cars are more expensive than horses (on average), yet consumers regard cars as more of a necessity than horses (that is, the same percentage increase in the prices of cars and horses causes a larger percentage decrease in the quantity demanded of horses than of cars).

Notice that in the above example, the price of the product increased by 5 percent, yet the quantity demanded of the product fell by only 2 percent. This is indicative of what we call a *necessity*. A *necessity* is a

product for which, when the price rises by 1 percent, the quantity demanded falls by *less than* 1 percent. This is the case of *price-inelastic demand*. These are goods that show little responsiveness to price changes. The absolute value of the price elasticity of demand for goods with price-inelastic demand is always less than one. Goods that are referred to as basic necessities have price-inelastic demand. An extreme case of price-inelastic demand is when the elasticity is exactly equal to zero, which indicates no responsiveness to price changes. This is also referred to as *perfectly inelastic demand*. Figure 6.10 shows that the demand curve becomes a vertical line in that extreme case. The example used here is a diabetic patient's demand for insulin shots. Let's say that currently the individual receives four shots per day, as that is the prescribed

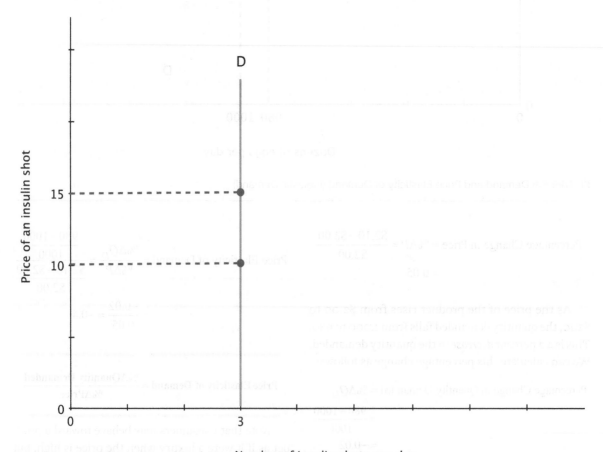

FIGURE 6.10 Perfectly Inelastic Demand

amount of shots, and pays $10 for each shot. If the price of a shot increases to $15, does that make this individual consume fewer insulin shots? The answer is no, because deviating from the prescribed amount of insulin shots can have serious health consequences for this individual. Here, zero elasticity indicates that the consumer shows absolutely no responsiveness at all to any price change.

NOTICE THAT if we had computed the price elasticity of demand in the other direction (i.e., a price decrease from $2.10 to $2.00 instead of a price increase from $2.00 to $2.10), we would have obtained a slightly different answer. Calculating the price elasticity of demand in this fashion yields a percentage change in price of −4.76 percent and a percentage change in quantity demanded of 2.04 percent. The resulting price elasticity of demand is −0.43 instead of the −0.4 shown here. The reason for the discrepancy is that the formula shown here is an algebraic approximation for the true elasticity. The proper formula for the price elasticity of demand is $(P/Q)(dQ/dP)$ where dQ/dP is the derivative of Q with respect to P. The smaller the change in price, the closer this approximation is to the true elasticity. Another alternative is to use the midpoint formula instead, which is shown below:

$$\varepsilon = \frac{\%\Delta Q}{\%\Delta P} = \frac{(Q_2 - Q_1)/0.5(Q_2 + Q_1)}{(P_2 - P_1)/0.5(P_2 + P_1)}$$

Some of the products with the most inelastic demand include (in the ascending price elasticity order): sugar, milk, gasoline, beer, cigarettes, marijuana and other illicit drugs, chicken, and so on.

Consider the case shown in figure 6.11. When the price of a movie ticket in figure 6.11 is $10, consumers are willing to buy 250 tickets per day. If the price of a ticket rises to $11, consumers will be willing to

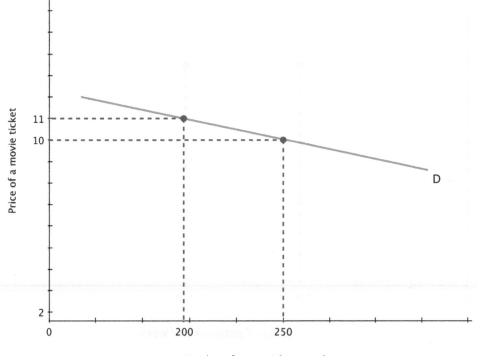

FIGURE 6.11 Demand and Price Elasticity of Demand (Elastic Demand)

purchase only 200 units per day. The increase in price from $10 to $11 is a 10 percent increase. The decrease in the quantity demanded from 250 to 200 is a 20 percent decrease. Thus, the price elasticity of demand for movie tickets is –20 / 10, or –2. This is the case of *price-elastic demand*. Among the product categories, luxury goods have price-elastic demand.

$$\text{Price Elasticity of Demand} = \frac{\%\Delta Q_D}{\%\Delta P} = \frac{\dfrac{200-250}{250}}{\dfrac{\$11-\$10}{\$10}}$$

$$= \frac{-0.2}{0.1} = -2$$

An extreme case of price-elastic demand is when the elasticity gets so high that it goes to infinity, which indicates very high or perfect responsiveness to price changes. This is also referred to as *perfectly elastic demand*. Figure 6.12 shows that the demand curve becomes a horizontal line in that extreme case.

Consider the product shown in figure 6.13. Suppose that the price of the product is initially $12. When the price of this product rises from $12 to $13, the quantity demanded falls from one hundred units per day to ninety-eight units per day. The percentage change in price is 8.3 percent, and the percentage change in quantity demanded is –2 percent. The price elasticity of demand is –0.24, which tells us that consumers regard this product as inelastic.

Now, suppose that the price of the product is initially $57. When the price of the product rises from $57 to $58, the quantity demanded falls from ten units per day to eight units per day. The percentage change

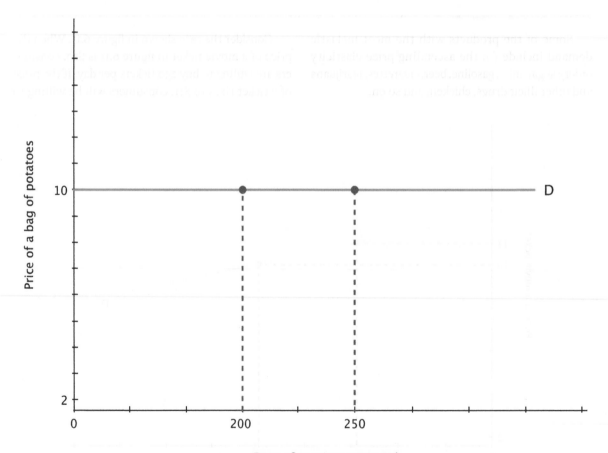

FIGURE 6.12 Perfectly Elastic Demand

in price is 1.8 percent, and the percentage change in quantity demanded is –20 percent. The price elasticity of demand is –11.1, which tells us that consumers regard this product as elastic.

In both cases, the product is the same. The only thing that has changed is the price. The lower the price of a product, the more consumers regard the product as a necessity. The higher the price of a product, the more consumers regard the same product as a luxury. This relationship does not, however, hold across products. Whether consumers regard one product as more or less of a necessity than a different product has little to do with the relative prices of the two products.

A middle-ground case is when demand is unit-elastic. This happens when a 1 percent increase in price leads to a 1 percent decrease in quantity demanded.

This is likely to happen somewhere near the middle of the demand curve.

Above the unit-elastic point on the demand curve in figure 6.13, the price elasticity of demand is greater than one in absolute value, which economists deem as elastic. Below that point, the price elasticity of demand is less than one, and economists deem it as inelastic. A peculiar thing about unit-elastic demand is that this is the only point on the demand curve that maximizes total revenue (price times quantity sold) for the seller. Below this point, the percentage increase in quantity sold is smaller than the percentage decrease in price, and total revenue falls. Above this point, the percentage decrease in quantity sold is larger than the percentage increase in price, and total revenue also falls.

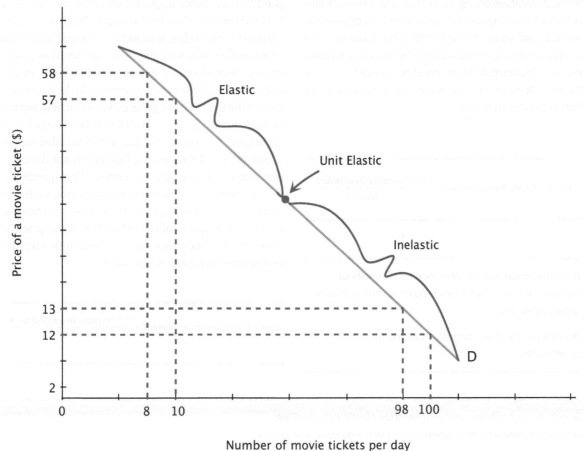

FIGURE 6.13 Different Demand Elasticities on a Linear Demand Curve

A FARMER'S CURSE   A good year for farmers, crop-wise, might end up being a bad year for farmers, profit-wise. Known as "farmer's curse," a sharp increase in crop supply may lead to a sharp drop in market price and, as a result, farmer's profit. For this to happen, consumers must be relatively unresponsive or inelastic to price decreases. The demand for food in general may exhibit this inelastic property: people have to eat even if the food is expensive, but people can only eat so much even if the food is cheap. This means very price-inelastic or steep-looking demand curves for food (see figure 6.9). If supply increases dramatically and quantity demanded barely budges, much of that supply increase will transfer into lower prices. As a result, farmers sell about the same quantity but at a much lower price.

The opposite happens when the demand curve is price-elastic or more horizontal. In this case, much of supply increase is transferred into higher quantity demanded, because people are very sensitive to price changes (even a small drop in price leads to a large increase in consumption).

There are also other demand elasticities we need to consider. The first of these is *income elasticity of demand,* which measures the responsiveness of demand to income changes. As we show below, it is found by dividing the percentage change in quantity demanded by the percentage change in income. This elasticity also helps us to distinguish between two types of goods. A *normal good,* as we defined in Chapter 3, has positive income elasticity, whereas an *inferior good* has negative income elasticity. A luxury good has not only positive income elasticity but also particularly high elasticity that is greater than one.

$$\text{Income Elasticity of Demand} = \frac{\%\Delta\text{ Quantity Demanded}}{\%\Delta\text{ Income}}$$

A normal good has positive income elasticity of demand. A luxury good has income elasticity that is greater than one.

An inferior good has negative income elasticity of demand.

Cross-price elasticity of demand measures the responsiveness of demand for a good, X, to a price change for another good, Y, where goods X and Y are related goods. As we show below, it is found by dividing the percentage change in quantity demanded for good X by the percentage change in the price of good Y. Goods can be related in two ways. They can be substitutes for each other, such as Pepsi versus Coke or tea versus coffee. When goods are substitutes, consumers choose between those goods, so an increase in the consumption of one means a decrease in the consumption of the other. Cross-price elasticity of demand for two substitute goods is positive. When the price of some good Y increases, the quantity demanded for the substitute good X increases. Goods can also be complements, such as coffee and cream. When goods are complements, they are consumed together, where an increase in the consumption of one means an increase in the consumption of the other. When the price of some good, Y, increases, quantity demanded for the complementary good, X, decreases.

$$\text{Cross - Price Elasticity of Demand} = \frac{\%\Delta\text{ Quantity Demanded for X}}{\%\Delta\text{ Price of Y}}$$

Goods are substitutes when cross-price elasticity is positive.
Goods are complements when cross-price elasticity is negative.

Price Elasticity of Supply

Price elasticity of supply is a measure of the strength of the relationship between price and quantity supplied. Price elasticity of supply measures the *change* in the quantity supplied of a product given a change in the price of the product. Consider now the supply for gasoline shown in figure 6.14. When the price of a gallon of gasoline is $5.00, producers are willing to supply 1,000 units (millions) of gasoline per day. When the price is $6.00, producers are willing to supply 1,100 units (millions) of gasoline per day.

Using the percentage change in price and the percentage change in quantity supplied, we can compute the price elasticity of supply as follows:

$$\text{Price Elasticity of Supply} = \frac{\%\Delta Q_s}{\%\Delta P} = \frac{\dfrac{1100 - 1000}{1000}}{\dfrac{\$6.00 - \$5.00}{\$5.00}}$$

$$= \frac{0.1}{0.2} = 0.5$$

$$\text{Price Elasticity of Supply} = \frac{\%\Delta \text{ Quantity Supplied}}{\%\Delta \text{ Price}}$$

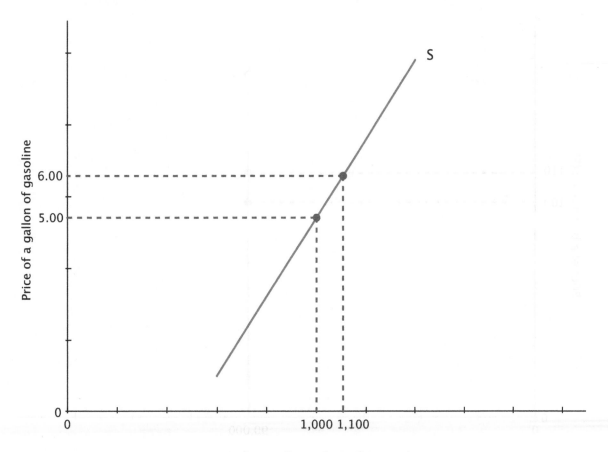

FIGURE 6.14 Supply and Price Elasticity of Supply (Inelastic)

In the above example, the price of the product increased by 20 percent, yet the quantity supplied increased by only 10 percent. This is the case of *price-inelastic supply.* Generally speaking, this occurs when the price increases by 1 percent, and the quantity supplied increases by less than 1 percent. An extreme case of price-inelastic supply is when the elasticity is exactly equal to zero, which indicates no responsiveness to price changes. This is also referred to as *perfectly inelastic supply.* Figure 6.15 shows that the supply curve becomes a vertical line in that extreme case. The example used here is the production of oil. Because of the nature of production, it is very difficult to increase the total production of oil in a given time period, especially in a short time period. If the price of a barrel of oil increases to $110, it doesn't generate any increase in oil production for the next day. Here, zero elasticity indicates that the producer shows absolutely no responsiveness at all to any price change in such a short time period.

Consider now the case shown in figure 6.16. When the price of a pound of cheese in figure 6.16 is $5, producers are willing to supply 1,000 pounds of cheese per day. If the price of cheese rises to $5.50, producers are now willing to supply 1,200 pounds per day. The increase in price from $5 to $5.50 is a 10 percent increase. The increase in the quantity supplied from 1,000 to 1,200 is a 20 percent increase. Thus, the price elasticity of supply for cheese is 20 / 10, or 2. This is the case of *price-elastic supply.*

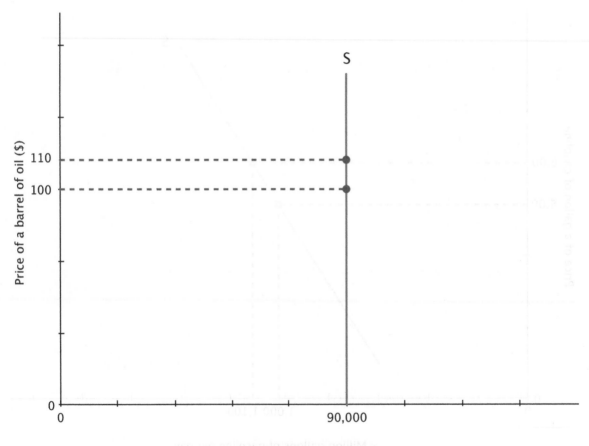

FIGURE 6.15 Perfectly Inelastic Supply

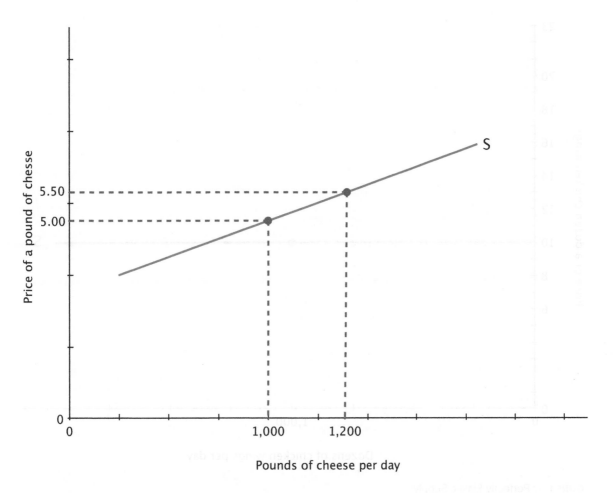

FIGURE 6.16 Supply and Price Elasticity of Supply (Elastic Supply)

$$\text{Price Elasticity of Supply} = \frac{\%\Delta Q_s}{\%\Delta P} = \frac{\dfrac{1200-1000}{1000}}{\dfrac{\$5.50-\$5.00}{\$5.00}}$$

$$= \frac{0.2}{0.1} = 2$$

An extreme case of price-elastic supply is when the elasticity gets so high that it goes to infinity, which indicates very high or perfect responsiveness to price changes. This is also referred to as *perfectly elastic supply*. Figure 6.17 shows that the supply curve becomes a horizontal line in that extreme case.

Determinants of Elasticity

Elasticity depends on a variety of factors and tends to increase over time. Price elasticity of demand, for example, increases as product scope narrows. The demand for soda at large is inelastic compared to the demand for a particular brand of soda. Price elasticity of demand increases when more substitutes become available. Price elasticity of demand is also high for products that make up a larger share of a consumer's budget (think housing vs. salt). Both demand and supply are more elastic in the long run than in the short run.

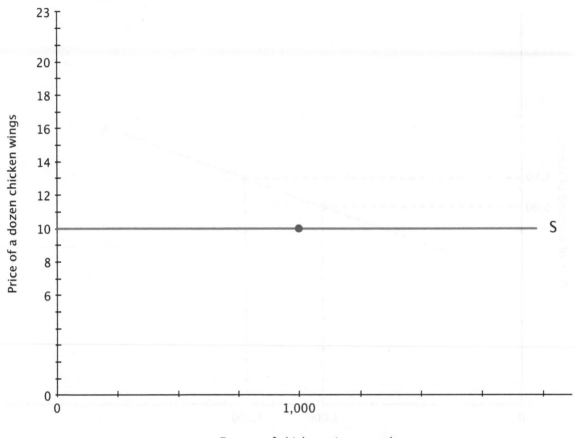

1,000

Dozens of chicken wings per day

FIGURE 6.17 Perfectly Elastic Supply

ON THE ELASTICITY OF DEMAND FOR ALCOHOL, DRUGS, AND TOBACCO Elasticity is a very nifty concept, with so many interesting applications. Consider the government's attempt to reduce the supply of illicit drugs in the presence of inelastic demand. The attempt to restrict drug supply leads to a large increase in the price without a significant reduction in drug use. Because drugs can be addictive, demand remains unresponsive (inelastic) to price changes. However, the criminalization of drugs makes this black market very lucrative for the sellers, giving rise to powerful drug cartels that solve their business disputes through violence. The government's war on drugs has led to countless lives lost due to violence and substandard drugs, broken families, incarceration of many productive individuals, and a heavy burden on taxpayers. The alcohol prohibition era in the 1930s in the United States teaches us that policies that try to prevent an exchange between willing buyers and sellers could be ineffective. The more inelastic the demand for some good, the harder it will be to stop people from consuming it.

CONCLUSION

In this chapter, we pointed out that market prices embody incentives, which guide individual behavior in a predictable fashion much like traffic signals induce an orderly flow of transportation. Economists use consumer surplus and producer surplus to measure the gains from exchange to consumers and producers. Total surplus or society's gain from exchange is maximized at the market equilibrium. Various government policies, like price controls and product bans, may push the market participants away from the equilibrium, reducing societal wellbeing. How strongly consumers and firms respond to changes in prices and other factors is captured in the measure economists call elasticity. Understanding the concept of elasticity can aid in designing more pragmatic policies.

DISCUSSION QUESTIONS AND PROBLEMS

1. Can total surplus tell us anything about the relative distribution of the economic gains for producers and consumers?

2. How responsive are the consumers and producers of oil to its price change in the short run versus the long run?

3. How will a binding rent ceiling on apartments affect the consumer, producer, and total surpluses if the supply of apartments is perfectly inelastic?

4. What would happen to a firm's total revenue if it were to increase the price of its product, while still remaining on the inelastic portion of the demand curve?

5. Would the producers of inferior goods be more likely to experience higher or lower sales if people's incomes were to fall?

7 Taxation and the Market

FAMOUS TAX QUOTES

- The art of taxation consists of plucking the goose as to obtain the largest possible amount of feathers with the least possible amount of hissing. (Jean Baptiste Colbert)
- The hardest thing in the world to understand is the income tax. (Albert Einstein)
- Why shouldn't the American people take half my money from me? I took all of it from them. (Edward Albert Filene)
- The lottery is just a tax on people who are bad at math. (Anonymous math teacher)
- What is the difference between a taxidermist and a tax collector? The taxidermist takes only your skin. (Mark Twain)
- It's a game. We [tax lawyers] teach the rich how to play it so they can stay rich— and the IRS keeps changing the rules so we can keep getting rich teaching them. (John Grisham, The Firm)
- Academicians and politicians have finally come to understand that it's the after-tax rate of return that determines people's behavior. (Arthur B. Laffer)
- The tax code, once you get to know it, embodies all the essence of life: greed, politics, power, goodness, charity. (Sheldon S. Cohen)
- It is a signal advantage of taxes on articles of consumption that they contain in their own nature a security against excess. (Alexander Hamilton)

FIGURE 7.1 Unfinished Structures and Property Tax Avoidance in Greece

The above quotes[1] reveal that taxation is a complex topic. The preamble to the US Constitution states that the government should "provide for the common defense, promote the general Welfare, and secure the Blessings of Liberty to ourselves and our Posterity." Even this narrow scope of government requires raising a substantial amount of revenue. Should the government be financed with taxes or voluntary contributions? Some see taxation as a coercive revenue tool that seems to violate the whole notion of individual freedom. However, the problem with voluntary contributions is that some individuals will choose not to contribute in hopes that the good Samaritans will pick up the tab. Free riders will effectively chip away at the rights of contributors and undermine the system of voluntary payments for public goods. The free-rider problem is so serious that even countries with well-established government funding systems constantly struggle with tax avoidance (legal) and tax evasion (illegal). Tax avoidance is particularly pernicious in Greece, where homeowners can avoid paying property taxes on finished structures by leaving rebar permanently protruding from their houses (see figure 7.1).[2]

1 J. L. Yablon. "As Certain as Death. Quotations About Taxes." *Tax Analysts* (2010). Available at: http://www.taxanalysts.com/www/freefiles.nsf/Files/Yablon2010.pdf/$file/Yablon2010.pdf

2 Photo source: author's photo.

This example demonstrates that the system of voluntary payments will most likely fail to raise enough revenue due to free riders. As the US Supreme Court Justice Oliver Wendell Holmes Jr. put it, "taxes are what we pay for civilized society."

What Is a Tax?

A TAX is a compulsory transfer of resources from an individual to the government. Taxes are commonly levied on income, wealth, and consumption.

A *tax* is a compulsory transfer of resources from an individual to the government. Taxes can take various forms, from the traditional income, profits, sales, property, and wealth taxes to exotic taxes, such as a tax on beards in ancient Russia. Great Britain is known for a flurry of odd taxes throughout its history that target particular items, such as fireplaces, windows, bricks, hats, candles, wig powder, wallpaper, and televisions. From 1885 to 1923, Canada collected the Chinese Head Tax per Chinese immigrant until Chinese immigration into Canada was banned altogether. Some taxes are less coercive than others: state lottery is a quasi-tax because it is not a compulsory payment but still is a source of government revenue. Taxes could also be imposed on international trade, such as import tariffs and export taxes. Regardless of what form a tax takes, the concept of elasticity we covered in the previous chapter can tell us who truly pays taxes and how inefficient they can be.

An *income tax* is a tax on money that a person earns. An income tax can be regressive, proportional, or progressive. In the United States, the federal income tax is progressive, meaning that people with higher incomes are taxed at a higher rate (in 2013 the lowest statutory tax rate was 10 and the highest was 39.6 percent). A *profits tax* is tax on the profit a firm earns. The two are not analogous. "Income" to a person is not the same thing as "profit" to a firm. Profit is revenue *minus* expenses. So, profit for the firm is analogous to *savings* for a person. In the United States, the federal government, most states, and some local governments collect corporate income taxes. According to the Tax Foundation, a tax policy think tank, US corporations face the highest statutory corporate income tax rate in the world at 39.1 percent.[3] In comparison to Europe, the American central government taxes income (and by extension savings) relatively heavier than consumption.

Wealth taxes are taxes on things already owned. For example, states and many municipalities (governments of a lesser scope than state governments—i.e., counties, cities, townships, etc.) charge property taxes. A *property tax* is a wealth tax that people must pay based on the value of certain pieces of property they own. In West Virginia, county governments charge wealth taxes on the value of people's homes, land, cars, and (interestingly) dogs.

Sales taxes and excise taxes are similar in that they are both taxes levied on products when they are purchased. A *sales tax* is a tax on the *value* of a product. An *excise tax* is a tax on the *quantity* of a product. Most states impose sales taxes, which are collected at the time consumers purchase products. These taxes are calculated as a percentage of the total purchase amount. For example, if you purchase a $30 pair of jeans and the sales tax is 6 percent, you must pay an additional $1.80 in tax. If you purchase the same pair of jeans somewhere else for $20, you pay only $1.00 in tax. By law, the federal government cannot impose sales taxes. It can, however, impose excise taxes. Look closely at the fine print on a gas pump the next time you buy gas. You will probably see a statement saying that the price includes a $0.30 (or thereabouts) tax for each gallon of gas. This is an excise tax. If you buy ten gallons of gas for $1.20 per gallon, you pay $3.00 in tax. If you buy ten gallons of gas for $1.40 per gallon, you

---

3 K. Pomerleau and A. Lundeen, "The U.S. Has the Highest Corporate Income Tax Rate in the OECD." *Tax Foundation* (January 27, 2014). Available at: http://taxfoundation.org/blog/us-has-highest-corporate-income-tax-rate-oecd

still pay $3.00 in tax. The tax is levied on the quantity of the product purchased, not the value of the product.[4]

Tariffs are like sales and excise taxes, but they are levied on imports. In the United States, tariffs can be levied only by the federal government.[5] It is an interesting historical footnote that, according to the Constitution, the federal government may impose tariffs on imports only, not on exports. The reason for this is that the Southern states (which at the time of the formation of the United States were primarily exporters) were afraid that the Northern states (which would hold more votes in Congress) would impose export tariffs to raise revenue. These export tariffs, it was argued, would impact the Southern states more adversely. Thus, the Southern states made it a condition of their ratifying the Constitution that the federal government not be allowed to impose tariffs on exports.

The term "flat tax" is being used in modern politics to describe a tax that is the same percentage of income for all people. Technically, this type of tax is not a flat tax, but a *proportional* tax. A *proportional tax* is a tax that charges the same percentage of income to all people. For example, everyone pays a tax equal to 20 percent of their income. A *flat tax* (also called a "poll tax") is a tax that charges the same dollar amount to all people. For example, everyone pays $1,000 per year, regardless of their income. A *progressive tax* is a tax that charges a higher percentage of income to people with higher incomes and a lower percentage of income to people with lower incomes. For example, people who earn more than $50,000 pay 40 percent of their income, and people who earn less than $50,000 pay 20 percent of their income. A regressive tax is the opposite of a progressive tax. A *regressive tax* charges a higher percentage of income to people with lower incomes and a lower percentage of income to people with higher incomes. For example, people who earn more than $50,000 pay 20 percent of their income, and people who earn less than $50,000 pay 40 percent of their income.[6]

Taxation can be viewed as a practical and just tool for ensuring an adequate provision of public services. Economist Charles Tiebout argued that with locally provided public goods, people will determine how much government they want by voting with their feet. However, public goods such as national defense may not be possible to provide at the local level, leaving it up to the central government to decide how much to tax and spend. In either case, taxation could protect individual rights to public goods by preventing some people from free riding on the contributions of others. As a practical matter, it appears that "in this world nothing can be said to be certain, except death and taxes."[7]

Taxation is often used to transfer resources from one group to another. Specifically, a democratic system

---

A LUMP-SUM TAX, SOMETIMES CALLED A POLL TAX, is a fixed fee collected from all individuals regardless of their income.

---

of government might be prone to redistributing income from the rich to the poor. In the words of Alexis de Tocqueville, "a democratic government is the only one in which those who vote for a tax can escape the

---

4 Taxes are the principal reason why gasoline is so much more expensive in Europe than in the United States. In most European countries, the price of gas (before taxes) is the same (or lower) than the price of gas in the United States. After applying the taxes, however, the price of gas in European countries is three to five *times* greater than the price of gas in the United States. In the United States, taxes on gas equal approximately $0.35 per gallon.

5 In fact, at one point in our history, New York state came close to threatening to secede from the United States because the federal government told New York that it must stop levying tariffs on imports from Canada. The case went to the Supreme Court, which held that the levying of tariffs was a right reserved to the federal government.

6 It is argued that some sales taxes (for example, a sales tax on food) are regressive. Because people will tend to spend about the same amount of money on groceries, they will also pay about the same amount of tax on groceries. The more income a person has, however, the lesser percentage of income the tax represents.

7 Benjamin Franklin, in a letter to Jean-Baptiste Leroy, 1789.

obligation to pay it."[8] A telling statistic from the Tax Policy Center indicates that 43 percent of American households paid no federal income taxes in 2013.[9]

TYPES OF INCOME TAXES

FLAT TAX:	Everyone pays the same dollar amount.
PROPORTIONAL TAX:	Everyone pays the same percentage of their incomes.
PROGRESSIVE TAX:	People with higher incomes pay a higher percentage of their incomes.
REGRESSIVE TAX:	People with higher incomes pay a lower percentage of their incomes.

The federal income tax, which tends to burden more higher-income households, and the sales tax, which tends to burden more lower-income households, raise the important question of tax fairness. As Russell B. Long, US senator from Louisiana, put it: "Don't tax you, don't tax me, tax that fellow behind the tree!" Who should bear the burden of taxation and to what degree? At the same time, we also wonder if some taxpayers

Taxation and Fairness

Who should pay taxes is a matter of fairness. How people respond to taxation is a matter of efficiency.

Economists often cite the great tradeoff between fairness and efficiency.

Economists usually invoke the ability-to-pay (vertical and horizontal) and benefits-received principles of equity or fairness when they talk about taxes. The ability-to-pay principle in its vertical form suggests that people who are able to pay more should pay more in taxes. This principle of equity supports progressive income taxation. Horizontal-equity principle suggests that people in identical economic circumstances should pay identical taxes. The benefits-received principle

decide to work and invest less or move to another state or even country in response to higher taxes, or whether a certain public service would be provided properly if tax rates and revenues were low. These points illuminate the tradeoff between fairness and efficiency of taxation. As you can see, the issues surrounding taxation can be very complex and controversial.

suggests that people should pay taxes in proportion to the benefits they derive from government programs.

Who truly pays taxes? It is always individuals who bear the burden of any tax, never firms or corporations. There is no such thing as corporations' bearing tax burden. The individuals who actually pay corporate income taxes could be the consumers, workers, or firm owners. How much they pay in taxes is determined by the elasticity of demand and supply. Consider a typical sales tax that is officially paid by the retail stores. When you buy a pack of gum at a store, you may see that the final price you pay for that gum has increased by the amount of the tax. In fact, the sales receipt shows that it is you who actually pays that tax. But isn't the tax officially levied on the sellers? Yes, and this is why economists emphasize the difference between statutory (legal) tax incidence and economic (true) tax incidence. Who actually suffers as a result

---

8 Alexis De Tocqueville, *Democracy in America, Volume 1*. Charlottesville, VA: University of Virginia Library, 2000. http://web.archive.org/web/20081201215034/http://etext.lib.virginia.edu/toc/modeng/public/TocDem1.html

9 Tax Policy Center, "Who Doesn't Pay Federal Taxes?" n.d., http://www.taxpolicycenter.org/taxtopics/federal-taxes-households.cfm.

of a tax (economic incidence) may have nothing to do with who officially is charged with paying a tax (statutory incidence).

A PRIMER ON TAX POLICY IN THE UNITED STATES AND AROUND THE WORLD

Nations rely on multiple taxes to finance government operations. Taxes are typically levied on earnings, consumption, and wealth. Earnings are typically taxed through personal, payroll, capital gains, and corporate taxes. Consumption taxes are usually levied on the sale of goods and services, while gift, inheritance, estate, and property taxes are usually designed to tax accumulated wealth.

What unites many countries is strong reliance on personal income and consumption taxes for generating government revenue. The US federal government, for example, collects more than 80 percent of its revenue through personal income and payroll taxes. In contrast, many European countries rely more heavily on national sales taxes or value-added taxes (VAT). Most economically developed nations raise a large share of total revenue through a progressive income tax, under which individuals with higher incomes typically face higher tax rates. In contrast, a regressive tax is the one where people with lower incomes face higher tax rates, which is often the case for consumption taxes.

Tax Reform

The US federal tax code has become extraordinarily complex over the years. It is estimated that Americans spend about 6.1 billion hours a year preparing their taxes.[10] The Internal Revenue Service employs more than ninety thousand and the private sector more than three million full-time workers to comply with the federal tax code. More than 4,600 changes were made to the federal tax code between 2001 and 2013, amounting to more than one change per day. The Tax Foundation reports that the number of words in the US tax code related to the income tax grew from 172,000 in 1955 to 1,286,000 in 2005.[11] The number of pages in the instruction booklet accompanying the personal income tax form 1040 increased from 2 in 1935 to 142 in 2005.[12] A simplex tax code is not only easier to enforce but also easier to comply with, which can save the nation a tremendous amount of time and resources.

Tax Burden (Tax Incidence)

Statutory tax incidence (burden) describes who legally pays a tax, while economic tax incidence (burden) describes who effectively suffers from paying a tax.

When the government imposes a tax, it creates a differential between the price the consumer pays for the product and the price the producer receives. For example, a consumer who buys a $20 pair of shoes on which there is a 6 percent sales tax ends up paying a total of $21.20. The producer, however, receives only

---

10 "Billions and billions of hours burned – on taxes," Face the Facts USA. A Project of the George Washington University (April 14, 2013). Available at: http://www.facethefactsusa.org/facts/billions-and-billions-hours-burned-taxes

11 J. S. Moody, Dr. W. P. Warcholik, and S. A. Hodge, "The Rising Cost of Complying with the Federal Income Tax," Tax Foundation Special Report, December 2005, No. 138, p. 4.

12 D. Keating, "A Taxing Trend: The Rise in Complexity, Forms, and Paperwork Burdens," National Taxpayers Union Policy Paper 120, April 17, 2006.

$20. The difference of $1.20 goes to the government. While the consumer pays a price of $20, the cost to the consumer is $21.20. Thus, the producer price of the product is $20, while the consumer price of the product is $21.20. When the government imposes a tax on a product, the person who *pays* the tax is not necessarily the person from whom the tax is *collected*. For example, the government may impose a $2.00 tax on cigarettes. This tax is *collected* from the consumer at the time the cigarettes are purchased. To determine who *pays* the tax, we must examine the producer price of cigarettes before and after the tax. If the producer price of cigarettes before the tax was $5.00 and the producer price of cigarettes after the tax is still $5.00, the consumer has *paid* the $2.00 tax (the total cost of the cigarettes to the consumer is $7.00—$2.00 more

than before the tax was imposed). If, on the other hand, the producer price of the cigarettes before the tax was $5.00 and the producer price of cigarettes after the tax is $3.00, the producer has *paid* the $2.00 tax (the total cost of the cigarettes to the consumer is $5.00—the same as before the tax was imposed). Thus, while the government can control *from whom the tax is collected*, the government cannot control *who pays the tax*. Who actually ends up paying the tax depends on what happens to the producer price of the product after the tax is imposed. This in turn is determined by the elasticity of demand and supply, as we have shown in chapter 6.

Consider the imposition of a tax on gasoline, as shown in figure 7.2. The free-market equilibrium price of a gallon of gasoline is $3.00. In equilibrium, 360 million gallons are sold every day. Now, suppose

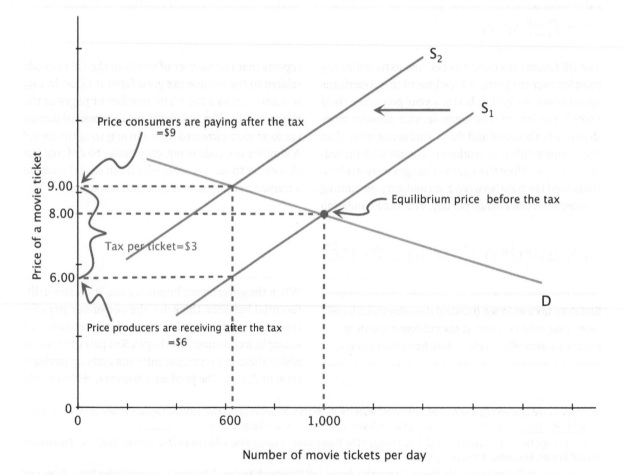

FIGURE 7.2 Tax on Producers with Inelastic Demand

that the government imposes a $3.00-per-gallon excise tax on gasoline. What does this do to the price of gasoline? The tax is initially a burden on producers and acts like an increase in cost of production for producer. As we have seen before in chapter 4, this would shift the supply curve to the left, as shown in figure 7.2. The producer price (the price of the product) falls to $2.00, while the consumer price (the price of the product plus the tax) rises to $5.00. The difference between the consumer price and the producer price ($3.00) is the tax.

According to figure 7.2, the price producers are receiving for gasoline is $2.00. Following the price of $2.00 over to the supply curve shows us that producers are willing to offer three hundred million gallons of gasoline per day. The price consumers are paying for gasoline is $5.00 ($2.00 plus $3.00 tax). Following the price of $5.00 over to the demand curve tells us

that consumers are also willing to buy three hundred million gallons per day. Thus, despite the difference between the consumer and producer prices, the market is in equilibrium—quantity demanded equals quantity supplied.

Notice that the majority of the burden of the taxation is being borne by the consumer. When the government imposed the $3.00 tax, the price consumers paid (plus the tax) rose by $2.00 (from $3.00 to $5.00), while the price that producers received fell by $1.00 (from $3.00 to $2.00)—of the $3.00 the government collects on every gallon of gasoline, consumers are paying $2.00 and producers are paying $1.00.

Consider now the case of imposing a $3.00 tax on movie tickets, as shown in figure 7.3. Before the imposition of the tax, the price of a movie ticket was $8.00 per ticket, and one thousand tickets were sold

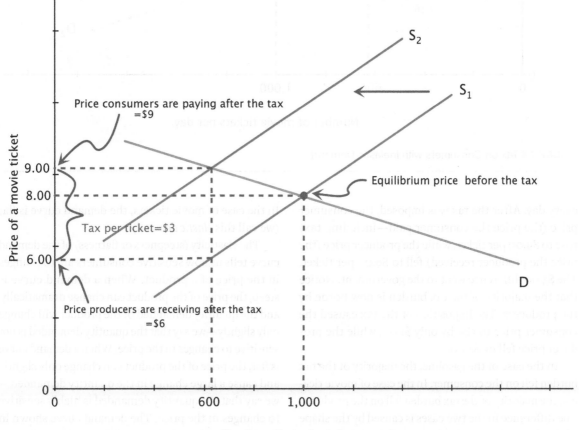

FIGURE 7.3 Tax on Producers with Elastic Demand

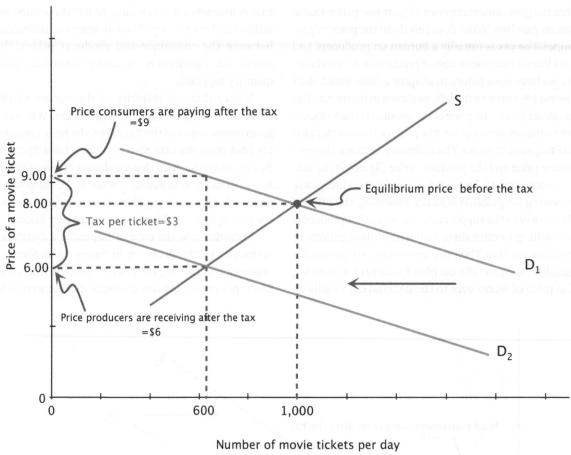

FIGURE 7.4 Tax on Consumers with Inelastic Demand

every day. After the tax was imposed, the consumer price (the price the consumer paid—including tax) rose to $9.00 per ticket, while the producer price (the price the producer received) fell to $6.00 per ticket. The $3.00 difference went to the government. Notice that the majority of the tax burden is now borne by the producers. The imposition of the tax caused the consumer price to rise by only $1.00, while the producer price fell by $2.00.

In the case of the gasoline, the majority of the tax burden fell on the consumer. In the case of movie tickets, the majority of the tax burden fell on the producer. The difference in the two cases is caused by the shape of the demand curve. In the case of the gasoline, the demand curve is steep (we call this *inelastic demand*).

In the case of movie tickets, the demand curve is flat (we call this *elastic demand*).

The elasticity (steepness or flatness) of the demand curve tells us how sensitive consumers are to changes in the price of a product. When a demand curve is steep, the price of the product can change dramatically, and the quantity demanded of the product will change only slightly—we say that the quantity demanded is not sensitive to changes in the price. When a demand curve is flat, the price of the product can change only slightly and cause a large change in the quantity demanded—we say that the quantity demanded is highly sensitive to changes in the price. The demand curve shown in figure 7.2 is relatively steep, while the demand curve in figure 7.3 is relatively flat. Notice that the majority of the tax burden for the product in figure 7.2 falls on

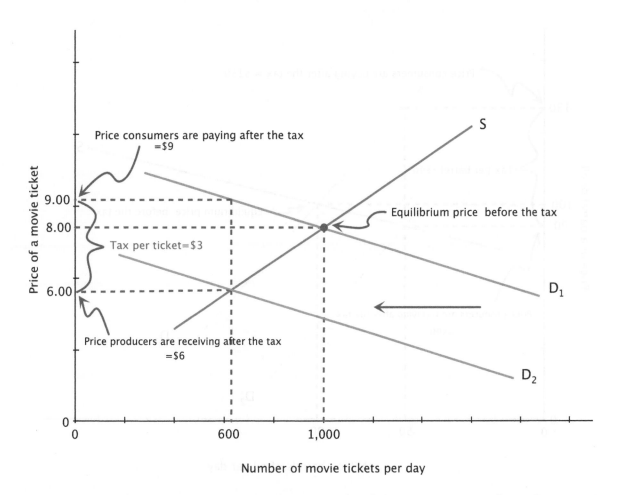

FIGURE 7.5 Tax on Consumers with Elastic Demand

the consumer, while the majority of the tax burden for the product in figure 7.3 falls on the producer. It is the case that the more sensitive consumers are to changes in the price of a product (i.e., the flatter the demand curve), the more of the tax burden will be borne by the producers.

We can do a similar exercise by imposing the tax on consumers while keeping the examples and the tax rates used in figures 7.2 and 7.3 the same. These are shown in figures 7.4 and 7.5. With the tax on consumers, it is now the demand curve that changes. A tax reduces the purchasing power of a consumer and acts like a decrease in income. Therefore, the demand curve shifts to the left, indicating a decrease in demand. While the shifts are different, the incidence results are the same. The tax incidence result in figure 7.4 is

the same as the tax incidence result in figure 7.2, while the tax incidence result in figure 7.5 is the same as the tax incidence result in figure 7.3.

In the next two figures, we show how the tax incidence or real tax burden on consumers rises as supply becomes more elastic. In figure 7.6, much of the tax burden, officially paid by consumers, effectively falls on suppliers due to relatively inelastic supply. However, in figure 7.7, firms with more elastic supply are able to shift much of the same tax burden onto consumers.

If supply is perfectly elastic and demand is not, the entire burden of a tax is shifted onto consumers in terms of a higher price, even though the seller is officially charged with a tax. When demand is just as elastic as supply, the tax burden is likely to be borne by both sides of the market equally, regardless of who

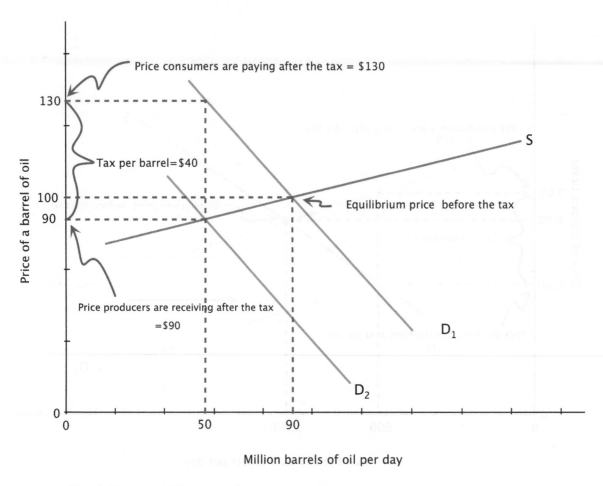

Price of a barrel of oil

Price consumers are paying after the tax = $130

130

Tax per barrel=$40

S

100
90

Equilibrium price before the tax

Price producers are receiving after the tax
=$90

D₁

D₂

0

0   50   90

Million barrels of oil per day

FIGURE 7.6 Tax on Consumers with Inelastic Supply

is officially responsible for paying a tax. If consumers are officially responsible for paying the entire tax, it is still split in half between consumers and producers.

The rule of thumb for any tax is this: the more inelastic side of the market will pay more in taxes, regardless of who is officially paying the tax.

The more responsive party (either consumers or producers) with elastic demand or supply bears a smaller share of the tax burden.

The less responsive party (either consumers or producers) with inelastic demand or supply bears the greater share of the tax burden.

Taxation and Efficiency

As we learned in the previous section, elasticity rather than law determines who truly pays taxes. But

elasticity also determines how much harm a tax can inflict on the market. How much people scale back on

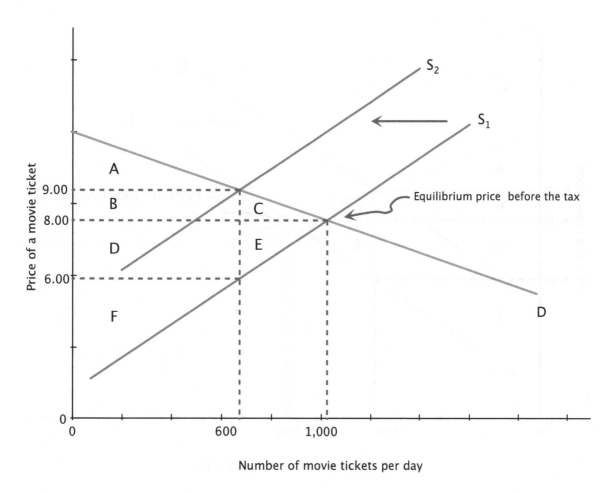

FIGURE 7.7 Tax on Consumers with Elastic Supply

production or consumption of something as a result of a tax-induced price increase would indicate how inefficient a tax can be. Consider two very different markets: one with rather elastic demand and supply and another with inelastic demand and supply. The same tax levied in each market will produce very different results. A tax levied in an elastic market will result in much lower production, tax revenue, and efficiency compared to an equivalent tax levied in an inelastic market. If people cannot easily change their behavior in response to a tax, they not only end up paying more of a tax but also undertake the taxed activity nearly as much as before. In sum, the elasticity concept also helps us understand how much deadweight loss (inefficiency) will be created by a tax.

Let us now revisit the excise tax (a tax on the purchases of a specific good or service) and examine it in light of what we know about consumer and producer surplus. Figure 7.8 shows the market for movie tickets. In the free-market equilibrium, tickets sell for $8.00, and one thousand tickets are sold each day. In the free-market equilibrium, the consumer surplus is area ABC and the producer surplus is area DEF. That is, the net benefit the consumer receives from buying and consuming the product is the same as he gets from the amount of money represented by area ABC. The net benefit the producer receives from manufacturing and selling the product is the amount of money represented by area DEF. The society surplus (the overall benefit society receives from this market) is the sum of the surpluses: area ABCDEF.

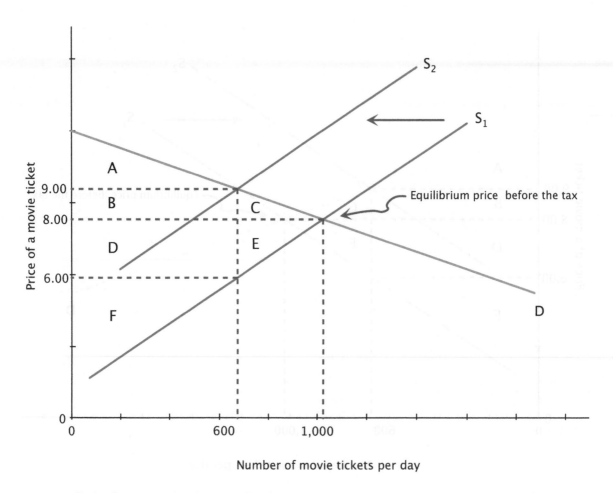

FIGURE 7.8 Excise Tax and Deadweight Loss (Elastic Demand)

Now, suppose that the government imposes a $3.00 excise tax on movie tickets.[13] The producer price of tickets (the price the producer receives) falls to $6.00. The consumer price of tickets (the producer price plus the tax) rises to $9.00. The $3.00 difference in the two prices goes to the government. After the tax is imposed, the consumer surplus becomes area A (the area above the consumer price, below the demand curve, and to the left of the quantity sold). The producer surplus becomes area F (the area below the producer price, above the supply curve, and to the left of the quantity sold). The revenue the government receives from the tax is $3.00 times six hundred units sold, or area BD

(the tax takes area B away from the consumer and gives it to the government, and takes area D away from the producer and gives it to the government). The society surplus is the consumer surplus plus the producer surplus *plus* the revenue the government receives from the tax. In the case of the tax, the overall benefit society receives from this market—the society surplus—is the area ABDF. What happened to areas C and E? These are no longer accounted for and are called *deadweight losses*. A *deadweight loss* is a type of opportunity cost—it is an amount of net benefit a market could have generated, but didn't. The deadweight loss area in figure 7.8 is also the area of a triangle where the base of the

---

13 Recall that an *excise tax* is a tax on the number of units sold, while a *sales tax* is a tax on the value of the product sold. While the figure depicts an excise tax, the same qualitative results discussed here are obtained when one considers a sales tax.

triangle can be thought of as the tax rate (or the difference between consumer price and producer price), and the height is the change in equilibrium quantity from before to after the tax.

Why did the market fail to generate the net benefit represented in areas C and E? The answer is actually quite profound. When the government imposed the tax, it distorted the price of movie tickets. So what? Well, price—it turns out—is far more than a number on a sticker. The free-market price of a product sends a signal to the economy as to how important the product is.

Now imagine that there is a town where the residents are almost addicted to movies, and they show very little responsiveness to movie ticket prices. That market is depicted in figure 7.9, where the demand

curve is now very steep, reflecting the price-inelastic demand. Starting from the same market equilibrium point of $8.00 per ticket and one thousand tickets sold per day, the same $3.00 tax would have a significantly different impact on the market. The number of tickets sold still decreases and the price per ticket still increases, but the magnitude of the changes is quite different. The market equilibrium price increases a lot, by $2.50, but the number of tickets sold decreases by only one hundred tickets. Because deadweight loss is mainly about the lost opportunity in terms of net benefit from an economic transaction, that loss would be much smaller in this case compared to the case with elastic demand shown previously in figure 7.8. This is best seen in the quantity sold in the market. In figure 7.8, the number of tickets sold goes down from

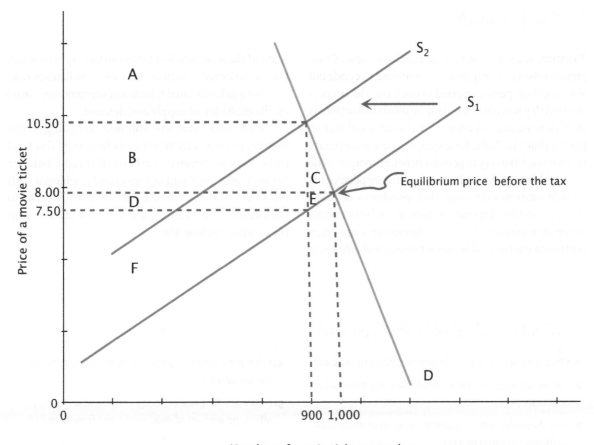

FIGURE 7.9 Excise Tax and Deadweight Loss (Inelastic Demand)

one thousand tickets per day to six hundred tickets per day, whereas in figure 7.9 it goes down from one thousand to nine hundred tickets per day. Notice also that the deadweight loss area (or triangle) C + E shown in figure 7.9 is indeed smaller than C + E in figure 7.8.

Deadweight loss rises exponentially with a rise in the tax rate. For example, doubling a tax leads to a quadrupling of deadweight loss. If the government wants to raise a lot of tax revenue efficiently (i.e., with minimal deadweight loss), it should tax inelastic items much more and elastic items less or not at all. This idea is known as the inverse elasticity rule and was proposed by economist Frank Ramsey. Of course, people who are inelastic in the production or consumption

of these items will bear most of the tax burden and will be strongly opposed to these taxes. This is why the government often tries to avoid taxing necessities like food too high, but has no problem taxing "sin" goods such as alcohol, tobacco, and gambling. There is also a practical alternative to differentiated taxation: broad-based taxes. The idea is to keep tax rates low, but tax virtually all goods and services that exist in order to generate sufficient revenue with the lowest deadweight loss. Taxation, it appears, is as much of an art as it is science.

A DEADWEIGHT LOSS is an amount of net benefit a market could have generated but did not.

CONCLUSION

Taxation is a very complex and divisive topic. Complexity arises not only from a convoluted tax code but also from how people respond to taxation. The concept of elasticity reveals not only how much distortion or inefficiency a tax can create but also who will end up paying that tax. Take, for example, the US corporate income tax. Contrary to popular belief, corporations do not pay this tax. The tax burden is borne by people that include consumers through their purchases of goods and services that corporations provide and others work for or own corporations. Divisiveness of a tax often centers on the tradeoff between fairness and efficiency:

some of the most efficient taxes can be very regressive. One of the interesting tax rules, called the Ramsey rule, calls for a differentiated taxation of commodities based on the elasticity of supply and demand.

While taxes that are imposed according to the Ramsey tax rule can be very efficient, they also tend to be very regressive. Perhaps, the right balance between efficiency and fairness can be achieved with the so-called broad based tax system, which seeks to tax virtually everything but at very low rates to keep the deadweight loss low.

QUESTIONS AND PROBLEMS

1. What are the main categories/items subject to taxation?

2. Can we separate the fairness and efficiency dimensions of taxation?

3. How do economists measure the amount of distortion/ inefficiency created by a tax?

4. What is the relationship between deadweight loss and the size of a tax?

5. How does the price elasticity of demand and supply affect the amount of deadweight loss from taxation?

Mathematical Model

Comparing the Effects of a Sales Tax and an Income Tax

Verbal Description: A consumer consumes leisure, a privately produced product, and a publicly produced product. The time the person does not spend in leisure is spent working at a job. The person consumes as much of the privately produced product as he desires and can afford. The amount of the publicly produced product the person consumes is determined by the government (i.e., the person consumes whatever amount of the public product the government produces). The government taxes the person both an income tax (on wages the person earns) and a sales tax (on the person's purchases of the private product) and uses the tax revenue to produce the public product. Determine how the usage of a sales tax versus an income tax affects the person's consumption of leisure and the private product, as well as the person's utility.

Definitions: Let L be the percentage of the person's time spent in leisure. Let X be the quantity of the private product the person purchases. Let Y be the quantity of the public product provided by the government. Let t be the proportional income tax rate. Let s be the sales tax rate. Let w be the wage the person earns for working 100 percent of the time. Let PX be the price of a unit of product X. Let PY be the price of a unit of product Y (i.e., it costs the government PY per unit to produce the public product).

Assumptions: Let the person's utility function be $U = LXY$. Assume that the government has a balanced budget (i.e., total government expenditures on product Y equals total tax revenues).

Setup: L and X are choice variables. Y, w, PX, PY, t, and s are parameters.

Procedure: First, determine the person's budget constraint accounting for the taxes. That is, the person's budget constraint should take the following form:

$$\text{Gross income} - \text{Income tax} = \text{Cost of } X + \text{Sales tax}$$

Second, determine the amount of Y the government will produce (hint: we have assumed that the government spends on Y exactly the amount of money it takes in as taxes).

Third, find formulae that show the quantity of X and the amount of L the person will consume as functions of the parameters.

Fourth, determine the *tax equivalence* relationship between t and s. That is, find t as a function of s, such that the amount of Y the government produces and the amount of X the person consumes are both constant. Substitute this equation for t in the person's consumption equation for X.

Fifth, examine how the person's consumption of X changes as s goes from 0 to 1. Note that, according to the tax equivalence relationship, as s approaches 0, t approaches 1, and as s approaches 1, t approaches 0.

8 Externalities, Public Goods, and Asymmetric Information

The smog in Beijing, China, highlights the potential tradeoff between economic development and cleaner environment, indicating that people in poorer countries might be willing to tolerate more pollution.[1]

---

1 Copyright © McKay Savage (CC by 2.0) at http://commons.wikimedia.org/wiki/File%3AChina_-_Beijing_1_-_Tiananmen_Square_(130829277).jpg.

Scientists estimate that the Earth's average temperature has increased by almost 1.4 degrees Fahrenheit over the past century. Over the next one hundred years, the Earth is projected to warm up somewhere between 2 and 11 degrees.[2] Even small increases in the Earth's temperature can lead to significant changes in climate, bringing with it severe droughts and rising sea levels. Many scientists believe that higher carbon dioxide emissions from human economic activity are partly to blame for this warming trend. Rapid deforestation, overfishing, and environmental degradation in general suggest that humanity might be unwilling or unable to tackle these important issues. This chapter examines the instances when the free market may fail to deliver the socially desired outcome and whether the government can fix it.

Market Failure

Market failure is a situation when the level of unregulated market activity is inefficiently high or inefficiently low. Much of the time, competitive free markets tend to produce the efficient level of output, where the benefit of producing another unit of something, usually called the *marginal benefit*, is offset by its expense, called the *marginal cost*. In other words, nothing extra can be gained by changing this level of activity, making it efficient for individuals and society as a whole. However, this may not always be the case. The market fails to achieve efficiency when it produces at a level where society's marginal benefit is not equal to its marginal cost. This could happen in the presence of externalities, public goods, monopoly, and asymmetric information, which are discussed in this chapter. In general, inefficiency occurs when something prevents people from bearing the full benefit or cost of their actions.

Government intervention might be able to steer the market to the efficient level of output. The most successful government policies, such as the cap-and-trade system or carbon taxes, tend to rely on the price mechanism in pushing markets toward the efficient level of output. One of the most successful environmental policies in the United States has been the Clean Air Act of 1970. This act and its consecutive amendments have dramatically improved the air quality and health outcomes in the country. Similar policies could be used to reduce carbon emissions, perhaps the largest negative externality the world has ever seen. But this requires international cooperation and unequally shared sacrifices. One might argue that the government should ban all pollution. Such a plan, however, would make virtually all production prohibitively expensive. Therefore, the optimal or efficient level of pollution is not zero.

Externalities

Externality is an uncompensated cost or benefit imposed on society by the behavior of optimizing individuals. Externalities can be positive (a benefit to society) or negative (a cost). Positive externalities that accompany the consumption of vaccines and education, for example, tend to be underproduced in a free market because individuals do not internalize the full benefit of their actions. Conversely, negative

MARKET FAILURE is a situation where the level of unregulated market activity is inefficiently low or high.

externalities, such as pollution, tend to be overproduced in a free market because individuals do not bear the full cost of their actions. Production externality,

2 US Environmental Protection Agency, "Climate Change: Basic Information," last updated March 18, 2014, http://www.epa.gov/climatechange/basics/.

whether it is positive or negative, stems from the actions of producers, while consumption externality stems from the actions of consumers.

Externalities arise because individual property rights are not clearly defined. In the case of pollution,

---

EXTERNALITY is an uncompensated cost or benefit imposed on society by the behavior of optimizing individuals.

EXTERNALITY can be negative or positive and it can arise from the production or consumption of something.

---

it is unclear who owns the air: do the people who breathe the air own it (so the factory should compensate the people for polluting the air), or does the firm own it (and should people pay the firm in exchange for breathing)? Because the ownership of the air cannot be clearly defined, someone (either the people or the firm) is being cheated out of payments that are rightfully theirs. In other words, air is a common resource, which means that it suffers from the same tragedy of the commons problem as do public lands, oceans, and rivers. The lack of private property rights gives rise to a negative externality, such as the tragedy of the commons.

Here's another example. Suppose there is a firm upstream from your house that dumps toxic waste into the river. This waste kills the fish (which wash up on your lawn), it makes the air stink, it makes your dog sick, and so on. The firm has imposed the cost of the pollution on you by forcing you to deal with the consequences of the pollution. Because the firm does not clean up the pollution, it can produce its product at a lower cost. Thus, the (marginal) cost to the firm of producing another unit is not the same as the (marginal) cost to society of having another unit of that good produced. Whenever the social marginal cost (benefit) is not the same as the private marginal cost (benefit), an externality arises.

Figure 8.1 shows the market for the product produced by the firms that pollute. The supply and demand curves intersect at point A. In equilibrium, the price of the firms' product is $4, and two thousand units are sold every day. The industry's supply curve is also the private marginal cost (PMC) curve, because the

firm is not incurring the cost of pollution. The social marginal cost (SMC) curve, which is the sum of PMC and marginal damage from pollution (MD), shows the cost to society of the firms' production, or what the PMC should truly be. The costs to society include (a) the costs to the firms (because the firms are members of society) and (b) the pollution caused by the firms. The demand curve shows the benefit to consumers from consuming the product. Because the consumers are members of society, the demand curve also shows the social marginal benefit (SMB) of the consumers' consumption. The marginal benefit to society is the same as the marginal benefit to the consumers (i.e., the market demand), because the pollution is generated by production, not consumption.

Notice point B in the figure. When the firms produce two thousand units of product per day, the marginal cost to society of producing one more unit per day is $8, but the marginal benefit to society of producing one more unit per day is only $4. This says that if the firms were to decrease their total output by one unit per day, the benefit to society would decrease by $4, but the cost to society would decrease by $8. Thus, if the firms decreased their total output by one unit per day, society would be $4 per day better off! In fact, as long as the marginal cost to society is greater than the marginal benefit to society, society as a whole is better off producing less of the product. The optimal amount of production is the amount at which the marginal cost to society is equal to the marginal benefit to society—this occurs at 1,500 units of output per day (point C). In a free-market system, firms may not achieve the efficient level of output and pollution because the firms are making production decisions without taking into account the costs that they are imposing on society, resulting in deadweight loss (DWL) or inefficiency equal to the shaded triangle in the figure.

Suppose that you live next door to a woman who keeps a beautiful garden. In this garden are many flowers, which bloom all through the summer. From your porch, you have a delightful view of the woman's garden. This is an example of a positive externality— the woman is providing you with an uncompensated benefit. Although you may be quite happy with this benefit, it is not good for society any more than the

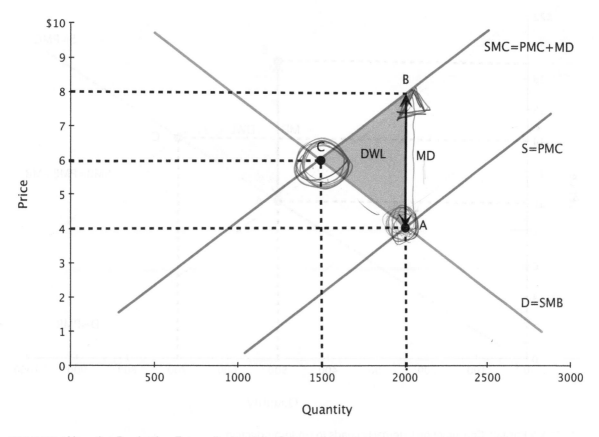

FIGURE 8.1 Negative Production Externality Leads to Overproduction

pollution in the previous example. How can flowers be as bad as pollution? It is not that the flowers are bad—what is bad is that the woman may not plant the socially efficient quantity of flowers. We call this a positive consumption externality because it is a benefit accruing onto society from the consumption of a product.

Figure 8.2 shows the market for flowers. The free-market equilibrium is found at point A, at the intersection of the demand (private marginal benefit, or PMB) and supply (private marginal cost, or PMC) of flowers. According to the diagram, there will be five hundred flowers sold each day at a price of $10 each. In equilibrium, the marginal cost to the firms of producing one more flower per day is $10, and the marginal benefit to the consumers of consuming one more flower per day is $10. When a consumer purchases and plants a flower, however, the flower also benefits the neighbors because it beautifies the

neighborhood (i.e., a positive consumption externality occurs). Thus, when there are five hundred flowers sold each day, social marginal benefit (SMC) to society of consuming one more flower per day is $19, the sum of private marginal benefit (PMB) of $10 and external marginal benefit (MB) of $9. Notice that the production of the flowers does not impose any benefits on society, only the consumption, hence the industry's supply curve is the same as the marginal social cost curve.

What does this mean? If society's utility increases the equivalent of $19 when one more flower is consumed each day, but society's costs increase only $10 when one more flower is consumed each day, then society is $9 better off per day if it increases its consumption of flowers by one unit per day. In fact, as long as the marginal benefit to society of another flower is greater than the marginal cost to society of another flower, society should consume another flower. This

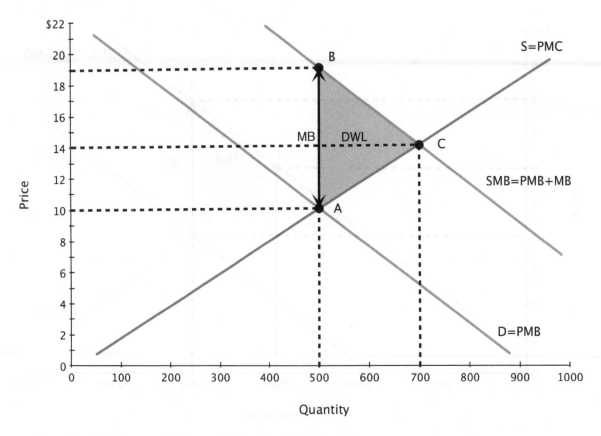

FIGURE 8.2 Positive Consumption Externality Leads to Underproduction

implies that the free-market equilibrium at point A is inefficient, resulting in deadweight loss equal to the shaded triangle. The efficient output of flowers is found at point C (seven hundred flowers per day), where the marginal benefit to society of one more flower ($14) just equals the marginal cost to society of one more flower. We can see that in the presence of a positive

consumption externality, less than the efficient amount of the product is sold at the free-market equilibrium.

For the market to be efficient in the presence of externalities, whether it is emitting pollution or planting flowers, people must bear (internalize) the full cost or benefit of their actions. There are two fundamental ways in which that can be done: either through private efforts or government intervention.

Decentralized Solutions to Externalities

Are free markets doomed to be inefficient in the presence of externalities? Not necessarily, points out Elinor Ostrom, the Nobel Prize laureate in economics. In her analysis of forest harvesting in sixteenth-century Switzerland and seventeenth-century Japan, for example, she noticed that these communities developed social norms or agreements that helped them mitigate negative externalities, such as the tragedy of the

commons. In other words, she found that groups of people, resembling neither the state nor the market,

---

COASIAN SOLUTION is an attempt by private parties to internalize an externality through bargaining and negotiations.

---

can develop institutions to address the fundamental cause of externalities: the lack of private property rights over certain resources.

Yet externalities can exist even in the presence of well-defined property rights. Ronald Coase, another Nobel Prize laureate in economics, argues that in this case if nothing prevents people from trading, the efficient level of externality can be reached through bargaining. The following example illustrates the logic behind the so-called Coase theorem, or the Coasian solution. A large positive externality exists in the pollination industry: beekeepers unintentionally increase farmers' harvest through pollination, while farmers' orchards unintentionally boost beekeepers' honey output. It would make sense for both types of businesses to cooperate in order to internalize this positive externality. And they do! Beekeepers rent out their hives to farmers for a fee, which turns an uncompensated benefit (i.e., externality) into a compensated one, allowing both parties to become more efficient. The surprising aspect of the Coasian solution is that it does not matter who has the property rights or who pays whom: the externality would still be internalized if beekeepers had to pay farmers for allowing beehives on their property. The same logic applies to a negative externality, such as pollution: a party affected by the pollution may pay the polluter, as unfair as it sounds, for reducing the harmful emissions, or the polluter may have to compensate the wronged party for the inflicted harm. Either way, bargaining should lead to an efficient level of externality. However, the Coasian solution can fail to work in the presence of high transaction costs. For example, when too many people are involved, the cost of reaching an agreement can be quite high, especially if there is a holdout problem, where the individual with a decisive vote stifles bargaining by demanding excessive compensation. For these reasons, it is unlikely that large externalities, such as carbon dioxide emissions, can be internalized through individual bargaining.

Centralized Solutions to Externalities

The failure of the Coasian solution in some situations opens the door for government intervention as the alternative solution to market failure. The government can intervene in two different ways: (1) directly regulate the quantity of emissions (i.e., command and control) or (2) use the price mechanism in the form of a cap-and-trade system or its analytical equivalent—corrective taxes and subsidies—in order to steer the market toward the efficient level. Economists typically prefer the latter type of regulation because it is more likely to achieve the efficient level of the regulated activity at a lower cost to society. In a cap-and-trade system, the government issues a limited number of pollution permits (i.e., the right to pollute), effectively assigning property rights over pollution and allowing people to trade them. Essentially, tradable pollution permits allow companies to emit a certain amount of pollution into the air for a fee. Companies that can reduce emissions at a lower cost than paying for permits will sell their permits to companies that need them. If society determines that there is too much polluting, people adversely affected by the pollution will seek to purchase the permits so that they are not used. This increase in the demand for permits causes the price of permits to rise. Firms that pollute heavily will then face a higher price for additional permits, giving them incentives to pollute less. The end result is a more efficient (lower) level of pollution.

The US Clean Air Act, later augmented with a cap-and-trade system, has led to significant reductions in sulfur dioxide and other pollutants, with the benefits of cleaner air exceeding the compliance costs by a factor of thirty to one. The Environmental Protection Agency (EPA) estimates that from 1970 to 2012, aggregate national emissions of the six common pollutants

PIGOUVIAN SOLUTION is a collective attempt to force private parties to internalize an externality through taxes or subsidies.

have dropped on average by 72 percent.[3] EPA claims that by 2020, the Clean Air Act Amendments could prevent more than 230,000 early deaths. Similarly, the Kyoto Protocol, as of this writing ratified by 191 countries, with the exception of the United States, has also sought to reduce global emissions of greenhouse gasses through the use of a cap-and-trade system, albeit with limited success because of significant disagreements among some of the biggest carbon-emitting nations. The difficulty of achieving international cooperation on reducing carbon emissions paints a gloomy picture of our collective ability to deal with longer-term challenges such as climate change. Conversely, in a rare feat of international cooperation, the Montreal Protocol, signed in 1987, has led to a significant reduction in chlorofluorocarbon (CFC) emissions responsible for the depletion of the Earth's ozone layer.

Of course, no one is stopping countries from reducing pollution emissions unilaterally. Welcome to the Pigou club, named after a British economist, Arthur Cecil Pigou. The members of this informal group include many prominent economists who advocate the use of corrective taxes and subsidies as a way to internalize externalities. The Pigouvian solution to a negative (positive) externality is to institute a tax (subsidy) per unit of some good equal to the marginal damage (benefit) from that externality. Such a corrective tax or subsidy would force the agents to bear the costs or benefits of their actions and move the market equilibrium toward efficiency.

Figure 8.3 illustrates how a corrective tax set equal to the marginal damage (MD) from pollution could move the market toward the efficient level of output and associated pollution (point C), eliminating the deadweight loss from this negative production externality. If the tax in the amount of $4 per unit of this good is imposed on the producers, it moves the market supply curve, or PMC, to the left (a reduction in supply) and makes it equal to social marginal cost (PMC +

Tax = SMC), as shown in the figure. If the same tax is imposed on the consumers, it reduces the market demand, or PMB, resulting in the new intersection or equilibrium with PMC at the price of $2 and 1,500 units. Either way, the tax decreases the inefficiently high level of pollution and production at 2,000 units to the lower and efficient level of pollution and production at 1,500 units.

While the mechanics of the Pigouvian solution differ from the cap-and-trade solution, the two are solutions identical in their effects on the market because both solutions rely on the price mechanism. Many economists believe that higher taxes on fossil fuels in the United States could help reduce pollution and allow for efficiency-increasing tax cuts elsewhere. While this proposal offers very strong social efficiency benefits, it is not gaining political traction.

Still, not all hope is lost, even when national governments fail to enact appropriate corrective policies. Consider the illuminating case of Ecofiltro, a private Guatemalan company owned and managed by Philip Wilson. This for-profit company sells aesthetically pleasing and competitively priced water filters, which improve people's health and productivity. Ecofiltro already epitomizes Adam Smith's invisible-hand argument that private gain can promote societal well-being. But the story gets even better: no longer needing to boil water to sanitize it, people emit less carbon dioxide and cut down fewer trees for fuel. These positive externalities represent the additional benefits to society that the company, in theory, would underprovide because it receives no monetary compensation for it. This would typically be the end of the story, which is fortunately not true in this case. Being a recipient of the coveted Gold Standard Certification for clean production, Ecofiltro reaps the benefits from the positive externalities it provides by selling carbon credits in the Voluntary Carbon Market to other environmentally conscientious companies, such as Microsoft, for example. These incentives allow the company to sell more filters at a lower price, making clean water affordable even for the poorest of households. The case of Ecofiltro demonstrates that a combination of proper

3 US Environmental Protection Agency, "Progress Cleaning the Air and Improving People's Health," last updated April 22, 2014, http://www.epa.gov/air/caa/progress.html#breathe.

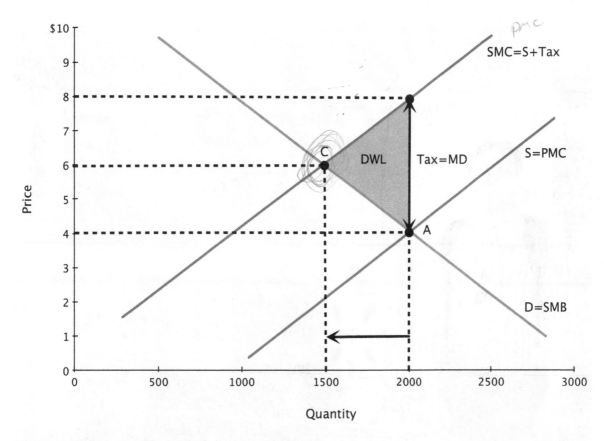

FIGURE 8.3 A Corrective (Pigouvian) Tax Leads to Efficiency

incentives and responsible private ownership have the potential to correct for some externalities.

Public Goods

Competitive free markets tend to produce a wide variety of private goods rather efficiently, but there is a class of goods, known as public goods, that the free market may not be able to provide efficiently or at all. A combination of two characteristics of a good, rivalry and excludability, determine how efficiently the free market may provide them. A rival good becomes less available when more of it is consumed. For example, if we are sharing a pizza and I eat more of it, there is less pizza left for you. In contrast, a non-rival good, such as sunshine, can be enjoyed by many of us without reducing its availability to others. An excludable good, such as pizza, is a product that cannot be acquired through a voluntary trade unless it is paid for. Conversely, a

PUBLIC GOOD is a type of good that is non-rival and non-excludable in consumption. A public good can sometimes be provided by the private sector, but is often provided by the government.

non-excludable good is a product that companies cannot effectively prevent people from consuming if they did not pay for it.

Most goods produced in the economy are both rival and excludable, which makes them pure private goods. Unlike a private good, a pure public good is both non-rival and non-excludable: by its nature, it can be denied to no one. National defense is a popular

Textbook author Pavel Yakovlev (left) and Ecofiltro owner and CEO Philip Wilson (right) pictured in front of the company's water filters.

example of a public good. Individuals inside an antimissile defense system, for example, cannot be selectively excluded from enjoying it, even if they did not pay for it. Another excellent example of a public good is a lighthouse. Once a lighthouse is operational, it alerts all ships to the presence of land, whether or not they paid for it. This non-excludable feature of public goods gives rise to the free-rider problem, which threatens the efficient provision of public goods in a free market. If private companies cannot find a cost-effective way of preventing people from consuming a good without paying for it, companies will not be able to collect enough revenue to cover their costs and will go out of business. In other words, the government tends to provide public goods such as national defense and lighthouses not because they are called public, but rather because they are likely to be underprovided in

FREE RIDERS threaten the private provision of a public good unless the private sector can exclude non-payers from consuming.

a free market because of free riders. The government overcomes the free-rider problem by forcing people to pay for public goods through taxes.

Recall that the market demand for a private good is derived through a horizontal summation of individual demands. In contrast, the market demand for a public good is derived through a vertical summation of individual demands. This means that instead of varying the quantity consumed for a given price, as it happens in a private good market, we now vary the price that each individual has to pay for a given quantity of public good. The implication here is that the government has to determine how much each individual will pay in taxes when providing a public good.

The paradox here is that individual optimization that usually leads to efficiency in a free market may create a market failure in public goods, while a coercive institution such as the government, which is not typically known for efficiency, may actually improve the market outcome. There may also be no conflict between individual freedom and government provisions of public goods. Recall that public goods tend to be underprovided because free riders do not contribute to the goods they benefit from. In other words, free riders take what is not theirs. By forcing people to pay for public goods through taxes, the government assigns implicit property rights and effectively internalizes this externality. This logic is easily seen in the case of computer software, which can be considered a public good. Once the firm manufactures and sells a single copy of its software, it becomes non-rival but also non-excludable, as it is costly for a company to prevent people from copying it. The illegal copying of proprietary software is another form of free riding that threatens the provision of valuable public goods. The aim of government intervention in the form of copyright or intellectual property laws is to establish and protect individual property. Thus, government intervention, either in the form of government-provided public goods or publicly financed but privately provided public goods, may improve efficiency.

Does the government always need to intervene to ensure the efficient provision of public goods? The successful operation of privately owned lighthouses in seventeenth-century England noted by Ronald Coase suggests that the answer is no. The private lighthouse owners overcame the free-rider problem through bargaining with port owners, much like the beekeepers and farmers in the earlier example: a portion of the ships' docking fees went to the lighthouse owners, on the assumption that the ships must have used the lighthouse to arrive in that port. Furthermore, if some public goods are rather localized, like a flower garden, people with strong private demands may obtain the efficient quantity of them, regardless of whether their neighbors contribute or not. For example, the father of one of the textbook's authors felt so strongly about having a paved road leading up to his house that he paid for it fully without any contribution from his neighbors, who undoubtedly benefit from using it. Thus, as we saw with externalities, public goods can sometimes be provided privately.

WATER AS AN ECONOMIC GOOD   Water is one of the most important resources we have on earth. It is certainly a scarce resource. This is particularly visible to those who live in drought areas of the world. At the same time there is quite bit of debate and controversy regarding the economic nature of water. Is it a human right? Is it a private good or a public good? Should the government intervene in the water markets? There are many good economic arguments revolving around these questions.

Monopoly

A *monopoly* is a market with a single supplier of a product for which there is no close substitute. For example, if pizzas and hot dogs are good substitutes, having a single pizza shop and hot dog stand in town does not constitute a monopoly, because the two businesses have to compete for the same customers. Still, the level of competition even with two firms may not be very strong. The lack of competition lowers efficiency, because companies do not have the incentive to innovate, guarantee quality, and keep prices near the cost of production. The government can increase competition by dismantling artificial monopolies or collusive agreements, as exemplified by US antitrust regulation in the form of the Sherman and Clayton Acts of 1890 and 1914, respectively. More often than not though, the government creates additional barriers to entry and reduces competition. For instance, regulations in many US cities require taxicab operators to purchase a permit, known as "the medallion" in the trade, in order to legally operate their business. The number

---

MONOPOLY is a market with a single producer (supplier) of a good.

---

of medallions is tightly controlled by the government, which protects the established taxi businesses by increasing the cost of market entry (a taxi medallion in New York City sold for more than $1 million in 2013[4]). Higher barriers to entry lead to fewer taxicabs and higher fares.[5] A telltale sign of the artificially created inefficiency is the prevalence of unlicensed taxi drivers, whom the government often tries to prosecute for trying to satisfy the unmet demand. It is hard to argue that policies like that are in the public interest.

There is one case, though, where government regulation in the form of price controls or government takeover of an industry might improve market efficiency. This may happen in the presence of a natural monopoly, an industry characterized by really high fixed costs, such that a single large firm can satisfy the entire market demand at a lower cost than several smaller firms. Economies of scale or cost spreading across more units of output gives a bigger firm the cost advantage over smaller firms, similar to splitting the rent with a roommate or reducing the cost of commuting through carpooling. Some of the highest fixed-cost industries include the airline, automotive, energy, utilities, and telecommunications industries. A natural monopoly may form in these kinds of industries, leading to anticompetitive pricing. Because breaking up these industries into smaller competing firms raises the cost of production, the government is left with either regulating the industry's price or taking over the natural monopoly and selling its product at a competitive price, which is often done with local utilities, such as electricity and water. The implementation of these policies, however, is easier said than done, because the government may not know the cost structure of the industry or its competitive price. Furthermore, government bureaucracies may lack the incentive to innovate and operate efficiently, which undercuts the justification for government intervention. A more detailed analysis of monopoly regulation is presented in chapter 12.

Asymmetric Information

Competitive free markets may also fail to achieve efficiency in the presence of asymmetric information, a situation where one party to an exchange has pertinent private information about the item to be traded and both parties are aware of that. The consequence of this information asymmetry is that the market price of a product or service may exceed its benefit, causing the market to underproduce it. The used-car market is a popular example of this problem. Contrary to the owners of used cars, buyers in this market have a hard time distinguishing between good and bad used cars of a similar make, known respectively as "peaches" and "lemons" in the trade. Not knowing which one is a good one, buyers might be tempted to go for a lower-priced one, only to find out that it is a lemon because the

---

ASYMMETRIC INFORMATION is a situation where one of the parties to an exchange has private information about the product or service that is relevant to both parties.

---

owners of reliable used cars are not willing to sell what they know to be good cars below their true value. The consequence of asymmetric information in the used car market is that it tends to be dominated by lemons, discouraging many individuals from buying a used car. This is a problem not only for the buyers but also for the sellers: too many buyers and sellers give up on the exchange, making the market inefficiently small.

---

4 Matt Flegenheimer, "$1 Million Medallions Stifling the Dreams of Cabdrivers," *New York Times*, November 14, 2013, http://www.nytimes.com/2013/11/15/nyregion/1-million-medallions-stifling-the-dreams-of-cabdrivers.html?_r=0.

5 S. Dompe and A. C. Smith, "Taxicab Cartels Restrict Entry into Market at the Expense of Consumers," Mercatus Center (November 24, 2014). Available at: http://mercatus.org/publication/taxicab-cartels-restrict-entry-market-expense-consumers.

Identified by George Akerlof, a Nobel Prize laureate in economics, this problem is generally known as adverse selection, which can be described as the prevalence of an inferior good, service, or outcome in the market. The adverse selection problem caused by asymmetric information is pervasive: it affects many markets, from labor to insurance. Employers and universities, for example, have a hard time determining whether a candidate they are interested in is a peach or a lemon.

While recent advancements in information technology have reduced the severity of asymmetric information in many markets, adverse selection still continues to plague the health and auto insurance markets. The adverse selection problem in unregulated insurance markets leads to cost spirals. Less healthy people are more likely to buy health insurance, which leads to a rise in insurance premiums. Higher insurance premiums price the relatively healthy people out of the market, leaving the insurance companies with an unhealthy pool of customers, which increases the cost of insurance even further. This upward spiral in insurance premiums leads to the underprovision of insurance, which is inefficient. In the United States, many firms provide their employees with health insurance automatically, which somewhat reduces the adverse selection problem. However, for more than 15 percent of uninsured Americans, who have to buy health insurance on the open market, adverse selection is a real problem. The government can solve the adverse selection problem in the health insurance market as it does in the auto insurance market by mandating universal coverage. When both healthy and unhealthy people have to buy insurance, the diverse pool of insured customers lowers the risk for insurance companies and prevents adverse selection from taking place. The Affordable Care Act signed into law by President Obama in 2010 seeks to eliminate the adverse selection problem by creating a health insurance mandate for the uninsured Americans.

However, a new problem known as the moral hazard stems from asymmetric information. *Moral hazard* can be defined as a situation where a party behaves in a socially inefficient manner because of perverse incentives. In the insurance market, moral hazard usually takes the form of irresponsible behavior by the insured, such as reckless driving, unhealthy lifestyle, or overconsumption of insurance. The author's auto insurance experience is illuminating. A car and deer collision resulted in some cosmetic damage to the car and its tire, which the insurance company paid to fix. The author did not turn down a new tire, although he would not have chosen to replace it in the absence of insurance. This is inefficient, because having insurance has altered individual behavior and cost society an extra tire. The extent of moral hazard in the health insurance market can be rather severe since people do not have strong incentives to conserve resources when insurance companies are paying for their treatments. The moral hazard problem is very much akin to the tragedy of the commons, where people overconsume the common resource. Thus, asymmetric information may lead to an underprovision of insurance in a free market (the adverse-selection problem) and its overconsumption in the regulated market (the moral hazard problem), simultaneously justifying and undercutting the case for government intervention in the market.

Government Failure

Nirvana is not for this world—governments may also fail to correct a market failure. Government regulation can create side effects that are as bad or even worse than the problem it is trying to correct, in which case the public has to choose between the lesser of two evils: government failure or market failure. To understand why governments may fail, we first need to understand how governments operate. The field of economics known as political economy or public choice seeks to explain why the government chooses to do what it does. The common assumption of self-interested, optimizing individuals applies equally to private individuals and public officials. The basic problem with the government system is that, in contrast to a competitive market, it puts private interest in conflict with public interest. In other words, the individuals in the

GOVERNMENT FAILURE is a situation where the government fails to correct a market failure.

private sector openly pursue their self-interest and, by doing so, promote the common good through competition. Meanwhile, public officials are supposed to promote the common good without regard for self-interest, which is pretty hard to do. This basic conflict of interests gives rise to corruption and various other abuses of power. Furthermore, the coercive nature of government raises some poignant philosophical questions about government involvement in the private affairs of its citizens. As Thomas Paine, the author of the famous *Common Sense* pamphlet, aptly put it, "government even in its best state is but a necessary evil; in its worst state an intolerable one."

This section focuses on several theories that seek to explain how the popular form of government known as representative democracy actually operates. The first and perhaps the most insightful theory stems from the rational voter model, which reasons that rational individuals will vote for a particular candidate when the benefits of voting exceed its costs. The costs of voting may not be trivial, while the benefits are typically slim. It has been reported that some individuals waited in line for seven hours to cast a vote in the 2012 US presidential election.[6] Furthermore, there is a real probability that an individual may get injured or killed in a traffic accident on the way to a voting station. And what about the benefits? First of all, how much different would your life be if the opposing candidate won the presidential election? Many individuals will probably not notice any real difference in their lives, which may explain why so many people are apathetic toward politics. Second of all, even if you really care about who wins the presidential election, *your particular vote*

is extremely unlikely to make a difference or, in economics jargon, unlikely to be decisive. One study has estimated that a voter in America had a one in sixty million chance of casting a decisive vote in the 2008 presidential election.[7] When dying in a car accident has higher odds than casting a decisive vote, it is rather puzzling that about 50 percent of Americans choose to vote in presidential elections. Are voters delusional, or are they really bad at math? Perhaps neither. Some economists believe that the voter turnout is so high because people simply enjoy expressing their preferences or opinions through voting, like they do through bumper stickers or sports teams' merchandise.

What makes the rational voter model important is its implication that individuals have very little incentive to be informed about their government given that an individual's vote is unlikely to make a difference in a large election. In other words, it is rational for voters to be ignorant. And the widely documented, shockingly low level of political knowledge among voters corroborates this hypothesis. For example, the results from the 2000 National Election Study indicate that 58 percent of survey respondents admit that they have heard "very little" or "nothing" about the USA Patriot Act, which has significantly increased law enforcement powers for the claimed purpose of fighting terrorism.[8] It gets even worse: slightly more than 50 percent of respondents know which party has control of the Senate, and about 30 percent can name either of their state's senators, while the vast majority of respondents fail to name any congressional candidate in their district at the height of a political campaign.[9] It is difficult to expect sound policies from a representative democracy that relies on such appallingly uninformed voters.

The ignorance issue is further compounded by the difficulty of observing and transforming voters' views, as ignorant as they might be, into sound policy. First,

---

6 Andrew Cohen, "No One in America Should Have to Wait 7 Hours to Vote," *The Atlantic*, November 5, 2012, http://www.theatlantic.com/politics/archive/2012/11/no-one-in-america-should-have-to-wait-7-hours-to-vote/264506/.

7 Gelman, Andrew, Nate Silver, and Aaron Edlin, "What Is the Probability Your Vote Will Make a Difference?" *Economic Inquiry* 50 (2012): 321–326.

8 Ilya Somin, "When Ignorance Isn't Bliss: How Political Ignorance Threatens Democracy," *Policy Analysis* 525 (2004), http://www.cato.org/sites/cato.org/files/pubs/pdf/pa525.pdf.

9 Michael X. Delli Carpini and Scott Keeter. *What Americans Know about Politics and why it Matters* (New Haven, CT: Yale University Press, 1996, p. 94) and W. Russell Neumann, *The Paradox of Mass Politics* (Cambridge, MA: Harvard University Press, 1986, p. 15)

people may not be able to quantify how much or what kind of government spending they want, which is called the preference knowledge problem. For example, do you know how much the federal government should spend on national defense to make you feel safe?

Second, people may not want to reveal their true preferences even if they know them, which is known as the preference revelation problem. Third, the government may not be able to translate voter preferences into a fair and efficient policy, known as the preference aggregation problem. The challenges in aggregating individual preferences were highlighted by Kenneth Arrow, Nobel prize-winning economist. Arrow's impossibility theorem postulates that the four essential features of any voting system are impossible to attain without violating at least one of them. Arrow's work implies that a democratic system of government will have to restrict some preferences in formulating a collective decision. Even the widely espoused majority voting system is far from being ideal, as it ignores the preferences of a sizable voting minority and may lead to inefficient and inconsistent policies.

For better or worse, simple majority voting is a very popular system, and it is important to understand how it works. Suppose that you have a society with three voters and two political candidates. Suppose that each voter uniquely prefers either the low, medium, or high level of government spending. The vote-maximizing strategy for each political candidate is to offer voters the medium level of government spending most preferred by the voter in the middle of the continuum (i.e., the median voter). If one candidate offers the low level of spending and the other candidate offers the medium level, the candidate offering the medium level will win the election by obtaining the needed votes from individuals preferring medium and high levels of

spending. This median voter model, based originally on Harold Hotelling's optimal business location model and applied to politics by Anthony Downs, suggests that a simple majority system is likely to implement the policy most preferred by the person located in the middle of the political spectrum. This may explain why politicians pander so much to the middle-class or centrist voters. Despite its elegance, the median voter model does not guarantee the efficient or fair outcome.

The presence of asymmetric information can make the already imperfect system of government even more fallible. Asymmetric information, which causes moral hazard, makes it very costly for the voters (principal) to ensure that their representatives (agents) serve their interest or do not engage in legislative shirking. Moral hazard or the conflict of interests that it creates has come to be known as the principal-agent problem. In a clever study, Ebonya Washington examines the voting patterns in Congress and finds that the gender of legislators' children influences the direction in which representatives stray from their constituents' preferences.[10] Lobbying may also cause politicians to enact policies that benefit a narrow group of individuals at the expense of the general public. Bailouts, trade barriers, and protectionist subsidies are glaring examples of legislation that falls prey to concentrated private gains at the expense of the general public. For example, American taxpayers currently spend more than $20 billion per year on farm subsidies, even though the average farmer's income exceeds that of the average American.[11] Most trade barriers seek to protect select domestic firms or industries from foreign competition at the expense of the majority of population. Such policies do not appear to be efficient or democratic, yet they can be found in virtually every representative democracy.

---

10 Ebonya L. Washington, "Female Socialization: How Daughters Affect Their Legislator Fathers' Voting on Women's Issues," *American Economic Review* 98 (2008): 311–332.

11 V. Smith, "The 2013 Farm Bill: Limiting Waste by Limiting Farm Subsidy Budgets." Mercatus Center (June 17, 2013). Available at: http://mercatus.org/publication/bloated-farm-subsidies-will-2013-farm-bill-really-cut-fat

CONCLUSION

We learned in this chapter that the market can fail to achieve the efficient outcome for society. The market fails when social costs or benefits are not aligned with the private ones. This may occur in the presence of externalities, which include the tragedy of the commons (a negative externality) and public goods (a positive externality), as well as natural monopolies and asymmetric information. Unfortunately, the government may also fail to improve the market outcome. As a result, economists argue that the choice should be made on a case-by-case basis given that sometimes the market and sometimes the government deliver the superior outcome.

DISCUSSION QUESTIONS

1. What are the main causes of market failure?

2. What are the main causes of government failure?

3. Why cap-and-trade system and pollution taxes are viewed as being analytically equivalent?

4. Compare and contrast the Pigouvian and Coasian solutions to externalities.

5. Are commercial radio stations a public or private good? Is there a market failure in that industry?

6. Is water a private good or a public good? What are some of the externalities associated with water? What is the industry structure in the provision of water in the United States and other countries?

Factor and Financial Markets

9

I t is estimated that Tim Cook, the CEO of Apple Inc., earned about $377 million in 2011. Tiger Woods and Robert Downey Jr. each purportedly earned more than $75 million between 2012 and 2013. The highest-earning professions in the United States are concentrated in the medical sector, according to the Bureau of Economic Analysis (BEA), with anesthesiologists and surgeons topping the list with an average salary of more than $230,000. Sadly, most of us earn much less. If you are a recent college graduate, your starting annual salary might be about $62,000 if you have a bachelor's degree in engineering and about $37,000 if you have a bachelor's degree in the social sciences.[1] According to the Bureau of Labor Statistics (BLS), the average personal income in the United States in 2012 was slightly more than $42,000. Many people earn even less than that. In 2012, 16 percent of Americans earned less than $11,720, the federal poverty threshold per person. Why is there such a drastic disparity in incomes? As usual, demand and supply can explain a large portion of the observed inequality in incomes.

In a free-market economy, a person earns a living by offering something of value to others in exchange for a payment. A voluntary exchange will occur only if both parties benefit from it. Households

FACTORS OF PRODUCTION (land, labor, and physical capital) are the inputs used to produce outputs such as goods and services.
FACTOR MARKET is a market where firms buy or rent the factors of produc-tion owned by households.

---

1 Susan Adams, "The College Degrees with the Highest Starting Salaries," Forbes, September 20, 2013, http://www.forbes.com/sites/susanadams/2013/09/20/the-college-degrees-with-the-highest-starting-salaries/.

supply factors of production or inputs, such as labor, land, and physical capital. If laborers value their time less than what employers are willing to pay them, workers get hired. At the competitive equilibrium, the wage rate reflects the value of labor acceptable to both sides of the market. A similar story could be told about physical capital: firms will accumulate machines, equipment, and structures up to the point where their prices equal their value. This demand-and-supply theory helps explain the distribution of income among workers and capital owners. The labor and capital factor markets are the focus of this chapter.

The Labor Market

The *labor market* is an interaction of workers and firms, respectively, supplying and demanding labor. Individuals exchange various things of value (skills, time, effort) in this market, typically for monetary compensation. The common form of compensation in the labor market is the *real wage rate*, which is the nominal (i.e., observed) wage rate adjusted for the cost of living. It is determined by the interaction of market demand and supply, the determinants of which are discussed in the next sections.

Work Decision and Labor Supply

Individuals face the basic tradeoff between work and leisure: more income can be earned by sacrificing some leisure. Therefore, the opportunity cost of leisure is forgone income, usually measured by the *real wage rate*. Holding everything else constant, a rise in the real wage rate increases the opportunity cost of leisure and may lead to a higher quantity of labor supplied. This is the law of supply in the labor market, which explains why the labor supply slopes upward, but only up to a point. Eventually, some individuals may reach a point where their labor supply may begin to bend backward, implying that they can reduce the quantity of labor supplied in response to higher wages (see figure 9.1).

This happens because a large increase in the equilibrium wage rate can lead to a higher standard of material well-being (known as the *income effect*), allowing people to earn higher income by working less. In this case, the income effect more than offsets the *substitution effect* (i.e., trading work for leisure), making workers consume more leisure even as the real price of leisure rises. In figure 9.1, the substitution effect dominates the income effect from point A to point B, implying that a higher hourly wage entices a greater *quantity* of labor supplied (not supply). The situation reverses in the range between points B and C, implying that a higher hourly wage may actually decrease the quantity of labor supplied, though we typically find most individuals on the positively sloping section of the labor supply curve (between points A and B).[2] In a seminal paper, Nobel Laureate in economics Edward Prescott argues that American laborers work 50 percent more, on average, than French, Italian, and German workers. Could this be due to significantly lower income tax rates in the U.S.? While the empirical findings are mixed, Prescott's finding highlights the substitution effect: higher income taxes reduce the disposable income of workers and, by extension, the opportunity cost of leisure.

Of course, people also differ in their preferences for work, which impacts the shape of their supply curves. It is not surprising that fewer people volunteer to do inherently difficult, unpleasant, or dangerous jobs, unless they are appropriately compensated for it. Economists call this wage premium a *compensating differential*, which means that higher wages compensate workers for doing risky, unpleasant, or unusual jobs. Some of the most unusual jobs purportedly include a "cuddler" (pays $1 to $4 per minute), chick "sexer"

---

2 This is why, going forward, we will graph labor supply as a positively sloped curve.

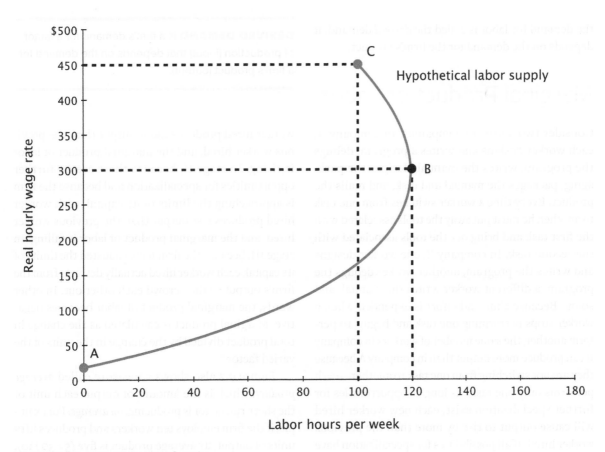

FIGURE 9.1 Hypothetical Labor Supply

(pays as much as $15,000 per month), line waiter (pays $36 per hour), and snake "milker" (average salary of $2,500 per month).

By horizontally adding up all individual supply curves, we can determine the market labor supply curve. There are three main shifters of the market labor supply curve: population, demographics, and available alternatives. Population growth either due to immigration or higher fertility means more workers in the market, which increases the market supply of labor (a rightward shift). Changing demographics, such as population aging and greater participation of women in the labor market, also affect the market labor supply. For example, a rise in the female labor force participation in the United States since World War II has increased the market labor supply. And, finally, changes in the alternatives to work, such as education, housework, black markets, taxes, and unemployment compensation, all can affect the market supply of labor. Holding everything constant, a greater (smaller) market supply of labor would decrease (increase) the equilibrium wage rate.

Labor Demand as Derived Demand

In a competitive market, each firm is a price taker, which means that any given firm cannot singlehandedly change the prevailing market wage rate. As a result, a firm's decision boils down to how much output it needs to produce and how many workers it needs to hire for this purpose. In other words, the more output the firm is able to sell, the more workers and other factors of production it will need to hire. This is why the demand for labor is called the *derived* demand: it depends on the demand for the firm's product.

> **DERIVED DEMAND** is a firm's demand for a factor of production (input) that depends on the demand for a firm's product (output).

Marginal Product of Labor

Consider two software companies. In company A, each worker designs and writes a program, debugs the program, writes the manual, designs the packaging, packages the manual and disk, and mails the product. Every time a worker switches from one task to another, he must put away the tools associated with the first task and bring out the tools associated with the second task. In company B, one worker designs and writes the program, another worker debugs the program, a different worker writes the manual, and so on. Because time and effort is expended when a worker stops performing one task and begins to perform another, the same number of workers in company B can produce more output than in company A because they are not switching from one task to another—each performs only one task. As long as opportunities for further specialization exist, each new worker hired will cause output to rise by more than the previous worker hired. If all possibilities for specialization have been exhausted, adding more units of some factor without changing other factors of production would cause the output to rise at a decreasing rate. Imagine a lumber company that has one hundred chainsaws (its physical capital) and one hundred workers (its labor). When this company hires one more worker, that worker must wait around until someone else goes on break in order to get a chainsaw. The more workers the company adds, the more time the additional workers must spend waiting around for a chainsaw. Thus, when other factors of production remain fixed, each additional worker hired increases output by less than the previous worker hired. We can extend the analysis by defining a very important measure called *marginal product* (MP), which is the *extra* output generated from employing one additional unit of the variable factor. For example, to say that the marginal product of labor is five means that an extra worker will increase the firm's output by five units.

Figure 9.2 shows a typical marginal product curve for a firm. In stage I, because of specialization, each worker hired produces more output than the previous worker hired, and the marginal product of labor is rising. In stage II, because there are no further opportunities for specialization and because the firm is approaching the limits of its capital, each worker hired produces less output than the previous worker hired, and the marginal product of labor is falling. In stage III, because the firm has exhausted the limits of its capital, each worker hired actually detracts from the firm's output as they crowd each other out. In other words, the marginal product of labor becomes negative. Marginal product is calculated as the change in total product divided by the change in the units of the varied factor.

Figure 9.2 also shows a measure called *average product*, which is the amount of output each unit of the short-run factor is producing, *on average*. For example, if the firm employs ten workers and produces fifty units of output, its average product is five ($5 = 50 / 10$). Average product and marginal product are similar, yet the difference is important. While marginal product measures the *extra output* generated by *one more* unit of the varied factor, average product measures the *average output* generated by *all* units of the varied factor. Here is another analogy: there is the same relationship between marginal and average product as there is between a test grade and a course grade. A test grade is a measure of the impact of *one* test, while a course grade is the average impact of *all* tests. Whenever marginal product is greater than average product, average product is rising. Whenever marginal product is less than average product, average product is falling. Hence, the marginal product curve always intersects the average product curve at the average product curve's maximum point. This intersection will always occur in stage II.

When deciding how much labor to hire, a firm compares the benefit of hiring another unit of labor (the value of the marginal product of labor) to its cost (the wage rate or compensation in general). The value of

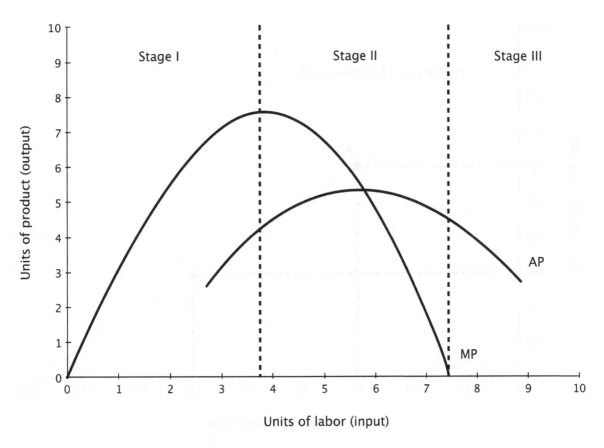

FIGURE 9.2 Marginal Product and Average Product of Labor

the marginal product of labor, also called the marginal revenue product of labor, or MRPL, is simply the product's market price (P) times the marginal product of labor (MPL). Together, they reflect a change in a firm's revenue from hiring another worker (i.e., its MRPL), which represents a firm's willingness to pay for labor. This is why MRPL is also a firm's demand for labor. Figure 9.3 shows a hypothetical downward-sloping demand for labor, which indicates that a decrease in the cost of labor from, say, $300 to $150 per hour increases the *quantity* of labor demanded (not demand) from 60 to 120 labor hours, holding everything else constant. This is the law of demand in the labor market: changes in the real wage rate cause movements up or down the labor demand curve.

A firm will continue to hire more workers up to the point where its MRPL becomes equal to the market's real wage rate. If the wage rate rises above MRPL, firms will be forced to reduce the number of workers until

MARGINAL REVENUE PRODUCT OR MRP is a factor's marginal product multiplied by a firm's output price. Sometimes it is called the value of the marginal product. **DEMAND FOR LABOR** is essentially the marginal revenue product of labor.

the equality between MRPL and wage rate is restored, because a reduction in the use of one input relative to other inputs increases its marginal product (in phases II and III). This is why the minimum-wage law that raises the wage rate above workers' MRPL increases unemployment by pricing lower-skilled labor out of the market. Therefore, the only real way to increase worker compensation is to increase worker productivity. A rise in worker productivity makes labor more attractive to firms, leading to a higher demand for labor and better worker compensation. When one of the nation's largest installers of auto glass, Safelite

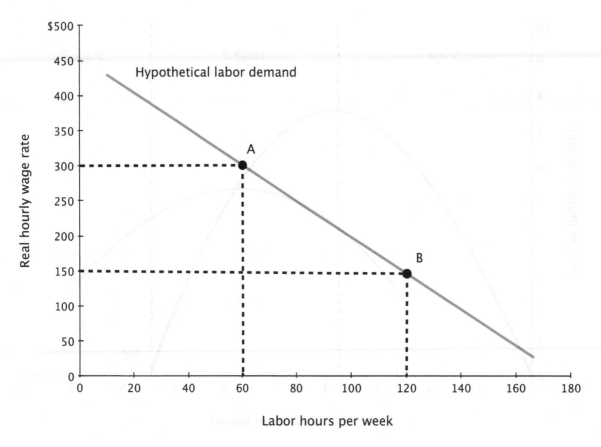

FIGURE 9.3 Derived Labor Demand Is Marginal Revenue Product of Labor

AutoGlass, changed its worker compensation system from an hourly wage to per glass installed, they saw a rise in worker productivity, which has led to higher profits and worker compensation.[3] According to the 2005 Economic Report of the President, average worker productivity and worker compensation have grown at about the same rate of about 2 percent per annum from 1959 to 2003.

To determine the market demand for labor, we horizontally sum all firms' demand curves. As with the market supply of labor, there are also three main shifters of the market demand for labor: product price, worker productivity (affected by technology and capital), and the number of firms in the market. Recall that product price (P) is a component of MRPL and,

by extension, the demand for labor. Therefore, higher product price means higher MRPL and market demand for labor. A rise in worker productivity, which can come from a variety of sources, including education and technological progress, increases MPL and, by extension, the market demand for this more productive labor. Finally, more firms and competition in a market imply a higher demand for labor. Holding everything else constant, a rise (fall) in the market demand for labor leads to higher (lower) worker compensation. For instance, competition for labor between Wal-Mart, TJ Maxx, Marshalls, and other big retailers has forced them to increase the base wage rate to $9 per hour.[4]

There is a peculiar theory in economics, known as the *efficiency wage* theory, which seeks to explain why

---

3 Edward P. Lazear, "Performance Pay and Productivity," *The American Economic Review* 90 (2000): 1346–1361.

4 Chelsey Dulaney, "T.J. Maxx Owner Lifts Worker Pay, Following Wal-Mart," *The Wall Street Journal*, February 25, 2015, http://www.wsj.com/articles/tjx-to-boost-pay-for-u-s-employees-to-9-an-hour-1424873150.

market wages and unemployment rates might exceed their equilibrium values. Anyone who has ever run a business would attest that finding or retaining qualified workers and making sure they show up to work are some of the top challenges facing a firm. According to the Conference Board of Canada, absenteeism in the workplace costs the Canadian economy at least $7.4 billion each year in direct costs and $37 billion in indirect costs, when lost productivity or the cost of replacement workers is factored in.[5] Such high costs may explain why firms may pay more in salary and benefits to their workers than their productivity justifies in order to reduce labor turnover and improve worker morale.

Differences in Wages

As noted in the beginning of this chapter, vast gaps in pay exist across occupations and for individuals within the same occupations. For example, numerous studies indicate that women in the United States earn somewhere around eighty cents for every dollar earned by men, which some advocates of equal pay interpret as evidence of gender discrimination. While discrimination may certainly exist and cause some of the observed wage gap, much of the gap can be explained by objective factors, namely, the market demand and supply. Economists argue that much of the pay gap can be attributed to the differences in three factors: education, experience, and job preferences. Because of childbearing duties and other reasons, women are more likely than men to have less experience, on average, and choose a different occupation, all of which affect pay. Putting the market supply and demand together, we can analyze how changes in relevant factors on both sides of the market affect the real wage rate and employment.

Figure 9.4 shows that a decrease in the market supply of labor (the shift from point A to B) and an increase in the market demand for labor (the shift from point B to C) both increase the wage rate but leave employment unchanged.

Furthermore, many economists argue that in a competitive market it is not in a firm's interests to discriminate against workers on subjective grounds as it limits the pool of qualified workers and raises employment costs, which is not good for profit. In other words,

competition can keep productivity-irrelevant discrim-

COMPENSATING DIFFERENTIAL refers to a wage premium needed to entice workers to perform an unpleasant, inconvenient or dangerous task. **MARGINAL REVENUE PRODUCT OF LABOR (MRPL)** is the main determinant of worker compensation.

---

ination to a minimum. However, this is not to say that firms will never discriminate. Worker discrimination (employees who refuse to work with other groups), customer discrimination (customers who refuse to be served by other groups), and negative feedback loops can preclude even a competitive market from eradicating discrimination. Negative feedback loops may reinforce certain gender and race stereotypes in the workplace and discourage certain groups from entering particular occupations. While any discrimination is unfortunate, there may not be a practical or fair solution to it. If one believes that some groups ought to be protected, why not be fair and extend protection to all groups of people (short, old, ugly, etc.)? If we want superficial equality in the labor market, one could make an argument for requiring advertising agencies and athletic teams to employ a representative ratio of physically unfit candidates. Moreover, mandating superficial equality may be unfair to the consumers who might like to be served by certain kinds of people,

---

5 Carissa Tanzola and Shana French, "Canada: Workplace Absenteeism—Much More Than the Cost of Doing Business," *Mondaq*, August 5, 2013, http://www.mondaq.com/canada/x/256130/employee+rights+labour+relations/ Workplace+Absenteeism+Much+More+Than+The+Cost+Of+Doing.

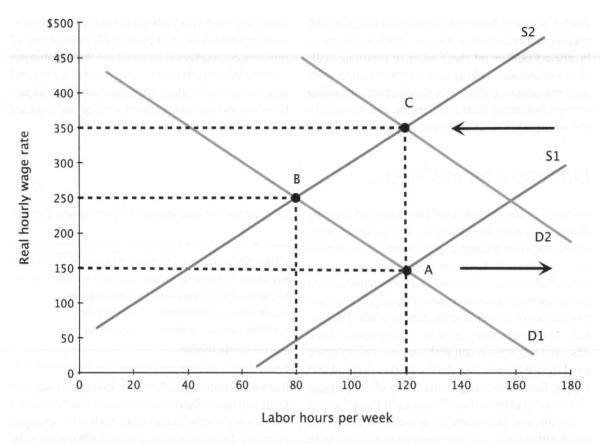

FIGURE 9.4 Changes in Labor Demand and Supply Affect Wages and Employment

say, young and attractive individuals. Or do their rights not matter?

But not all markets are competitive enough to ensure that compensation matches the value of worker productivity. In markets with low competition between firms, employers can pay workers below their MRPL. Coal-mining towns in West Virginia and Pennsylvania have been cited as examples of a monopsony (i.e., a single buyer) in labor markets. Monopsony leads to an inefficiently low amount of labor hired. In this case, labor unions can even out the bargaining power between firms and labor, thereby pushing the wage rate up to a competitive level. Princeton University economist Dani Rodrik finds[6] that more democratic

societies tend to have higher wage rates in manufacturing industries, which might indicate that organized labor is able to improve the bargaining process in its favor in more democratic nations. Economist Thomas Palley,[7] on the other hand, argues that democracy might improve workers' wages only indirectly through better labor standards, for example. Some studies also suggest that labor unions may increase workplace safety, much like safety regulations, and increase worker compensation.

However, some economists are skeptical of these findings. Interestingly, both occupational injury and worker unionization rates in the US private sector have been falling before and after increased safety

6 Dani Rodrik, "Democracies Pay Higher Wages," *Quarterly Journal of Economics* 114 (1999): 707–738.

7 Thomas Palley, "Labour Standards, Democracy and Wages: Some Cross-Country Evidence," *Journal of International Development* 17 (2005): 883–898.

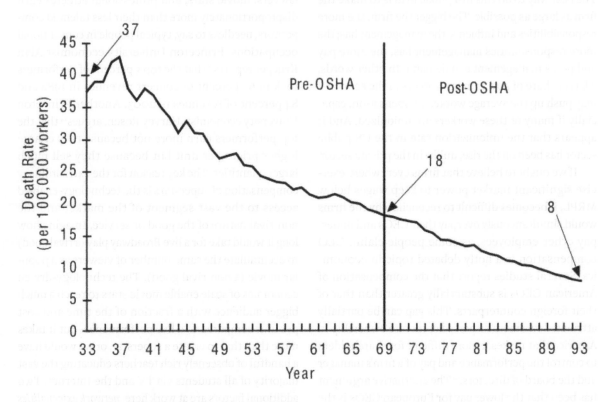

FIGURE 9.5 Workplace Safety Before and After OSHA[8]

regulations instituted by the Occupational Safety and Health Administration (OSHA). While there is some evidence that unionized workers generally earn more than nonunionized workers, the results might be misleading, because some union jobs may not have perfect equivalents in the nonunion sector.[8]Furthermore, even if labor unions succeed in raising worker compensation and safety, it may lead to higher unemployment or higher product prices. Those who lose their jobs or find themselves paying higher prices may find it unfair. On the other hand, several studies[9] find that higher economic freedom (i.e., fewer regulations and labor unions) leads to higher employment[10], average income, women's well-being[11], and less child labor. But economic freedom has also been linked to higher income inequality and obesity.

Yet another explanation for higher wages in more democratic societies is also plausible. In the case of a public or nonprofit firm, the people who control the company do not get to keep the profit the firm earns. As a result, people in charge of public companies may want to maximize job security, salary, perks, and power.

8 Thomas J. Kniesner and John D. Leeth. "Occupational Safety and Health Administration" in *Cato Handbook for Congress, Policy Recommendations for the 106th Congress* (1999): 409–417.

9 J. C. Hall and R. A. Lawson, "Economic Freedom of the World: An Accounting of the Literature," *Contemporary Economic Policy* 32 (2014): 1–19.

10 L. Heller and E. F. Stephenson, "Economic Freedom and Labor Market Conditions: Evidence from the States," *Contemporary Economic Policy* 32 (2014): 56–66.

11 M. D. Stroup, "Separating the Influence of Capitalism and Democracy on Women's Well-Being," *Journal of Economic Behavior & Organization* 67 (2008): 560–572..

The best way to do this in a public firm is to make the firm as large as possible. The bigger the firm, the more responsibilities and influence the management has; the more responsibilities management has, the more pay and perks management can demand. In other words, a larger share of government workers in the economy may push up the average worker compensation, especially if many of these workers are unionized. And it appears that the unionization rate in the US public sector has been on the rise, unlike in the private sector.

If we ought to believe that firms everywhere exercise significant market power to keep wages below MRPL, it becomes difficult to reconcile why the firms would simultaneously overpay their CEOs and underpay other employees, as some people claim. CEO compensation is a hotly debated topic in economics. Several studies report that the compensation of American CEOs is substantially greater than that of their foreign counterparts. This gap can be partially attributed to a more dispersed corporate ownership in America that makes it more difficult for shareholders to control the performance and pay of a firm's manager and the board of directors.[12] The alternative argument has been that the lower pay for European CEOs is the result of more envious attitudes in European societies. In any case, a consensus seems to be forming that the most questionable aspect of CEO compensation is the generous severance pay, or the "golden parachute." This form of compensation creates the perverse incentive to take excessive risks: if the company does well, the CEO is handsomely rewarded; otherwise, the CEO is guaranteed a cozy retirement with the golden parachute.

The new field of "superstar economics" pioneered by Sherwin Rosen seeks to explain why top executives, lawyers, movie stars, and professional athletes earn disproportionately more than their less talented competitors, needless to say, typical people in conventional occupations. Princeton University economist Alan Krueger reports[13] that the top 5 percent of performers took in 62 percent of concert revenues in 1982 and 84 percent of revenues in 2003. Another Princeton University economist, Harvey Rosen, argues[14] that the top performers earn more not because they charge higher prices per unit but because they sell much larger quantities. The key reason for the extraordinary compensation of superstars is the technology-enabled access to the vast segment of the market and the non-rival nature of the good or service. Imagine how long it would take for a live Broadway play (a rival good) to accumulate the same number of viewers as a popular movie (a non-rival good). The technology-driven economies of scale enable movie stars to reach a much bigger audience with a fraction of the time and cost per unit compared to a live performance. But it takes more than that to create a superstar, or we would have a handful of obscenely rich teachers educating the vast majority of all students via TV and the Internet. Two additional factors are at work here: *network externalities* and *superior talent*.[15] People may enjoy being a part of the same network or club, and a handful of "stars" makes it easier to find common ground in a company of friends. The superior talent requirement means that it is difficult to trade one really stellar performance by Jack Nicholson, for example, for several mediocre ones by Seth Rogen and still remain just as happy. Combined, these factors may explain why only a small number of people can earn such enormous wealth.

12 R. S. Thomas, "Explaining the International CEO Pay Gap: Board Capture or Market Driven?" *Vanderbilt Law Review* 57 (2004): 1171–1267.
M. J. Roe, "Some Differences in Corporate Structure in Germany, Japan, and the United States," *Yale Law Journal* 102 (1993): 1927–2003.
R. A. Posner, "From the New Institutional Economics to Organization Economics: With Applications to Corporate Governance, Government Agencies, and Legal Institutions," *Journal of Institutional Economics* 6 (2010): 1–37.
L. A. Bebchuk and J. M. Fried, "Executive Compensation as an Agency Problem," *Journal of Economic Perspectives* 17 (2003): 71–92.
L. A. Bebchuk and J. M. Fried, Pay without Performance (Cambridge, MA: Harvard University Press, 2004).

13 A. B. Krueger, "The Economics of Real Superstars: The Market for Concerts in the Material World," *Journal of Labor Economics* 23 (2004): 1–30.

14 S. Rosen, "The Economics of Superstars," *The American Economic Review* 71 (1981): 845–858.

15 S. Nüesc, *The Economics of Superstars and Celebrities* (Zurich: University of Zurich, 2007).

The Capital Market

In economics, *physical capital* refers to buildings, machines, equipment, and other manmade tools that can be combined with labor to produce various goods and services. As in the market for labor, the intersection of market demand and supply determines the rental price (rate) of physical capital.

Saving Decision and the Supply of Capital

The supply of capital comes from many of us deciding to save money rather than spend it. Most of us keep our savings in a bank, where the money hopefully earns some interest, or in the stock market for those with higher risk tolerance. What happens to saving when the real interest rate (i.e., the inflation-adjusted rate of return) on that saving increases? Similar to the relationship between the real wage rate and labor supply, there are two effects that ultimately determine how saving responds to the real interest rate. *Substitution effect* indicates that higher interest rate raises the opportunity cost of consuming your income today. That would induce the individual to save more and consume less now. At the same time higher interest rate would bring more to an individual from a certain principal amount that is saved. If there is already a targeted amount that the individual expects in the future, with a higher interest rate the individual can decrease the amount of saving now such that he/she can still get the same total amount in the future. That is the *income effect*. The individual feels richer than before with a higher interest rate, which would induce him/her to save less and consumer more now. If the substitution effect dominates the income effect, which many believe would be the case, the higher the real interest rate, the more we save. Much of this newly saved money is taken out by firms in the form of loans, bonds, or equity issues to purchase physical capital. The market supply of saving is simply the horizontal summation of individual saving curves. If more of us behave like the proverbial Ebenezer Scrooge, the market supply of saving would rise, leading to a lower interest rate and more investment in physical capital. The moral of the story here is that more saving allows entrepreneurs to pursue new business opportunities, leading to more output and employment. Much of the innovation that takes place in the financial industry has the effect of making the supply of capital cheaper or more abundant. To paraphrase Adam Smith, it is not from the benevolence of investors that we gain machines, factories, and jobs but rather from their regard for themselves. Yet, just like with the supply of labor, there is a theoretical possibility here for a backward-bending supply of capital. This means that, in theory, it is possible that a tax cut on capital income may either increase or decrease the supply of capital. Just like with the labor supply, many economists think that the substitution effect dominates the income effect and the supply of capital typically falls in response to higher capital gains taxes.

Marginal Product of Capital

Just as we saw with labor, the marginal revenue product of capital (MRPK) is a change in firm's revenue from employing one more unit of physical capital. Mathematically, MRPK is equal to the product's price times the marginal product of capital (MPK). The average and marginal products of capital typically exhibit the same general properties (i.e., the same three phases) as their labor equivalents in figure 9.2. The main lesson here is that adding more capital to a fixed number of workers eventually leads to a falling MPK. This is the

DEMAND FOR CAPITAL is essentially the marginal revenue product of capital. Note that the term "capital" in economics refers to machines, tools, and structures, not the financial capital like stocks and bonds.

same concept of diminishing marginal product that we have come across before.

Capital Demand as Derived Demand

Analogously to the demand for labor, the demand for capital is also derived demand because the number of units a firm can sell affects its demand for inputs such as labor and capital. Essentially, the MRPK translates into the demand for capital (see figure 9.6). Like other demand curves, it is also downward sloping. This is the law of demand in the capital market: a lower price increases the *quantity* of capital demanded (not demand). Because of the diminishing marginal product of capital, firms are willing to buy more capital only when its price falls. Adding up horizontally all firms' demand curves results in the market demand for capital. If capital becomes more productive, the market demand for capital increases (a rightward shift) and drives up its price. Conversely, higher taxes on capital reduce the market demand for capital, lowering its rental price (i.e., the real rate of return on investment). Taxes on capital can have a detrimental effect on employment and worker compensation too. Recall that capital investment increases worker productivity and pay. Taxes on capital tend to do the opposite.

Putting the market demand and supply of capital together, we can see how changes (shifts) in these curves affect the rental rate and investment in physical capital. For example, as shown in figure 9.7, a decrease in the demand for physical capital (the shift from

point A to B) and an increase in the supply of physical capital (the shift from point B to C) both reduce its price or rental rate, but leave the level of physical capital unchanged.

By following the changes in market demand and supply, we may deduce that the factors of production in competitive markets tend to get paid what they are worth to the market participants. If one factor of production was paid less than its marginal revenue product, firms would be interested in hiring more of this input, increasing the market demand for it and, by extension, its compensation. A profit-maximizing firm will hire various factors of production in optimal proportions such as to make its marginal products ratio (MPL/MPK) equal to its factor price ratio (w/r). The marginal productivity theory of income distribution developed by economists John Bates Clark and Philip Henry Wicksteed suggests that in a competitive market each factor of production earns the value of its marginal product, which is its contribution to society. In other words, labor and capital get paid what they contribute to production, as determined through voluntary exchange. This theory stands in stark contrast to the Marxist theory of class struggle. The inequality in the ownership of factors of production and their compensation is much at the root of public debate on economic inequality.

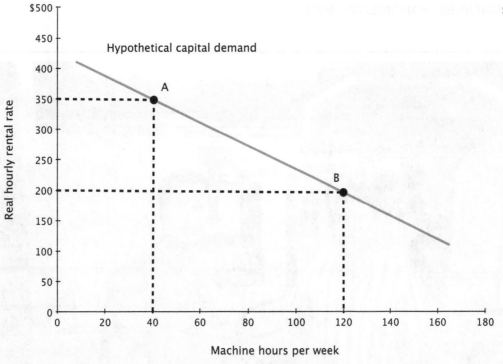

FIGURE 9.6 Derived Capital Demand Is Marginal Revenue Product of Capital

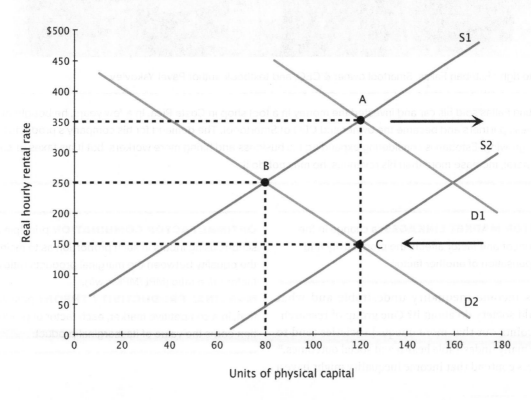

FIGURE 9.7 Changes in Capital Demand and Supply Affect Rent and Investment

Left to right: Esteban Fallas, Smartool owner & CEO, and textbook author Pavel Yakovlev.

Esteban Fallas sold his car and invested the money in a tool shop in Costa Rica. In a few years, he bought out his business partners and became the owner and CEO of Smartoool. The demand for his company's products has been growing. Esteban is considering expanding his business and hiring more workers, but if his taxes or costs, in general, increase more than his revenues, he may not do it.

FACTOR MARKET LINKAGES: a change in the amount of one factor affects the productivity and compensation of another factor.

OPTIMAL FACTOR COMBINATION principle prescribes using inputs in such proportion as to maintain the equality between the marginal products ratio and factor price ratio (MPL/MPK = w/r).

MARGINAL PRODUCTIVITY THEORY postulates that, in a competitive market, each factor of production earns the value of its marginal product.

Is income inequality undesirable and what should society do about it? One group of researchers points out that more unequal societies tend to have many undesirable health and social outcomes.[16] Others contend that income inequality might have a

---

16 R. G. Wilkinson and K. Pickett, *The Spirit Level: Why More Equal Societies Almost Always Do Better* (London: Allen Lane, 2009). Also see Thomas Piketty and Arthur Goldhammer, *Capital in the Twenty-First Century* (Cambridge, MA: Belknap Press, 2014).

spurious correlation with these outcomes, implying that income inequality is expected. Furthermore, if economic inequality reflects objective differences in productivity, altering it may not be desirable. Scholars also disagree about which type of economic inequality is more important—income, wealth or

The Financial Market

Much of the funding of new startups or existing firms' capital is done through financial markets. When a firm needs to raise money, it can do it in two ways: issue debt or equity. A partnership/proprietorship can borrow only by issuing debt. A corporation, on the other hand, can issue both debt and equity.

Issuing debt is, essentially, taking out a loan. When people and small firms take out loans, they go to a bank, and the bank loans them the money. When a large firm takes out a loan, it writes an IOU. The IOU is called a *bond*. A *bond* is a legal contract in which the borrower promises to make future payments to the lender. The bond represents a debt for the firm—something the firm owes in the future. Thus, when a firm takes a loan, we say that the firm *issues debt*. The firm sells the bond to a buyer. After a certain amount of time, the buyer of the bond takes the bond back to the firm, and the firm pays it off. Thus, the buyer of a bond is the *lender*, and the seller of a bond is the *borrower*.

When a firm issues debt, it must specify the *terms* (or attributes) of the bond. There are three attributes that must be specified: (1) the face value, (2) the coupon

consumption? Economists often invoke the tradeoff between efficiency and equity when asked about policies that may reduce income inequality. In short, people differ widely in their views on income inequality and what should be done about it.

rate, and (3) the expiration date. The *expiration date* is the date on which the bond expires—the date that the final payment on the bond comes due. The *face value* is the amount of money the borrower promises to pay the lender when the bond comes due. The *coupon rate* is an extra payment the borrower promises to pay the lender at periodic intervals (usually annually or semi-annually) between the time the bond is sold and the time it expires. This extra payment (called the *coupon payment*) is the coupon rate multiplied by the face value. For example, if a bond has a coupon rate of 10 percent and a face value of $2,000, the bond pays $2,000 when it expires plus $200 (10 percent times $2,000) at the end of each year.

For example, suppose that company A wants to borrow $900. On January 1, 1996, company A offers a bond for sale for $900. The bond has the following attributes: (1) face value = $1,000, (2) coupon rate = 8 percent, and (3) expiration date = December 31, 2000. Suppose that on January 1, 1996, company B purchases the bond. Payments between the two companies are as follows:

Date	Transaction	Description of Transaction
January 1, 1996	B pays A $900	The price of the bond.
December 31, 1996	A pays B $80	The first coupon payment (8 percent times $1,000).
December 31, 1997	A pays B $80	The second coupon payment (8 percent times $1,000).
December 31, 1998	A pays B $80	The third coupon payment (8 percent times $1,000).
December 31, 1999	A pays B $80	The fourth coupon payment (8 percent times $1,000).
December 31, 2000	A pays B $1,080	The last coupon payment *plus* the face value (8 percent times $1,000 plus $1,000).

Through the use of this bond, company B loaned company A $900. Company A paid back to company B a total of $1,400 (the $900 loan plus a total of $500 in interest). One might look at this loan and conclude that company B earned 56 percent interest on the loan it made to company A (56 percent = $500 / $900). This is actually *not* the case. Although company A paid a total of $500 in interest on a $900 loan, the $500 in interest was paid *over time* and thus is not the same as $500 at the time the bond was sold. To find out how much interest company B actually earns on the bond, one must compute the present value of the payments A makes to B.

Suppose it is January 1, 1996, and company B is deciding whether or not to purchase the bond. On December 31, 1996, A will pay B $80. Because this $80 is paid one year in the future, it is not the same as $80 today. If the prevailing risk-free interest rate is 5 percent interest per year, company B could calculate the present value of the first four $80 payments using the annuity formula and present value of the last payment of $1,050, using the lump-sum formula.

If you did the math right, *the total bond is worth $1,129.89 in today's dollars*. Buying this bond for $900 yields a total interest payment of $229.89 (today's value minus today's price of the bond). The true five-year return on this bond is 26 percent (26 percent = $229.89 / $900), not the 56 percent you might have thought earlier, because the present value of that $500 interest is only $229.89. More importantly, if company B instead puts $900 in a bank account that pays an annual interest rate of 5 percent for five years, it would have at the end of year 5 a total of about $1,149 compared to

a total of $1,400 from the bond. If the bond's default risk is zero, it is an attractive investment option for company B. If this is truly a good deal, it is unlikely to remain so for very long in a competitive market, as other companies will bid up the price of this bond. In general, the bond is said to sell at "a discount" when its purchase price is less than its face value, sell at "a premium" when it is the other way around, and sell at "par" when price is equal to face value. Bonds tend to sell at a discount when the market interest rises and at a premium when it falls in order to keep bonds competitive with the interest-bearing bank deposits.

According to the efficient-market hypothesis, for which economist Eugene Fama received the Nobel Memorial Prize in economics in 2013, competitive forces ensure that there are no obvious bargains in the stock or bond market. Otherwise, there would be unlimited arbitrage opportunity, and all of us would get rich by exploiting it. This is akin to the law of one price, which states that identical goods should sell at identical prices in different markets, holding everything else the same. The law of one price is easily observed in other competitive situations, such as roughly equal wait times in comparable lines at a grocery store, equal traffic speed in all lanes on a busy highway, and so on. Thus, whenever someone gives you a "hot stock" tip or makes you an offer that sounds too good to be true, it probably is too good to be true.

EFFICIENT-MARKET hypothesis maintains that, in a competitive market, traders with equal information will earn the same risk-adjusted rate of return.

Present versus Future Value

The popular saying that time is money could not be more correct. Knowing how to compare money over time can prevent you from making one of the common financial mistakes. Suppose that someone offers you a choice between (a) $1,000 to be paid to you today and (b) $1,000 to be paid to you one year from today. Most everyone would take the $1,000 today. This proves that *even in the absence of inflation* a dollar today is not the same as a dollar tomorrow. Why? Given a choice

between consuming a product now and consuming the same product later, everything else held constant, a person would rather consume it now. The reason has to do with the uncertainty associated with consuming in the future—events may transpire (i.e., accidents, death, etc.) that would cause us not to be able to consume in the future or greatly diminish the happiness we gain from consuming. If a dollar now is better than a dollar later, to entice someone to give up a dollar now, we must offer the person something in return. This something is called *interest*. *Interest* is an amount of money a borrower pays a lender to entice the lender to forgo purchasing products with the money until some future time. Borrowers must pay lenders interest to entice the lenders to loan their money, because lenders would rather have their dollars now than later. Lenders would rather have their dollars now than later because a dollar now is better than a dollar later. A dollar now is better than a dollar later because consuming now is better than consuming later. Consuming now is better than consuming later because later we might be dead.

So, we have determined that a dollar today is not the same thing as a dollar tomorrow, in the same way that a US dollar is not the same thing as a Canadian dollar. When we see something for sale in Canada, we can convert the price in Canadian dollars into a price in US dollars for comparison. We can make the same sort of conversion across time so that we can compare tomorrow's dollars and today's dollars. This conversion is known as finding the *present value* (PV). Present value tells us the value of a dollar received in the future in terms of dollars today. For example, suppose that you could put $100 in the bank for one year at 6 percent interest. At the end of year 1, you would get back $106 (FV is the future value of your savings):

$$FV = PV(1+r)^t = \$100(1+0.06)^1$$

In other words, having $106 one year in the future is like having $100 today. That is, the *discount rate*, or the amount of value that money loses over time, is 6 percent per year.[17] The present-value calculation is the reverse of the future-value calculation:

$$PV = \frac{FV}{(1+r)^t} = \frac{\$106}{(1+0.06)^1} = \$100$$

Suppose that you could put $100 in the bank for two years at 6 percent interest per year. At the end of the two years, you would get back $112.36. Thus, $112.36 two years in the future is the *same* as $100 today—the present value of $112.36 two years in the future is $100. The present value calculation is as follows:

$$PV = \frac{FV}{(1+r)^t} = \frac{\$112.36}{(1+0.06)^2} = \$100$$

A firm will always discount future profits by a factor equal to the rate of return the firm could have achieved on any other venture of equal risk. For example, consider a software company that has a choice of producing a new game versus a new business application. The game will bring large profits but for a short period of time. The business application will bring small profits but over a greater time period. If the firm produces the game, it will earn $20,000 profit in year 1, $17,000 profit in year 2, $12,000 in year 3, and no profit thereafter. If the firm produces the business application, it will earn $5,000 profit every year for fifteen years and no profit thereafter. The total profit from the game is $20,000 + $17,000 + $12,000 = $49,000. The total profit from the business application is ($5,000)(15) = $75,000. Which software should the firm produce? To answer that question, we must compute the present value of the profits for each type of software. Suppose that the interest rate is 10 percent per year for the next fifteen years. The present value of the profit from the game is as follows:

$$\frac{\$20,000}{1.1} + \frac{\$17,000}{1.1^2} + \frac{\$12,000}{1.1^3} = \$42,247$$

The present value of the profit from the business software is as follows:

$$\frac{\$5,000}{1.1} + \frac{\$5,000}{1.1^2} + \frac{\$5,000}{1.1^3} +$$
$$\cdots + \frac{\$5,000}{1.1^{15}} = FV\left(\frac{1-(1+r)^{-t}}{r}\right)$$
$$= \$38,030$$

---

17 It is possible that you would not be willing to part with $100 for one year in exchange for $106 at the end of the year. If this is the case, your subjective discount rate is higher than 6%. The market interest rate is a function of the average discount rates of all borrowers and lenders.

Thus, the firm will choose to produce the game instead of the business application. The moral of the story here is that comparing money directly over time without doing the present-value adjustment can lead to a very costly mistake!

The formula for calculating the present value of a one-time payment is $PV = \frac{FV}{(1+r)^t}$. For an annuity, as in the previous business software example, it is $PV = FV\left[\frac{1-(1+r)^{-t}}{r}\right]$. And for a perpetuity (a never-ending annuity), it is $PV = \frac{FV}{r}$. The perpetuity formula is a useful approximation for determining the current value of virtually any income-generating asset, whether it is a dividend-bearing stock share, a rental property, or a business venture. For example, suppose that you own a property that is expected to produce $10,000 of inflation-adjusted net income each year for the foreseeable future. If the real interest rate on a similar investment is 5 percent, the present value of this property should be around $10,000 / 0.05 = $200,000. The present value formula for perpetuity reveals another important relationship: the stock market booms when the real interest rate (r) falls due to the inverse relationship between PV and r.

the United States and many other countries. Furthermore, this gap has been rising simultaneously with the average standard of living in recent decades, suggesting that the rich got richer faster than the poor got richer.

The growing income and wealth inequality in many countries suggests that some fundamental institutional and economic forces might be fueling this trend. Even in the absence of superstar earners, inequality in a society may grow over time.

CONCLUSION

This chapter uses the tools of demand and supply to explain how the gains from exchange accrue to the factors of production, specifically labor and capital. The basic conclusion is that in a competitive market the level of compensation earned by each input depends on its marginal revenue product. There is no guarantee though, that the level of compensation earned by each input is going to be equal. In fact, it is common knowledge that there is a lot of economic inequality in

DISCUSSION QUESTIONS

1. What determines the labor wage rate?

2. Discuss what might cause the male-female wage gap.

3. What is the relationship between factor compensation and its productivity?

4. What are the substitution and income effects associated with changes in the real wage rate and the real interest rate?

5. How do capital gains taxes affect the demand for labor and capital?

6. What can the efficient-market hypothesis teach us about a "hot stock" tip?

PART 4

Market Structures

10

Capital, Technology, and Costs

Introduction

In this chapter, we discuss capital and technology. These are terms that economists use somewhat differently than do non-economists. Non-economists, particularly people in finance, tend to use the word, "capital" to refer to money. In economics, capital is not money. Capital is what a company uses to transform inputs into output. Roughly speaking, think of capital as buildings, land, and machinery. To non-economists, the term, "technology" usually means "computers." In economics, a computer is capital—something a business uses in transforming inputs into output. "Technology" refers to the sophistication of the production process. A production process that uses more advanced techniques or processes is said to have more advanced technology. Technology is usually intangible, whereas capital it usually tangible.

As you can probably guess, how much capital and technology a firm has influences how much the firm can produce, and so influences the firm's cost of production. And anything that influences the firm's cost of production will influence the price at which the firm can sell its product. In this chapter, we explore how capital and technology influence costs and price.

Have you ever wondered why you have a lot of options when it comes to choosing a restaurant, but fewer options when it comes to choosing an airline, and fewer options still (or possibly no options at all) when it comes to choosing a high-speed Internet service provider? What you are experiencing are differences in industry types. An industry is a collection of firms that produce similar products and that compete with each other. How much competition there is among the firms in an industry depends, in part, on the number of firms in the industry. The more firms there are, the more competitive the industry will tend to be. But the number of firms that can co-exist within an industry is largely determined by the cost of the capital and technology a

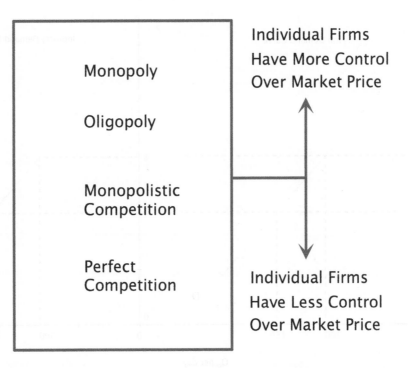

FIGURE 10.1 Industry Types

firm in the industry requires to produce its product. For example, the capital and technology a fast food restaurant requires costs much less than does the capital and technology that an airline requires. Other things equal, the more costly the capital and technology is, the more customers a firm will need for the firm to earn enough to afford the capital and technology. The more customers a firm requires, the fewer will be the number of firms that can co-exist in the industry.

Industry Types

An *industry* is the set of all firms that produce a particular product. What does and does not constitute an industry depends on the definition of the product. For example, one might speak of the beverage industry, which would include all firms that manufacture beverages, such as Tetley (tea), Folgers (coffee), Seagrams (liquor), Budweiser (beer), Taylor (wine), Minute Maid (juice), Coke, Pepsi, and so forth. One might also speak of the alcoholic beverage industry (a subset of the beverage industry), which would include Seagrams, Budweiser, Taylor, and so on. Or one might speak of the hot beverage industry, which would include Tetley, Folgers, and so forth. Or one might speak of the ready-to-drink beverage industry, which would include Budweiser, Coke, Pepsi, and so on. So, you see, before one can speak of an industry, one must clearly define what type of product one is considering. The industry, then, is the set of all firms that produce that product.

A firm can ask whatever it likes for its product. But when economists talk about, "price," they are not referring to what the firm asks. They are referring to what the firm and the consumer, together, agree on. For example, a car dealer can ask $80,000 for a Kia hatchback. But if no one is willing to pay $80,000, then that's not the price of the car. Similarly, a prospective buyer can offer

AN INDUSTRY is the set of all firms that produce a particular type of product.

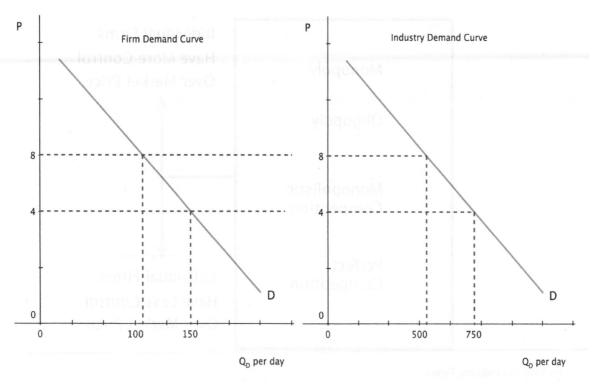

FIGURE 10.2 Firm Demand versus Industry Demand

$1,000 for the Kia, but if the dealer isn't willing to accept $1,000, then that's not the price of the car either. The price of the car is the number to which both the seller and the consumer agree. When you buy things from a store, you don't haggle over price as you might at a car dealership, but there is agreement and disagreement there as well. When you see a dozen eggs on the shelf with a $2 sticker, and you take the eggs to the front of the store to pay, you and the store have agreed on the price of $2.

An important question is how much control a firm has over the price of its product. A monopoly firm has much control over the price of its product because there is only one place consumers can get the product. If the monopoly firm asks a higher price, many consumers will agree to pay that higher price because their only option is not to purchase the product at all. A competitive firm

---

INDUSTRY structure refers to the degree of control individual firms in an industry have over the market price of their products.

---

has little control over the price of its product because there are many other places from which consumers can buy the product. If a single competitive firm asks a higher price, very few consumers will agree to pay the higher price because they can easily buy the product at a lower price from one of the firm's competitors. *Industry structure* refers to the degree of control individual firms in an industry have over the prices of their products.

There are four major types of industry structure: *monopoly, oligopoly, monopolistic competition,* and *perfect competition.* Monopoly firms have the most control over their prices. Oligopoly firms have less control over their prices than do monopoly firms. Monopolistically competitive firms have less control over their prices than do oligopoly firms. Finally, perfectly competitive firms have virtually no control over their prices. Where we need to distinguish between the price a firm asks, and the price to which a firm and consumer agree, we'll refer to the latter as the "market price."

There are also subtypes of industry structures that are hybrids of the four major types. For example, a duopoly is a hybrid of monopoly and oligopoly. Many industries that we call "monopolies" are really competition-monopoly hybrids. For example, prior to its breakup, AT&T was the only phone company in the United States, except in scattered rural areas where smaller companies, such as Quaker State Telephone, were allowed to provide phone service. The phone industry was comprised of one large firm (AT&T) and many very small firms. From AT&T's perspective, it was operating in a monopoly industry. From the small phone companies' perspectives, they were operating in a competitive industry, where AT&T represented the sum of all of their competitors.

For simplicity's sake, we shall restrict our discussion to the four major forms of industry structure. The differences in the types of industries manifest themselves in the degree of control a single firm in the industry has over the market price of the product it sells. In the case of a monopoly industry, the single firm has a tremendous degree of control over the market price of the product it sells. In the case of a purely competitive industry, the single firm has no control over the market price of the product it sells.

To discuss industry structure, we must introduce a new concept: the *firm demand curve*. You have already seen demand (also called *industry demand*) and seen that it depicts the relationship between the price of a product and the number of units the consumers will want to purchase. The firm demand curve (or *the demand curve faced by the firm*) depicts the relationship between the price of a product and the number of units the consumers will want to purchase from a specific firm. If you add up all the firm demand curves, you get the industry demand curve.

An example of the difference between a firm demand curve and the industry demand curve is shown in figure 10.2. Suppose that there are five identical firms in the industry. The demand for one firm's product is shown by the firm demand curve in the left panel. The demand for the industry's product (there are five firms in the industry in this example) is shown in the right panel. When the price of the product is $8, consumers want to purchase one hundred units per day from each of the five firms. Thus, when the price of the product is $8, the total quantity demanded of the industry is five hundred units per day (one hundred units per day times five identical firms). When the price

of the product is $4, consumers want to purchase 150 units per day from each of the five firms. When the price of the product is $4, the total quantity demanded of the industry is 750 units per day.

FIRM DEMAND is the demand for the output of a specific firm.

INDUSTRY DEMAND is the demand for the output of an entire industry.

When we say that a firm has a lot of control over the price it charges, we mean that it can ask and receive almost any price it wants. Of course, a firm can put any price tag it wants on its product, but if no one is willing to pay the price, the firm has not exhibited any true control. Now, consider the price elasticity of a firm's demand curve (as opposed to the price elasticity of the industry demand curve). The price elasticity is calculated in the same way as before. The difference is that the quantity demanded (Q_D) refers not to the total quantity demanded of the product, but the quantity demanded from a single firm. Suppose that there are 10,000 firms of the same size in an industry and that the equilibrium price of the firms' products is $10.00. If all the firms increase the quantity of the products they offer from 100 each to 150 each, the total output of the industry rises from 1,000,000 to 1,500,000. Because there is more product available, consumers are not willing to pay as much as before, and the equilibrium price drops to $8.00. The price elasticity of demand for the industry is as follows:

$$\text{Industry Price Elasticity of Demand} = \frac{\%\Delta Q_D}{\%\Delta P}$$

$$= \frac{\dfrac{1,500,000 - 1,000,000}{1,000,000}}{\dfrac{\$8 - \$10}{\$10}} = \frac{0.5}{-0.2} = -2.5$$

The price elasticity of demand for this product is greater than one (in absolute value), meaning that a 1 percent increase in the price of this product causes a greater than 1 percent decrease in the quantity demanded.

Now, suppose that only one firm increases the quantity of the product it offers from 100 to 150 units. Because this one firm represents only one ten-thousandth of the industry, we would expect the change in quantity to have little or no effect on the equilibrium price of the product. Let us suppose that the increase in quantity offered causes the equilibrium price to fall by $0.01. We can now examine the firm's price elasticity of demand—by how much the equilibrium price of the product changes when a single firm changes the quantity it offers. The firm's price elasticity of demand is as follows:

$$\text{Firm Price Elasticity of Demand} = \frac{\%\Delta Q_D}{\%\Delta P}$$

$$= \frac{\dfrac{150-100}{100}}{\dfrac{\$9.99-\$10.00}{\$10.00}} = \frac{0.5}{-0.001} = -500$$

The firm increased the quantity it offered by 50 percent, and the effect was just a one-tenth of 1 percent decrease in the equilibrium price! This firm has almost no control over the price of its product. The firm's price elasticity of demand tells us how much control a single firm has over the price of its product. The greater the firm's price elasticity of demand, the less control the firm has over the price of its product. The difference between individual firm and industry price elasticity of demand can reveal how competitive that industry is. In a competitive market with many small firms, the demand curve facing each firm is very elastic (i.e. nearly horizontal demand curve), but the industry's entire demand curve is less so. In contrast, a monopolist's demand curve and industry's entire demand curve are one and the same, and it tends to be rather inelastic.

Let us see what happens when there are only a few firms in the industry. Suppose that there are only three

PRICE ELASTICITY OF FIRM DEMAND measures the degree of control a single firm has over the market price of its product.
PRICE ELASTICITY OF INDUSTRY DEMAND measures the degree of control an industry has over the market price of its product.

firms in the industry; each produces one hundred units of output; the equilibrium price of the product is $10. Suppose that one of the firms increases the amount of product it offers from 100 units to 150 units. Because this firm is one-third of the industry, this increase is substantial. Let us suppose that the equilibrium price of the product falls to $8.50. The firm's price elasticity of demand is as follows:

$$\text{Firm Price Elasticity of Demand} = \frac{\%\Delta Q_D}{\%\Delta P}$$

$$= \frac{\dfrac{150-100}{100}}{\dfrac{\$8.50-\$10}{\$10}} = \frac{0.5}{-0.15} = -3.33$$

The firm's price elasticity of demand is much smaller (in absolute value) than in the previous example, indicating that this firm has much more control over the market price of the product than the previous firm. In fact, the 50 percent increase in output by the firm caused the market price to fall 15 percent—a substantial change.

THE GREATER THE FIRM'S price elasticity of demand (in absolute value), the less control the firm has over the price of its product.
THE GREATER THE INDUSTRY'S price elasticity of demand (in absolute value), the less control the industry has over the price of its product.

Short-Run and Long-Run Average Total Cost

When we constructed the cost curves, we were looking at the firm in the short run. Recall that in the short run, the firm can alter only the quantities of its short-run factors. The quantities of the firm's long-run factors must remain fixed. We shall now examine the firm in the long run and observe the effects of altering quantities of the long-run factors.

Consider the total product curve, labeled TP in figure 10.3. With this total product curve, the firm experiences the three stages of production, labeled I, II, and III. This total product curve shows the various amounts of output the firm can produce when it alters the quantities of its short-run factors. What happens if the firm increases the quantities of its long-run factors? With more long-run factors, the short-run factors can now produce more than before. Recall that the reason the total product curve is rising at a decreasing rate in stage II and decreasing in stage III is that the firm has a fixed amount of capital (a long-run factor), which is being completely utilized. When the firm reaches

stage III, it has exceeded the capacity of its capital, and increasing short-run factors further actually causes output to decline. If the firm increases its capital, it can employ more units of short-run factor before it begins to exceed the capacity of the capital. In short, increasing the quantity of a long-run factor causes the total product curve to shift up and to the right (to TP' in the diagram). Notice that when the firm's total product curve shifts to TP', the stages of production change from I, II, and III to I', II', and III'.

Just as the total product curve shifts, so too do the average and marginal product curves. When the firm increases the quantities of its long-run factors, the average and marginal product curves shift up and to the right, from MP and AP to MP' and AP' in figure 10.4.

Recall that the product curves are directly related to the cost curves—in fact, the cost curves and product curves tell the same story, but from different perspectives. The product curves describe the firm's

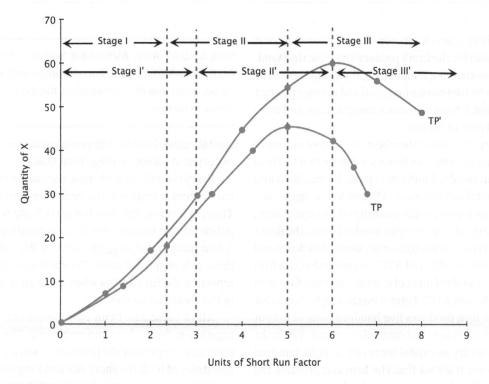

FIGURE 10.3 Total Product Curve

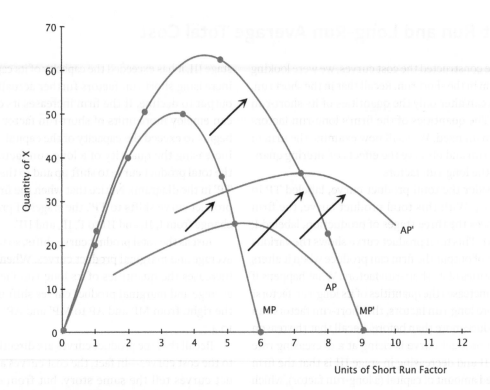

FIGURE 10.4 Marginal and Average Product Curves

productivity from the standpoint of factors; the cost curves describe the firm's productivity from the standpoint of output. So, if increasing the quantities of the long-run factors causes marginal and average product to increase, it must also cause marginal cost and average total cost to decline.

Figure 10.5 shows the effect on the cost curves of increasing the long-run factors. Suppose that the firm has seven hundred units of capital. Its marginal and average total cost curves are MC and ATC in figure 10.5. If the firm increases the quantity of its capital from seven hundred units to eight hundred units, the firm's marginal and average total cost curves shift down and to the right, to MC' and ATC'. Suppose that the firm has seven hundred units of capital (and therefore is on curves MC and ATC). Point A on the graph shows that when the firm produces five hundred units of output per day, its average total cost is $15 per unit. When the firm's quantity of capital increases to eight hundred units, point B shows that the firm can produce the same five hundred output per day, but at an average total cost of $11 per unit—increasing the quantity of

THE SHORT-RUN AVERAGE TOTAL COST CURVE (SRATC) is the firm's average total cost curve, given that the firm employs fixed quantities of long-run factors.

capital enabled the firm to produce the same amount of output at a lower average total cost.

Every time the firm changes the quantities of long-run factors it employs, the firm's cost curves shift. Thus, in a sense, the firm has an infinite number of potential cost curves—each corresponding to a different quantity of long-run factors. We call each of these a *short-run cost curve*. The short-run cost curves represent the firm's costs when it can alter quantities of the short-run factors only.

All of these short-run cost curves can be taken together to form a long-run cost curve. The long-run cost curves represent the firm's costs when it can alter quantities of both the short-run and long-run factors.

If we superimpose a number of short-run average total cost curves on a long-run average total cost

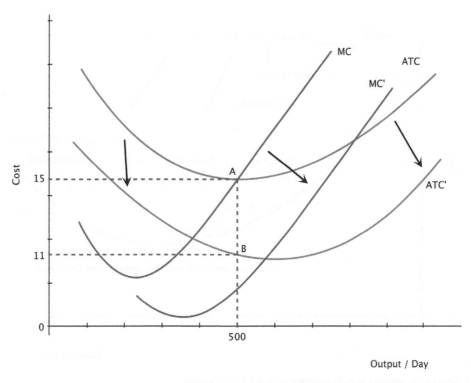

FIGURE 10.5 Marginal and Average Total Cost Curves

THE LONG-RUN AVERAGE TOTAL COST CURVE (LRATC) is the firm's average total cost curve, given that the firm can alter the quantities of both the short-run and long-run factors.

---

curve, we obtain a picture like that in figure 10.6. The large dark curve that holds all the smaller curves is the long-run average total cost curve. The smaller, lighter curves are short-run average total cost curves. Each short-run average total cost curve corresponds to a different quantity of capital. The short-run average total cost curve labeled "1,000 capital" is the firm's average total cost curve, given that it has one thousand units of capital. The short-run average total cost curve labeled "2,000 capital" is the firm's average total cost curve, given that it has two thousand units of capital, and so on.

Notice that the short-run average total cost curves decline from one thousand to five thousand units of capital. For quantities of capital greater than five thousand units, however, the short-run average total cost

curves increase—that is, the long-run average total cost curve is bowl shaped. Recall that the reason a short-run average total cost curve is bowl shaped is because average product is an inverted bowl shape—as the firm hires more workers, the average output of all workers rises (because of specialization) and then eventually falls (because of exhausting the limits of the capital). The long-run average total cost curve is similarly bowl shaped because, in the same way that too many workers can exhaust the limits of a fixed capital stock, too much capital can exhaust the limits of a fixed technology. Recall that *technology* refers to the technological complexity of the production process itself (not the materials used). A given level of technology can adequately support a limited amount of capital—too much capital, and the technology cannot effectively handle the size of the firm.

Consider the firm shown in figure 10.7. Let us suppose, for simplicity's sake, that the firm is in a purely competitive industry—thus, its profit-maximizing output quantity is also its efficient output quantity. We make this assumption so as to know how much

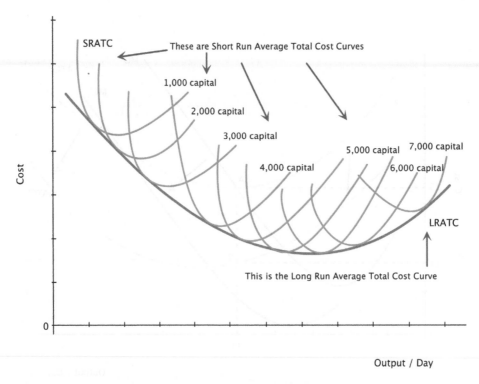

FIGURE 10.6 Short-Run versus Long-Run Average Total Cost Curves

the firm will produce without having to draw marginal revenue and marginal cost curves (which will greatly complicate this graph). Recall that the efficient output quantity is the minimum point on the average total cost curve. Suppose that the firm has two thousand units of capital. It should adopt two strategies, one short-run and one long-run. In the short run, the firm should produce at its profit-maximizing output quantity, which is found at point A—two hundred units of output per day. This output quantity will yield the firm an average total cost of $10 per unit. In the long run, the firm should increase its capital to five thousand units and produce four hundred output per day (point D). These output and capital levels will yield the firm an average total cost of $4 per unit. Let us return to the firm as it is now—two thousand units of capital and producing two hundred output per day (point A). Suppose that the firm increases its capital to four thousand units but does not alter its output. Producing two hundred output per day using four thousand units of capital puts the firm at point B on the graph—the firm's average total cost has actually risen (from $10 per unit

to $13 per unit). The firm has done the equivalent of building a new factory and not using it, or purchasing a new machine and letting it sit idle—of course, the firm's average total cost will increase. In addition to increasing its capital, the firm must utilize its new capital. Thus, if the firm increases its capital to four thousand units, it should also increase its output to 325 units per day. This puts the firm at point C on the graph and yields an average total cost of $5 per unit.

Notice that the lowest average total cost the firm can achieve is $4 per unit, and the way to achieve this is to produce four hundred output per day using five thousand capital. If the firm increases its capital beyond five thousand units, its average total cost will increase. We can describe point D as the *long-run efficient output quantity*—the output and capital levels at which long-run average total cost is minimum.

When the firm is producing at a low level of output, it experiences a high average total cost. Over the long-run, as it increases its output, its average total cost declines (i.e., the firm moves along the downward sloping section of the long-run average total cost curve).

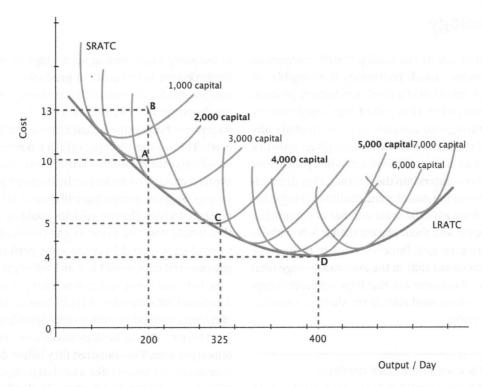

FIGURE 10.7 Long-Run Efficient Output

We call this decline in average total cost, *economies of scale*. People tend to understand economies of scale – we assume that bigger firms, for example big-box retailers, can offer products at a lower cost than can smaller firms, for example "mom and pop shops." What many people tend not to be aware of is the existence of *diseconomies of scale*. Diseconomies of scale are just as real and occur when, as the firm increases its output over the long-run, the firm's average total cost rises (i.e., the firm moves along the upward sloping section of the long-run average total cost curve). If there were no such thing as diseconomies of scale, then there would be only one firm and that firm would produce everything. In fact, examples of the effects of diseconomies of scale can be seen when large corporations choose to break up into smaller firms. For example, AOL Time Warner split into two companies (AOL and Time Warner). Sarah Lee split its meats division and beverage/bakery division into two separate companies. Some of these splits (like the AOL Time Warner) are described as being due to "differences in cultures within the company." But the humans (and

their psychological and cultural traits) are part of the company and impact the company's costs. To identify differences in "corporate cultures" as a reason for splitting a company in two is to describe the *reason* for the diseconomies of scale.

Finally, note that diminishing marginal returns and diseconomies of scale are not the same. Marginal returns refer to the impact of producing another unit of output. For example, to say that a firm is experiencing diminishing marginal profit means that the additional profit the firm earns from selling one more unit of output is less than the additional profit it earned from selling the last unit of output. Marginal returns refer to the *next* unit of output. Economies of scale refer to the average cost of all the units a firm is producing. For example, to say that a firm is experiencing diseconomies of scale means that increasing the quantity of output will cause the average total cost (over all the units produced) to increase.

Technology

People often equate "technology" with computers. Computers are capital. Technology is intangible—it is the sophistication of a firm's production process. For example, when Henry Ford first organized car manufacturing into assembly lines, he dramatically increased the number of cars that a given quantity of capital and labor could produce. When people first organized computers into the Internet, they dramatically improved the quantity and quality of things that could be done with the same number of computers. Technology is less about objects than it is how those objects are arranged. Improvements in technology cause a downward shift in the long-run average total cost curve, in the same way that improvements in capital cause a downward shift in the short-run average total cost curve.

THE LONG-RUN EFFICIENT OUTPUT QUANTITY is the output and long-run factor levels at which long-run average total cost is minimum.

Where technology (and also capital) is concerned, timing is important. It is possible that a given increase in technology can come at such a high price that the improvement in the costs of production may never compensate for the cost of the technology. For example, despite government subsidies of electric vehicles, 99 percent of cars in the United States are still gas-powered. The reason electric vehicles haven't caught on—despite the subsidies—is that the technology isn't evolved enough to make the investment worth the savings. Suppose it costs $10 trillion to develop a technology by which electric vehicles could be produced that would cost the same as gas-powered vehicles to produce, would deliver the same performance as gas-powered cars, would last as long as gas-powered cars, but would cost half as much to operate. In 2013 Americans consumed about 134.5 billion gallons of gasoline, which would amount to total spending of about $500 billion.[1] This technology would save drivers $250 billion per year. Two-hundred fifty billion dollars per year in savings sounds like a lot, but it requires a $10 trillion investment. In other words, the $250 billion return is less than a 3 percent return on the $10 trillion investment. For such a low return, it isn't worth it to make the investment. The $10 trillion investment would be better spent elsewhere.

The Determinants of Industry Structure

What is it that causes some industries to be purely competitive and others to be monopolies? It is interesting to note that the factors that determine industry type have nothing to do with the desires of the firm. A purely competitive firm may desire to be a monopoly, but all the money and physical plants in the world will not make it so. Similarly, the government may wish that a certain industry were purely competitive instead of a monopoly. The government can break up the monopoly into a very large number of very small producers, but if the government is not vigilant about enforcing the breakup, the firms will coalesce back into a monopoly. This tendency for a group of firms to form one industry type or another is caused by two factors: (1) the industry demand for the firms' products and (2) the shape of the firms' long-run average total cost curves. The first factor is determined by consumers; the second is determined by the physical requirements of producing the product and the cost of the factors used in production—neither factor can be altered by the firm itself.

Figure 10.8 shows the long-run average total cost for a representative firm in an industry (we can assume that all the firms are identical) and the industry

---

1   US Energy Information Administration, "How Much Gasoline Does the United States Consume?" last updated May 13, 2014, http://www.eia.gov/tools/faqs/faq.cfm?id=23&t=10.

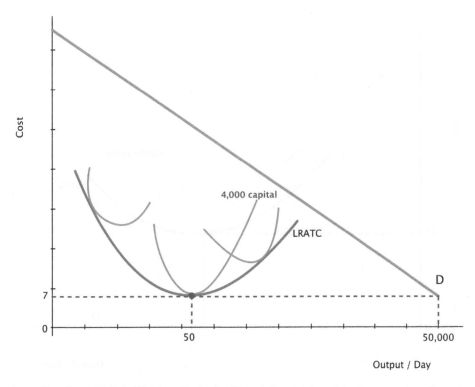

FIGURE 10.8 Long-Run Average Total Cost and Industry Demand

demand for the output of all the firms in the industry. According to the long-run average total cost curve, the lowest price a firm in this industry could ever conceivably charge for its product is $7 per unit. Further, if a firm in this industry is going to charge $7 per unit and not incur a loss, it must produce exactly fifty units of output per day and do so using four thousand units of capital. If it produces any other quantity of output or utilizes any other quantity of capital, its average total cost will rise above $7 per unit, and it will incur a loss. Now, if all the firms in this industry are identical and they all charge $7 per unit for their output, the total industry demand for this product is fifty thousand units per day (we obtain this number by tracing $7 per unit over to the industry demand curve). If the firms are not to incur a loss, each must produce fifty output per day. To achieve equilibrium (quantity demanded equals quantity supplied), there must be one thousand firms (fifty thousand output per day = fifty output per day per firm times one thousand firms). This is either a purely competitive or monopolistically competitive industry—many firms, all of them small.

Consider the firm shown in figure 10.9. Again, let us assume that all the firms in this industry are identical. According to the long-run average total cost curve, the lowest price a firm in this industry could ever conceivably charge for its product is $12 per unit. Further, if a firm in this industry is going to charge $12 per unit and not incur a loss, it must produce exactly one thousand units of output per day and do so using four thousand units of capital. If it produces any other quantity of output or utilizes any other quantity of capital, its average total cost will rise above $12 per unit, and it will incur a loss. Now, if all the firms in this industry are identical and they all charge $12 per unit for their output, the total industry demand for this product is one thousand units per day (we obtain this number by tracing $12 per unit over to the industry demand curve). If the firms are not to incur losses, each must produce one thousand output per day. To achieve equilibrium (quantity demanded equals quantity supplied), there must be one firm. The industry is natural monopoly.

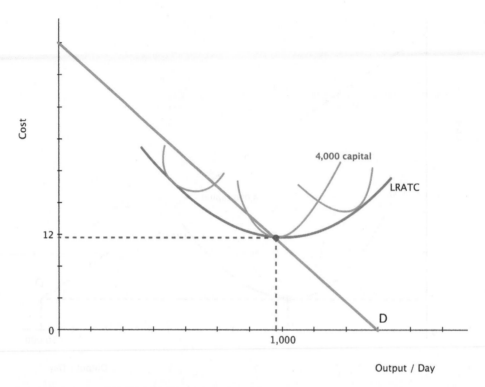

FIGURE 10.9 Long-Run Average Total Cost (Natural Monopoly)

Note that if the monopoly did charge $12 per unit and produce one thousand units per day using four thousand capital, it would make zero economic profit (its average total cost would be the same as its price). The monopoly will cut back its output below the one thousand level, so as to create a shortage and cause the price to rise (we have seen this already in our discussion of the monopoly industry). Suppose that the monopoly cuts its output back to five hundred units per day, and the price rises to $30 per unit. According to figure 10.9, another firm could enter the industry, obtain four thousand units of capital (which would enable the entrant to obtain an average total cost of $12) and undercut the monopoly's price. This is guaranteed not to happen. Why? Because the monopoly could match the entrant's price cut, which would leave the entrant with zero economic profit. If the entrant makes zero economic profit, it is not worth it for him to enter the industry. Thus, even if the monopoly is charging a price higher than the minimum price it

could charge, and even if other firms could enter the market and charge less than the monopoly is currently charging, they will not enter because of the threat that the monopoly would match their price cut and so leave them with zero economic profit.

Long-run average total cost curves, which have minimum points near the industry demand curve, arise because of very large startup costs. How is it that the monopoly could enter this industry, but other firms cannot? Remember that the monopoly is the pioneer (the first firm in the industry). When the monopoly entered the industry, it had to overcome very large startup costs. When an entrant attempts to enter the industry, it must overcome the same very large startup costs plus competition from the existing firm. It is this added factor of competition from the pioneer that makes it unprofitable for other firms to attempt entry into the monopoly industry.

Consider, however, that what is now a monopoly may not always be. Over time, the industry demand curve may shift right because of a violation of the ceteris paribus assumptions for demand. This shift could open up a large enough gap between the minimum point on the long-run average total cost curve and the industry demand curve for another firm (or firms) to enter.

CONCLUSION

As firms hire inputs and produce product, they experience two forces internally: specialization and congestion. Small firms employ so few units of input that increasing the quantity of inputs causes the firm's output to rise exponentially. This exponential growth is the result of specialization of the inputs within the firm. For example, the single worker in a one-person firm must perform all the work: production, selling, accounting. Hiring additional workers allows the workers to specialize, which makes them more productive. The increased productivity means that three workers can produce more than three times what one worker can produce. As the firm employs more units of one input, holding everything else constant, the firm may experience congestion: as the firm hires more workers, they get in each other's way. Whereas the force of specialization caused the firm's output to accelerate as the firm hired more workers, the force of congestion causes the firm's output to decelerate as the firm hires more workers.

These dual forces of specialization and congestion apply to all firms, regardless of what they produce. Specialization and congestion are what produce the bowl-shaped average cost curves. When the force of specialization is stronger than the force of congestion, the firm's cost per unit falls as the firm increases its output. We call this a movement along the short-run average cost curve. As the firm increases its output, the force of specialization weakens and the force of congestion strengthens. When congestion becomes strong enough, the cost curve turns up – as the firm continues to increase its output, its cost per unit starts to rise.

The firm can overcome congestion by investing in more capital. As the firm's capital (buildings, land, machinery) increases, the force of congestion diminishes, and the firm can once again cause its cost per unit to decline by increasing output. Because capital can only be altered in the long-run, we call this a movement along the long-run average cost curve. Economies of scale occur when the firm is on the downward sloping portion of the average total cost curve. Diseconomies of scale occur when the firm is on the upward sloping portion.

Finally, the longer the range of economies of scale is, the fewer firms will be able to co-exist in the industry. When diseconomies set in at low (compared to demand) levels of output, the industry will be comprised of a large number of small firms. When diseconomies set in at high (compared to demand) levels of output, the industry will be comprised of a small number of large firms.

DISCUSSION QUESTIONS

1. An entrepreneur starts a firm in a highly competitive industry and ends up earning near zero economic profit. Not satisfied with this, the entrepreneur hires an extremely talented CEO, and instructs the CEO to transform the firm into a monopoly. Making use of what you have learned in this chapter, discuss whether this might be possible.

2. How do economies of scale affect the composition and competitiveness of an industry?

3. Consider a firm and the industry in which it exists. Discuss what it means if the firm's price elasticity of demand is greater (in absolute value) than the industry's price elasticity of demand.

4. The term, "sustainable," while popular in the business lexicon, isn't well defined. Discuss whether the term "sustainable" can be more clearly defined using the concept of efficiency.

11

Perfect and Pure Competition

Introduction

Some consider the taco stand to be Mexico's version of fast food. It's a unique culinary experience not to be missed on a trip to the United States' southern neighbor. Half the fun of visiting new places and meeting new people is eating out and sampling the local cuisine. In Mexico, more than 85 percent of its people regularly eat at local taco stands. These can range from little street carts to larger and more established buildings. Pedro has operated his family's taco stand on the streets of Puerto Vallarta since he was seventeen years old. While he would love to raise the price of his tacos from 80 pesos to 100 pesos (roughly $1), it is unlikely to happen. A few unknowing tourists might pay that price; however, the majority of his regular patrons are local and would quickly take their business to the next taco stand less than three hundred feet down the street. We will discover that the degree of competition in product markets is a major determinant of product prices, quality, and availability. As we have learned in previous chapters, all businesses are trying to make a profit, but profits are constrained by the amount of competition the firms face.

When McDonalds offered boxes of 50 chicken nuggets for $9.99 (20 cents per nugget), Burger King responded by offering 10 chicken nuggets for $1.49 (15 cents per nugget). What caused Burger King and McDonalds to start fighting over nugget prices? It was competition from other restaurants. Both Burger King and McDonalds are losing customers to "fast-casual" restaurants like Chipotle. The competition from the fast-casual restaurants caused McDonalds to fight back by dropping the price of chicken nuggets in an attempt to lure customers. But this move not only pulled in customers who would have otherwise gone to a fast-casual restaurant, but also customers who would have otherwise gone to Burger King. This new competition from McDonalds forced Burger King to drop the price of its chicken nuggets.[1]

---

1 For more on this topic, see: www.bloomberg.com/news/articles/2015-01-12/burger-king-revives-15-cent-nuggets-in-price-war-with-mcdonald-s.

Attributes

A perfectly competitive industry has the following attributes:

1. There are many firms.
2. All the firms are small.
3. The firms produce a homogeneous product.
4. There is free entry to and exit from the industry.
5. Buyers and sellers have complete information.

"Many" firms simply means many in relation to the number of consumers. If there are two consumers, ten firms could be considered many. If there are one hundred consumers, ten firms might not be considered many. The number of consumers does not necessarily have to be larger than the number of firms for there to be "many" firms. The term is not so much a statement of *quantity* so much as a statement of the *quality* of the interactions of the consumers and producers.

"Small" means that no individual firm has any effect on the market price. When a small firm increases its output, the market price does not decline, because the firm's quantity of output is so small relative to the market as a whole that the firm's increase in output goes unnoticed in the larger market. Similarly, when a small firm decreases its output, the market price does not rise.

"Homogeneous" means that consumers believe that the output of one firm in the industry is qualitatively identical to the output of every other firm in the industry. The opposite of homogeneous is heterogeneous. An industry's products are heterogeneous when consumers believe that the outputs of the various firms are qualitatively different. Notice that it doesn't matter whether the firms' outputs are objectively the same or different. What matters is what consumers believe. Two products might be objectively different, but if consumers believe that the products are identical, consumers will behave in the same way they would if the products were objectively identical. Similarly, two products might be objectively identical, but if consumers believe that the products are different, they will behave as if the products were objectively different.

For example, bottled water sells for around three hundred times the price of tap water because consumers believe that bottled water is superior to tap water. However, repeated studies have shown that there is no objective difference between bottled water and tap water, or among different brands of bottled water. The product that bottled water companies sell is heterogeneous, not because the water is objectively heterogeneous, but because consumers believe that it is heterogeneous.

Conversely, there may be objective qualitative differences among firms' outputs, yet consumers might be unaware or even might ignore them. For example, over time, beer companies have spent a lot of money advertising small differences in their beers: fire-brewed beer, ice-brewed beer, short-neck bottles, long-neck bottles, labels you can write on, cold-activated cans, and vortex bottles. Each of these differences makes one manufacturer's beer qualitatively different from the others. However, over time, consumers end up not caring and therefore behaving as if the differences don't exist. We know this because beer manufacturers have to keep coming up with new minor differences that they can advertise. If, over the long run, a specific difference mattered to consumers, manufacturers would continue to advertise that difference.

"Free entry to and exit from the industry" means that existing firms can leave the industry and entrepreneurs can move into the industry. "Free," in this context, does not mean costless. An entrepreneur who, for example, wants to open a fast-food restaurant will incur startup costs for physical space, advertising, furniture, and equipment. But these costs are all normal costs associated with starting a business, so we would say that the entrepreneur has "free entry" to the industry. If, however, the entrepreneur must obtain a government license or pay off local criminals to start a business, we would say that there is not free entry to the industry. Notice that private licensing is not a barrier to entry. For example, to open a McDonald's restaurant, an entrepreneur must pay McDonald's Corporation an upfront fee plus a portion of the restaurant's annual revenue. This is not a barrier to entry.

The entrepreneur is paying McDonald's Corporation for the marketing benefits that go with the use of the McDonald's brand name. The difference between private licensing and government licensing (which can be a barrier to entry) is that when the entrepreneur pays for private licensing, he is freely choosing to pay in exchange for receiving a benefit. For example, the entrepreneur who does not want to pay the McDonald's licensing fee could look for another franchise or could open an independent restaurant. In the case of government licensing, the entrepreneur does not have the option to pay and, typically, is not receiving something of value in exchange for the fee.

If we include the fifth attribute, "complete information," we have a perfectly competitive industry. In a purely competitive industry, buyers and sellers are unaware of all prices being asked and offered elsewhere. For example, if drivers are aware of gas prices at stations along routes they typically drive, but are unaware of gas prices at stations down side streets that they don't travel, the retail gasoline industry (assuming it is a competitive industry) will be purely competitive. The more knowledge buyers and sellers have of prices elsewhere in the industry, the more different subsets of the industry will have to compete with each other.

For example, suppose that there are four gas stations along your route between your home and school. Those four gas stations must compete with one another for your business, so their prices will tend to be similar (allowing for differences in other things, such as whether they have good coffee, how crowded they tend to be, etc.). Gas stations that are not along your route have less ability to compete for your business because you are less likely to be aware of how much they are charging. Conversely, suppose that you want to buy a pack of blank DVDs on eBay. You can easily see what every single seller is charging for blank DVDs. The retail DVD industry on eBay will look more like perfect competition, while gas stations will look more like pure competition.

Pricing

A firm in pure or perfect competition will not charge a higher price for its product than its competitors charge. Suppose that there are ten thousand firms in a perfectly competitive industry, each of which charges $15 per unit for its product. If one of the ten thousand firms prices its product at $15.01, no consumers will buy from that firm because (1) there are many other firms from which to buy, and (2) the output of all firms is identical. You might think that while there are many firms, they are spread out over a large area, so that consumers cannot easily get from one store to another. But this violates the concept of "many firms." By spreading the firms out over a large area, there are now fewer firms available to any given consumer. Thus, there are no longer "many firms." You might argue that the single firm could get away with charging $15.01 if its product were of a higher quality. But this violates the concept of "homogeneous product." By altering the quality of its product (assuming that the consumers perceive the quality change), the firm's product is no longer the same as the products of the other firms. In short, in a purely competitive industry, no single firm will charge more than its competitors does. In a perfectly competitive industry, no single firm will charge more than do the competitors of which consumers are aware.

A single firm also will not charge less than its competitors do. The only reason a firm would lower the price of its product is so that it could sell more units. In fact, the firm that lowers its price intends for the percentage increase in unit sales to be greater than the percentage decrease in price, so that the firm makes more revenue. When a firm is small, it has no effect on the market price. This means that the firm can offer as many units of its product as it likes at the going market price, and there will always be someone willing to buy the units. Because the firm is small relative to the market, no matter how many units it produces, the firm does not produce enough to create a surplus of the product. If the firm wants to sell more units, it merely needs to produce more output. So, in a perfectly competitive industry, individual firms will not charge less than their competitors do.

If a single firm in a perfectly competitive industry will not charge less than its competitors and will not charge more, the firm will charge the same price—the

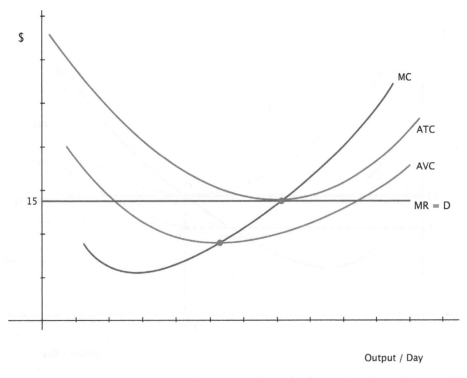

FIGURE 11.1 Perfectly Competitive Firm in the Long Run

equilibrium price. We say that such a firm is a *price taker*—that is, the firm has no control over the market price of its product. Of course, the firm can *ask* whatever price it likes. The price the firm asks is irrelevant. What matters is the price that the consumer is willing to pay and that the firm is willing to accept. That is the market price.

Figure 11.1 shows an example of a perfectly competitive firm in the long run. The firm's demand curve (that is, the demand for the output of this specific firm) is horizontal, meaning that this firm can sell as many units of output as it likes at the going market price. Other things being the same, the more control a firm has over the price of its product, the steeper the firm's demand curve is. Because the perfectly competitive firm has no control over the price of its product, the firm's demand curve is flat. We also described this as a marginal revenue curve—the amount by which the firm's revenue changes when it sells one more unit of output (i.e., if the equilibrium price of the firm's product is $15, every time the firm sells one more unit of output, its revenue rises by $15). The firm's demand curve and marginal revenue curve are horizontal

because no matter how much output the firm produces, the equilibrium price (and, hence, the firm's marginal revenue) remain unchanged.

What can we deduce about the firm from the diagram? Consider figure 11.2, which shows our firm in a little more detail. We know (by the sixth principle of economics) that the firm will produce the output quantity at which marginal revenue and marginal cost are equal. According to the figure, this occurs at 150 units of output per day. Point A on the graph is the point at which the marginal revenue and marginal cost curves cross. If the firm produces 150 units of output per day, we know that the firm will sell this output at $15 per unit. We find this figure by starting at 150 units of output per day on the horizontal axis and tracing this point straight up until we hit the demand curve (at point A). When we hit the demand curve, we trace to the left and find a figure of $15. In fact, no matter how much output this firm produces, it will sell it at $15 per unit. If the firm produces 150 units of output per day, we also know that the firm will spend $9 per unit of output on short-run factors. We find this figure by

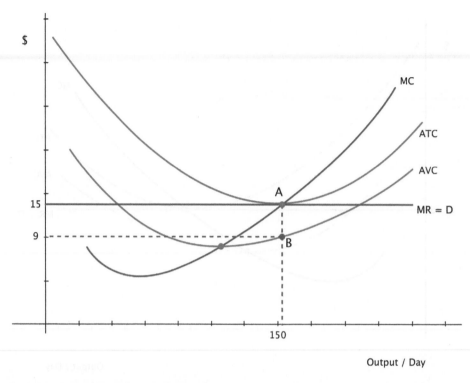

FIGURE 11.2 Perfectly Competitive Firm in the Long Run

starting at the output quantity of 150 units per day and tracing this point straight up until we hit the average variable cost curve (at point B). When we hit the average variable cost curve, we trace to the left and find a figure of $9. If the firm produces 150 units of output per day, we know that the firm will spend $15 per unit of output on short- and long-run factors combined. We find this figure by starting at the output quantity of 150 units per day and tracing this point straight up until we hit the average total cost curve (at point A). When we hit the average total cost curve, we trace this point to the left and find a figure of $15. While the average fixed cost curve is not shown on the graph, we know that AFC = ATC – AVC, or the firm's average fixed cost is $6 ($6 = $15 – $9) per unit of output. We also know that the firm's total cost is $2,250 ($2,250 = 150 × $15), the firm's variable cost is $1,350 ($1,350 = 150 × $9), and the firm's fixed cost is $900 ($900 = 150 × $6).

Notice something interesting about the profit-maximizing output quantity: the point where the MR and MC curves cross (profit-maximizing output) is also the point where the ATC curve is minimum. To this

minimum point on the ATC curve, we give a special name: the *efficient output quantity*. The *efficient output quantity* is that output quantity at which the firm's average total cost is minimum. When the firm produces at this output quantity, it is utilizing its resources in the most efficient way possible. Remember that the goal of a firm is not to be efficient but to maximize profit (we shall see later that it is possible to maximize profit without being efficient). When a firm's profit-maximizing output quantity and efficient output quantity coincide, the firm will produce at the efficient output quantity, because the efficient output quantity happens to be the same as the profit-maximizing output quantity. We call such a firm *efficient*.

THE PROFIT-MAXIMIZING OUTPUT QUANTITY is that output quantity at which the firm's profit is at maximum.
THE EFFICIENT OUTPUT QUANTITY is that output quantity at which the firm's average total cost is at a minimum.

Notice something else: the price the firm charges for its output ($15) is the same as the firm's average total cost ($15). This means that the firm's revenue ($15 per unit times 150 units) is the same as the firm's total cost ($15 per unit times 150 units). This firm is making zero profit. How can a firm that makes zero profit survive? Remember that when economists speak of cost, they mean economic cost, and economic cost includes opportunity cost. A firm may be making substantial accounting profit, yet still be making zero economic profit. Consider this: suppose that our firm's average accounting cost is $12.44 per unit. This means that the money the firm earns is $2,250 per day ($2,250 = 150 × $15), and the amount of money the firm spends is $1,866 per day ($1,800 = 150 × $12.44). Shouldn't this mean that our firm makes an economic profit of $384 per day? Not necessarily. Suppose that the owner of the firm invested $1 million in the startup of the firm. Instead of starting the firm, the owner could have put the $1 million into a variety of stocks and bonds, which would represent the same risk as the firm. Suppose that the owner could have earned (on average) 14 percent interest on those stocks and bonds. This 14 percent interest would have earned the owner (approximately) $140,000 per year, or $384 per day. The fact that the owner did not put his money into the stocks and bonds means that the owner missed an opportunity to earn $384 per day from the stock market. This is an opportunity cost. So, although the firm is making an accounting profit of $384 per day, it is making an economic profit of $0 per day—in other words, the amount of accounting profit the firm is earning is *no more than could be earned if the startup money had been invested elsewhere.*

Now, suppose that the owner could have invested the $1 million in the stock market and earned an average of 16 percent interest. This means that the owner, had he invested the money in stocks instead of starting the firm, would have earned $438 per day. If the owner instead uses the money to start the firm, although he earns an accounting profit of $384 per day, he incurs an economic loss of $54 per day ($54 = $438 – $384). That is, the amount of accounting profit the firm is earning is $54 per day *less than could have been earned had the money been invested elsewhere.*[2] The rules we used in analyzing this firm apply to all firms, regardless of the type of industry in which they reside. The rules are summarized as follows:

Now, this zero economic profit may just come from the way we drew the picture of the perfectly competitive firm. While the cost curves all must have the standard shapes shown, and the marginal revenue and demand curves must be horizontal (in a perfectly competitive industry), the positions of the curves can be played with a bit. How do we know how high or how low to draw the marginal revenue and demand curves?

RULES FOR ANALYZING A FIRM

1 To find the profit-maximizing output quantity, find the point where the MR and MC curves cross, and trace this point down to the horizontal axis.

2 To find the price the firm will charge for its output, start at the profit-maximizing output quantity, and trace this point up to the firm's demand curve and then left to the vertical axis.

3 To find the firm's average total cost, start at the profit-maximizing output quantity, and trace this point up to the ATC curve and then left to the vertical axis.

4 To find the firm's average variable cost, start at the profit-maximizing output quantity, and trace this point up to the AVC curve and then left to the vertical axis.

5 To find the firm's efficient output quantity, find the point where the MC and ATC curves cross (this is also the minimum point on the ATC curve) and trace this point down to the horizontal axis

---

2 It is true that if the owner invested the money in the stock market, he would still have the original $1 million in addition to whatever interest he earned. In equilibrium, however, when he invests the $1 million in the startup of the firm, he can at any point sell the assets of the firm for the same $1 million.

6 The economic profit the firm earns is the area below the firm's price, above the firm's average total cost, and to the left of the firm's profit-maximizing output quantity. If average total cost is above price, the area bounded by these three measures is an economic loss.

7 The firm is efficient if its profit-maximizing output quantity is the same as its efficient output quantity. This occurs when the firm's marginal cost is equal to market price.

The answer comes from the market. Figure 11.3 shows the market for the product produced by a perfectly competitive industry on the left and a single firm in the industry on the right. On the left, we see that the equilibrium price of the product is $15 per unit—this is the price at which industry demand and industry supply intersect. We trace this price to the right, and this determines the location of the marginal revenue and demand curves for the single firm. According to figure 11.3, at a price of $15 per unit, the total number of units sold by the industry is 1.5 million per day. Because each individual firm is producing 150 units of output per day, in equilibrium there must be ten thousand firms (10,000 firms = 1.5 million output per day / 150 output per firm per day).

Suppose that we draw our firm as incurring an economic loss. Figure 11.4 shows the perfectly competitive firm again; this time the demand and marginal revenue

curves are shifted downward. From following the rules for analyzing the firm, we see that the firm's MR and MC curves cross at point A, so the firm will produce 140 units of output. If we follow the firm's profit-maximizing output quantity up to the average total cost curve (point B), we see that the firm's average total cost is $15.10. We also note that the firm is not efficient, because the efficient output quantity (found where the MC and ATC curves cross at point C) is 150 units per day. Further, this firm is incurring an economic loss. Does the economic loss have to do with the fact that the firm is inefficient? No. The firm's profit-maximizing output quantity is 140 units per day—this means that even though the firm is incurring a loss, its loss is the smallest possible when it produces 140 units per day. Visualize what would happen to the "economic loss" box shown if the firm were to produce 150 units per day: the box would become just slightly shorter (as

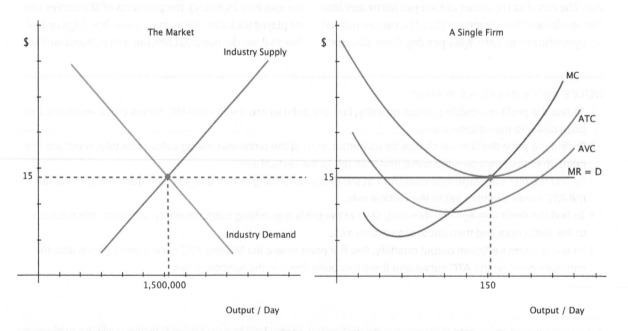

FIGURE 11.3 Perfectly Competitive Industry: Market and Single Firm

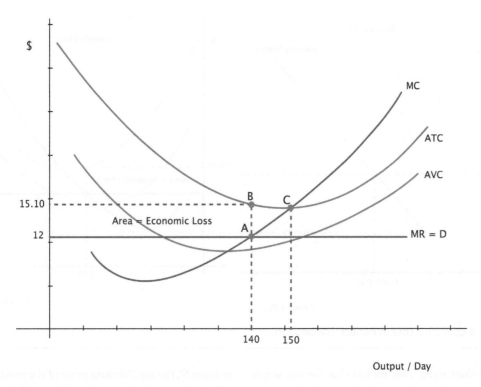

FIGURE 11.4 Economic Loss for a Perfectly Competitive Firm

the average total cost dropped from $15.10 to $15), but would become significantly wider (as the output rose from 140 units to 150 units). In fact, when the firm produces 140 units per day, its economic loss is $434 per day ($434 = $12 ×140 − $15.10 ×140). If the firm were to produce 150 units per day, its economic loss would rise to $450 per day ($450 = $12 ×150 − $15 ×150).

The conditions that would cause all firms to take an economic loss are shown in figure 11.5. The left panel of the figure shows that the equilibrium price of the product is $12. Following the $12 price over to the right panel, we see that the profit-maximizing output quantity for a single firm in this industry is 140 units of output per day. However, when a firm produces 140 units of output per day, its average total cost is $15.10 per unit of output—the firm is incurring an economic loss. Notice also that in equilibrium there are twelve thousand firms (12,000 = 1,680,000 / 140).

What happens when firms in a perfectly competitive industry incur economic losses? The firms eventually cease to exist—they move to another industry, producing a more profitable product, or their

owners shut them down completely and invest the money elsewhere, or they go bankrupt. Because the firms in a perfectly competitive industry are small, if one firm ceases to exist, there is no effect on the market. However, if many firms cease to exist, there is an effect on the market. In fact, when many perfectly competitive firms cease to exist, the ceteris paribus assumption for supply requiring that the number of producers remains fixed is violated. When the number of producers decreases, the industry supply curve shifts to the left. How far will the supply curve shift? The supply curve will continue to shift to the left until firms stop leaving the industry. Firms will stop leaving the industry when the accounting profit their owners can make elsewhere is no larger than the accounting profit their owners can make in this industry—that is, when the firms' economic profits are zero.

Figure 11.6 shows what happens to the industry and the remaining firms when a large number of firms leaves the industry. As the firms leave the industry, the industry supply curve shifts to the left. As the supply curve shifts left, the equilibrium price

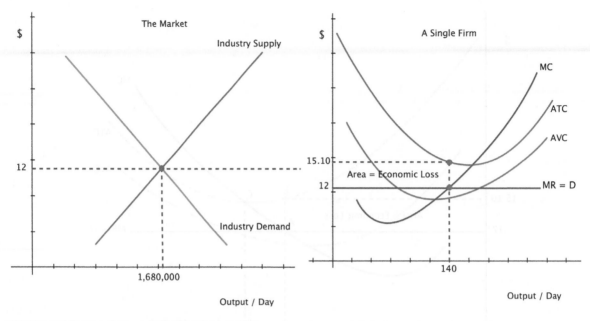

FIGURE 11.5 Economic Loss in Perfect Competition

of the product rises. This means that for the single firm shown in the right panel, the marginal revenue and firm demand curves are rising. Firms continue to leave the industry until the industry supply curve reaches S' in the left panel. When the supply curve

reaches S', the equilibrium price of the product is $15. When the equilibrium price of the product is $15, the firms in the right panel maximize their profits by producing 150 units of output each. This earns the firms zero economic profit. Because the owners of the firms

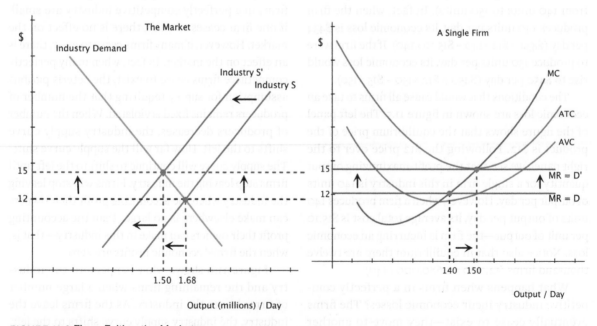

FIGURE 11.6 Firms Exiting the Market

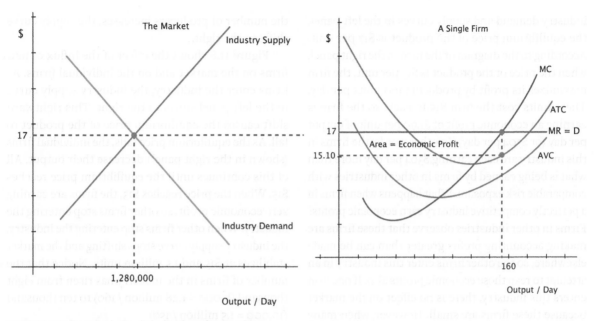

FIGURE 11.7 Economic Profit in Perfect Competition

are earning no less profit in this industry than they would anywhere else, firms stop leaving the industry, the industry supply curve stops shifting, and the equilibrium price stabilizes at $15. Notice that by the time the industry supply curve stabilizes, the number of firms in the industry will have fallen from twelve thousand (12,000 = 1.68 million / 140) to ten thousand (10,000 = 1.5 million / 150).

Figure 11.7 shows a firm in a perfectly competitive industry earning an economic profit. According to the

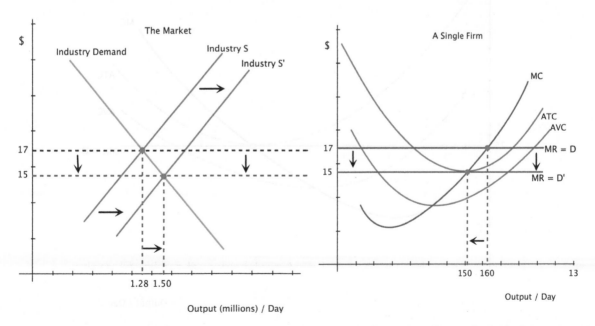

FIGURE 11.8 Firms Entering the Market

industry demand and supply curves in the left panel, the equilibrium price of the product is $17 per unit. According to the diagram of the firm in the right panel, when the price of the product is $17 per unit, the firm maximizes its profit by producing 160 units per day. These units cost the firm $15.10 each, so the firm is earning an economic profit of $1.90 per unit of output per day (or $304 per day). In other words, the firms in this industry are each earning $304 per day more than what is being earned by firms in other industries with comparable risk exposure. What happens when firms in a perfectly competitive industry earn economic profits? Firms in other industries observe that these firms are making accounting profits greater than can be made elsewhere, so the other firms enter this industry in an attempt to reap those economic profits also. If one firm enters this industry, there is no effect on the market because these firms are small. However, when many firms enter this industry, collectively, they violate the ceteris paribus assumption for supply, which requires that the number of producers remains constant. When

the number of producers increases, the supply curve shifts to the right.

Figure 11.8 shows the effect of the influx of new firms on the market and on the individual firms. As firms enter the industry, the industry supply curve in the left panel shifts to the right. This rightward shift causes the equilibrium price of the product to fall. As the equilibrium price falls, the individual firms (shown in the right panel) decrease their output. All of this continues until the equilibrium price reaches $15. When the price reaches $15, the firms are earning zero economic profit, so other firms stop entering the industry. When other firms stop entering the industry, the industry supply curve stops shifting and the market stabilizes at $15 and 1.5 million units. Notice that the number of firms in the industry has risen from eight thousand (8,000 = 1.28 million / 160) to ten thousand (10,000 = 1.5 million / 150).

This analysis proves that the perfectly competitive firm will make zero economic profit in the long-run. If a situation ever arose in which perfectly competitive firms were making economic profit or incurring

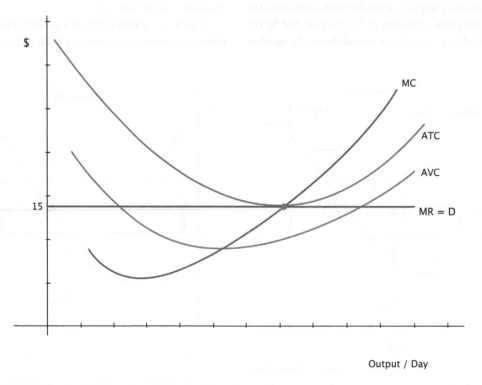

FIGURE 11.9 Perfectly Competitive Firm in the Long Run

economic loss, firms would enter or leave the industry until the economic profit of the remaining firms was again zero. Thus, the proper representation of a perfectly competitive firm is that shown in figure 11.9, in which the marginal revenue and demand curves are tangent to the average total cost curve. Notice that when the perfectly competitive firm is drawn this way, the profit-maximizing output quantity (the point where MR and MC intersect) is the same as the efficient output quantity (the minimum point on the ATC curve). Thus, we can conclude that (1) perfectly competitive firms make zero economic profit in the long-run, and (2) perfectly competitive firms are efficient in the long-run.[3]

ENTREPRENEURIAL ACTIVITY IN THE UNITED STATES

A competitive market environment is expected to be open to high level of entrepreneurship. If that is indeed the case then the recent drop in entrepreneurial activity in the U.S. can be seen as a worrying trend. A recent report by the Kauffman Foundation (http://www.kauffman.org/newsroom/2014/04/entrepreneurial-activity-declines-again-in-2013-as-labor-market-strengthens) indicated a decrease in entrepreneurial activity in 2013 despite a strengthening labor market. Additionally, entrepreneurial activity varies significantly across states. One would first wonder why there is a drop in entrepreneurial activity in the U.S. in recent times. One would also be curious about why entrepreneurship varies so significantly across states.

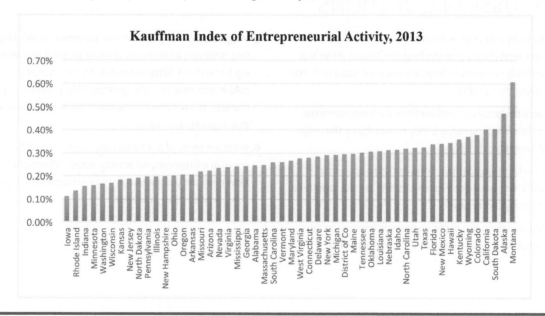

Source: The Kauffman Index of Entrepreneurial Activity, 2013.

---

3 Profit maximizing output occurs where MR = MC. Efficient output occurs where ATC is minimum. When the output at which MR=MC is the same as the output at which ATC is minimum, the firm will be efficient. In a perfectly competitive industry, firms will produce the level of output where P = MR = MC = ATC. The point here is that the firm does not pursue efficiency. It pursues profit. When the firm achieves efficiency, it is because of a happy coincidence that profit max output and efficient output are the same.

CONCLUSION

A perfectly or purely competitive industry is one in which there are many firms producing (essentially) identical products. These conditions mean that there is intense competition among firms within the industry. A firm in this industry can't pursue profits by raising its price above that of its competitors. Because its product is identical to the products of all the other firms, the firm that raised its price would lose its customers to the competitors. A firm in this industry also can't pursue profits by lowering its price below that of its competitors. The point of lowering price is to increase unit sales. Because there are many firms, the market is very large compared to the firm. If the firm wants to sell more, all it need do is to produce more. There is no need to lower its price. All of this means that the firm has no control over the price of its product. To pursue profits, the firm must concentrate its efforts on reducing its costs. Because of this, in the long-run, firms in a perfectly competitive industry will be efficient – they will seek out the output levels that drive their average total costs to the lowest possible level.

DISCUSSION QUESTIONS

1. Perfectly competitive firms produce a socially efficient level of output in the long run. Does it mean that perfectly competitive firms are not concerned with maximizing their profits?

2. Since perfectly competitive firms earn zero economic profit in the long run, are they constantly on the verge of bankruptcy?

3. If perfectly competitive firms earn zero economic profit, why would entrepreneurs ever choose to enter a perfectly competitive?

4. Discuss whether it might be possible for a perfectly competitive industry to evolve into a monopoly.

5. Imagine a perfectly competitive supermarket industry that discovers a better and cheaper method of preserving frozen food. What will this do to the price of food sold in supermarkets, the quantity of food sold in supermarkets, the number of supermarkets, and the profits that supermarkets earn?

6. What are some of the factors that explain the differences in entrepreneurial activity across different states? How does the U.S. fare in terms of entrepreneurship compared to other countries?

Monopoly

12

I n the mid to late 1800s, Western Union was one of the country's largest and most profitable monopolies. After acquiring smaller telegraph companies, Western Union was the first company to provide transcontinental telegraph communication. Although the cost of stringing telegraph wires across the entire continent was very high, Western Union earned enough revenue from providing telegraph services to make the investment profitable. However, potential competitors could not earn a profit doing the same thing because they would incur the same high cost as Western Union but capture fewer customers. Because of this, Western Union faced little serious competition. Yet, when the telephone replaced the telegraph, AT&T replaced Western Union as the leading telecommunications monopoly. When cellular phone service replaced many landlines, AT&T lost its position as a telecommunications monopoly. As Internet services, like Skype and Google, handle more voice and video calls, cellular phone companies are losing their hold on telecommunications markets. The interesting conclusion is that, while tremendous startup costs can enable some companies to establish themselves as monopolies, continued innovation can jeopardize that monopoly status.

In most locations throughout the US, consumers do not have many choices for cable Internet service providers. In many locations, there is only one. The absence of competition allows these firms to extract monopoly profits by restricting the quantity of bandwidth to your home and charging you a higher price. How do we know this? Look at what happens when a competing firm enters the market. In 2013, Time Warner Cable customers in Kansas City suddenly saw a 50% boost in their cable Internet service and a 30% reduction in their monthly cable bills. Why? Because Google selected Kansas City as a location to test market Google Fiber – a product that promises faster Internet service than cable service and at a significantly lower price.[1]

Attributes

Let us now move to the opposite extreme of industry structures: the monopoly. While a perfectly competitive industry has so many producers that each one, individually, has no effect on the market, a monopoly industry has only one producer, and that producer has a substantial effect on the market. The monopoly industry has the following attributes: (1) there is one firm, (2) the firm produces products without a close substitute, and (3) there might be significant barriers to entry into the industry.

ATTRIBUTES OF A MONOPOLY INDUSTRY

1 There is one firm.
2 The firm produces products without a close substitute.
3 There might be significant barriers to entry into the industry.

Recall that "small" means that a single firm has no effect on the market price. Conversely, to say that a firm is "large" means that the single firm does have an effect on the market price. If a large firm increases its rate of production, it creates a surplus, and the price of the product falls. If the firm reduces its rate of production, it creates a shortage, and the price of the product rises. Of course, a monopoly, like any other firm, can *ask* whatever price it wants. When we say that the price of the product rises or falls, we mean the price that *consumers are willing to pay*.

If there is free entry to the monopoly industry, we say that the monopoly is a *natural monopoly*. In the case of a natural monopoly, economic forces are such that other firms will not want to enter the industry and compete with the monopoly. If there is not free entry to the monopoly industry, we say that the monopoly is an *artificial monopoly*. That is, the only reason the firm is a monopoly is because of some sort of governmental regulation. Given the choice, other firms would enter this industry and compete with the single firm.

The US Post Office is a good example of an artificial monopoly. By law, only the US Postal Service may deliver first-class mail in the United States. Private companies, such as UPS and FedEx, are permitted to deliver packages but not letters (one can send a letter via these services, but it must be enclosed in a package). Because private companies can earn profit delivering packages, it is likely that they could also earn profit delivering first-class mail—if it were legal to do so. So, while first-class mail delivery is a monopoly industry, it is so because of the law rather than because of economic forces.

Natural monopolies evolve when a firm's average cost per unit declines over a long range of outputs. For example, as of early 2014, Google's asset value was $120 billion. Roughly speaking, this is what it cost to build Google. Amortizing the $120 billion cost to build Google over (to pick a reasonable number) twenty years gives us a cost of $16 million per day. What is Google's per-query cost? If Google answered one million queries daily, its per-query cost would be $16 million divided by one million, or $16 per query.

---

1 Source: http://finance.yahoo.com/q/ks?s=GOOG+Key+Statistics.

Using the same infrastructure, if Google answered ten million queries per day, its per-query cost would drop to $1.60. But Google currently answers almost six billion queries per day.[2] This makes its per-query cost around three-tenths of one cent. One reason Google is (almost) a monopoly in the search-engine industry is that its average cost per unit continues to decline over a large number of queries. So long as its average cost declines as its output increases, it will be able to charge a lower price than smaller competitors can and therefore prevent the potential competitors from entering the industry.

A NATURAL MONOPOLY is a monopoly that exists due to significant economies of scale.
AN ARTIFICIAL MONOPOLY is a monopoly that exists because of government regulation.

Natural monopolies have this in common: the startup costs are large, but once up and running, the cost of adding one more customer, or producing one more unit, is small. Airlines are a good example: the cost of buying a plane and renting space at an airport is significant. The incremental cost of putting one more person on an already existing plane is small. The cost of building an electricity power plant is huge. Once built, the incremental cost of providing electricity to one more house is small. This is known as economies of scale.

There are very few examples of pure natural monopolies. Most natural monopolies are actually hybrid industries that are dominated by a single large firm, yet also contain smaller firms. Natural monopolies tend not to be permanent because they face competition from new technologies. Accounting for 70 percent of the market, IBM was a near-monopoly in the computer industry in the 1960s and 1970s.[3] As emphasis shifted from hardware to software, monopoly profits in computer hardware dissipated as potential monopoly profits in software grew. This shift saw Microsoft replace IBM as the dominant firm. As emphasis is now shifting from on-the-computer software to cloud software, Google is emerging as a possible replacement to Microsoft as the dominant firm. What this illustrates is the fact that while a natural monopoly may face little or no competition within its industry, it does face competition from competing industries and new technologies. In this case, software came to be more important than hardware, and now cloud services are becoming more important than on-the-computer software.

Prior to its breakup, AT&T was a monopoly.[4] Other companies were free to enter the telephone industry and compete with AT&T, yet none chose to—the revenue the potential competitors expected to earn had they competed with AT&T were less than the costs they expected to incur starting up and running their own telephone companies. AT&T was a natural monopoly. Despite the fact that the government broke up AT&T into the five regional telephone companies, the same economic forces that caused AT&T to exist as a monopoly provided incentive for the regional telephone companies to reconsolidate. Thus, the government had to mandate that the regional companies not merge. When the government rescinded the laws that prevented mergers between the regional companies, economic forces caused the companies to re-consolidate.[5]

When we introduced marginal revenue, it was within the context of a perfectly competitive industry. In that context, we noted that marginal revenue could be thought of as the price of the firm's product. For example, if a firm sells its product for $10 per unit,

---

2 Source: http://www.statisticbrain.com/google-searches/

3 Rachel Konrad, "IBM and Microsoft: Antitrust Then and Now," *CNET*, June 7, 2000, http://news.cnet.com/2100-1001-241565.html.

4 Actually, prior to AT&T's breakup, the telephone industry in the United States was a perfect competition-monopoly hybrid. There were a number of much smaller telephone companies that mainly serviced rural areas that AT&T did not find it profitable to service. AT&T, because of its colossal size (in comparison to these other firms), exercised about the same amount of monopoly control over pricing that it would have had these firms not existed. The smaller firms, for their part, acted as if they were in a perfectly competitive industry where AT&T was to them what the sum total of all the other small firms in a perfectly competitive firm would have been.

5 New York Telephone merged with Bell Atlantic and Mid-Western Bell merged with Pacific Telesis.

every time the firm sells another unit of product, its revenue rises by $10—thus, the marginal revenue is $10. We call such a firm a *price taker* because the firm cannot influence the market price for its product. This is not the case in the context of the other industry types. Consider the case of a monopoly. A monopoly sells its product for $10 per unit. The firm produces 1,000 units per day. What happens if the firm decides to increase its output by one unit to 1,001 units per day? Because the monopoly is a large firm, its actions affect the market. When the monopoly increases its output, it creates a surplus of the product, and the price of the product falls. So, while the monopoly can sell 1,000 units per day at a price of $10 each, if it were to increase its output to 1,001 units per day, the resulting surplus would cause the price of the product to fall to $9.98. The result is that the monopoly's price is $10, but its marginal revenue is $9.98—if the firm sells one more unit of output, it does not get $10 but only $9.98. Thus, the monopoly's marginal revenue is always less than the price of its product. We call this type of firm

a *price setter* because the firm can influence the market price of its product by altering how much it produces.

Recall that the more control a firm has over the price of its product, the steeper the firm's demand curve is. Because a monopoly has a great degree of control over the price of its product (caused in part by the absence of competitors), the monopoly's demand curve will be downward sloping. Because the monopoly's marginal revenue is always less than the price of its product, the monopoly's marginal revenue curve will be downward sloping and will be steeper than the demand curve. In fact, because the monopoly is the entire industry, the firm's demand curve is the industry demand curve.

Notice in figure 12.1 that the monopoly's demand curve is downward sloping and that its marginal revenue curve is steeper than the demand curve. It is always the case (regardless of the industry type) that the marginal revenue curve and the demand curve intersect on the vertical axis, and the marginal revenue always intersects the horizontal axis at one-half the

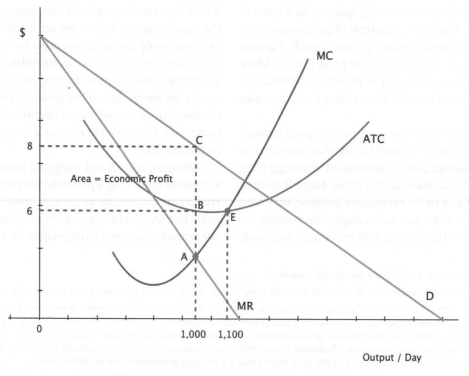

FIGURE 12.1 Monopoly Decision Making and Profit

distance that demand intersects the horizontal axis.[6] If the demand curve is horizontal, as in the case of the perfectly competitive industry, these rules imply that the demand and marginal revenue curves will be overlapping (as was the case in the diagrams of perfect competition).

Following the rules for analyzing a firm, we find the point at which the MR and MC curves intersect (point A) and follow this down to the horizontal axis to find the profit-maximizing level of output (one thousand units per day). We find the firm's average total cost by following the profit-maximizing output quantity up to the point at which it intersects the ATC curve (point B) and follow this across to the vertical axis to find $6 per unit. To find the price the firm will charge, we start at the profit-maximizing level of output and follow this up to the point at which it intersects demand (point C) and follow this across to the vertical axis to find $8 per unit. The firm's efficient output quantity is found by locating at the point at which the ATC curve is minimum (point E) and following this down to the horizontal axis (1,100 units per day). The firm's economic profit is the area below price, above the average total cost ($6, not the average total cost curve), and to the left of the profit-maximizing output quantity.

From our analysis, we can see that the monopoly makes an economic profit and is inefficient. How is it that the monopoly is maximizing its profit if its average total cost is not as low as possible? What would happen to the monopoly's profits if it were to produce at the efficient output quantity?

Notice what would happen if the monopoly produced at the efficient output level instead of the profit-maximizing output level. This is shown in figure 12.2. When the monopoly produces 1,100 units per day (the efficient output), its average total cost drops from $6 per unit to $5.90 per unit. However, because the monopoly is producing more units and because it is a large firm (whose actions affect the market price), the increase in output causes a surplus of product on the market, which causes the price of the monopoly's product to fall from $8 per unit to $7 per unit. So,

now the monopoly is producing more output at a lower average total cost, but it is selling the output for less. Graphically, the monopoly's profit when it produces 1,100 units per day is areas E, B, and C, but when the monopoly produces 1,000 units per day, its profit is areas A and E. Increasing output from 1,000 units per day to 1,100 units per day gains areas B and C but loses area A—and area A is larger than areas B and C combined. We can directly compute the monopoly's profit under each scenario. When the monopoly produces 1,000 units of output, the equilibrium price is $8 and its average total cost is $6. This means that the monopoly makes $2 economic profit per unit of output. On 1,000 units per day, that is $2,000 economic profit per day. When the monopoly produces 1,100 units of output, the equilibrium price is $7 and its average total cost is $5.90. This means that the monopoly makes $1.10 economic profit per unit of output. On 1,100 units per day, that is $1,210 economic profit per day. Thus, the monopoly is better off producing at the profit-maximizing output quantity, despite the fact that doing so makes it socially inefficient.

Intuitively, the monopoly makes more profit when it reduces its output from the efficient output level to the profit-maximizing level, because what the monopoly gains from the resulting price increase more than makes up for what it loses because of selling fewer units and incurring a slightly higher per-unit production cost.

We have stumbled on one reason why, in the United States, monopolies are regulated. The need for regulation has nothing to do (as is commonly believed) with the fact that the monopoly can charge any price it wants. In fact, the monopoly can't "charge any price it wants." The price it can charge is dictated by consumer demand. If the monopoly asks too high a price, consumers can choose not to purchase at all. The supposed need for regulation has to do with the monopoly's inefficiency. The fact that the monopoly is not producing at its efficient output level means that it is using some of society's resources (labor, machinery, land, etc.) inefficiently. That is, if these resources

---

6 The proof goes as follows. Suppose a firm faces the demand curve $P = a - bQ$, where P is the price of the product and Q is the quantity demanded (a is the vertical intercept of the demand curve and b is the slope). The firm's total revenue is $TR = PQ = aQ - bQ^2$. Marginal revenue is the partial derivative of total revenue with respect to output. Thus, $MR = d(TR)/dQ = a - 2bQ$. Notice that the equation for the marginal revenue curve gives the same intercept as that of demand and a slope of twice the magnitude.

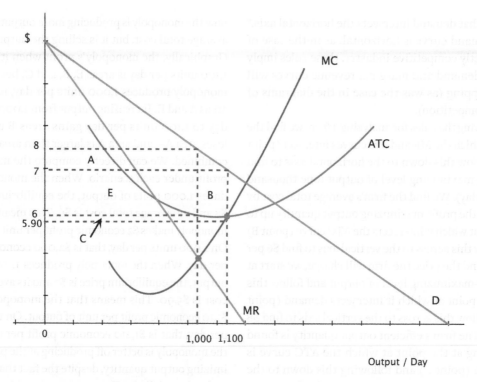

FIGURE 12.2 Monopoly and Inefficiency

were used by an efficient firm instead of an inefficient one, the resources would produce more product than they are producing now (in this example, 1,100 units instead of 1,000).[7]

Price Discrimination

Monopolies (and oligopolies, and sometimes monopolistically competitive firms) can engage in what is called *price discrimination*. Price discrimination occurs when the firm charges different prices for different units of the same product. For example, look at the two quotes below for a flight from New York's JFK airport to Los Angeles. Both flights leave on a Wednesday and return the next day. Both flights depart in the middle of the month (the 19th in both cases). Both flights are on the same carrier. Both flights are nonstop. Both flights depart just before 7:00 a.m. and arrive just after

10:00 a.m. But the prices are markedly different. In the first example, the coach price is $417. In the second it is $207. Why?

These quotes were given on February 16. That means that the $417 price was for a flight that departed three days in the future, while the $207 price was for a flight that departed more than one month in the future. Why would the flight that departed sooner be more expensive? There is a good argument that, if anything, it should be *less* expensive. After all, the airline has to pay the pilots and crew, it has to pay for fuel, it has to

---

7 Interestingly, only large monopolies are targeted for regulation. There are specific instances of small monopolies—firms that, because of geographic constraints imposed on the consumers, are monopolies. Prior to Amazon, college bookstores were good examples of small monopolies. Because many students lacked transportation or the information required to locate other textbook sellers, college bookstores had no competitors and so operated as small monopolies. Because movie theaters prohibit people from bringing in food from the outside, their concession stands operate as small monopolies.

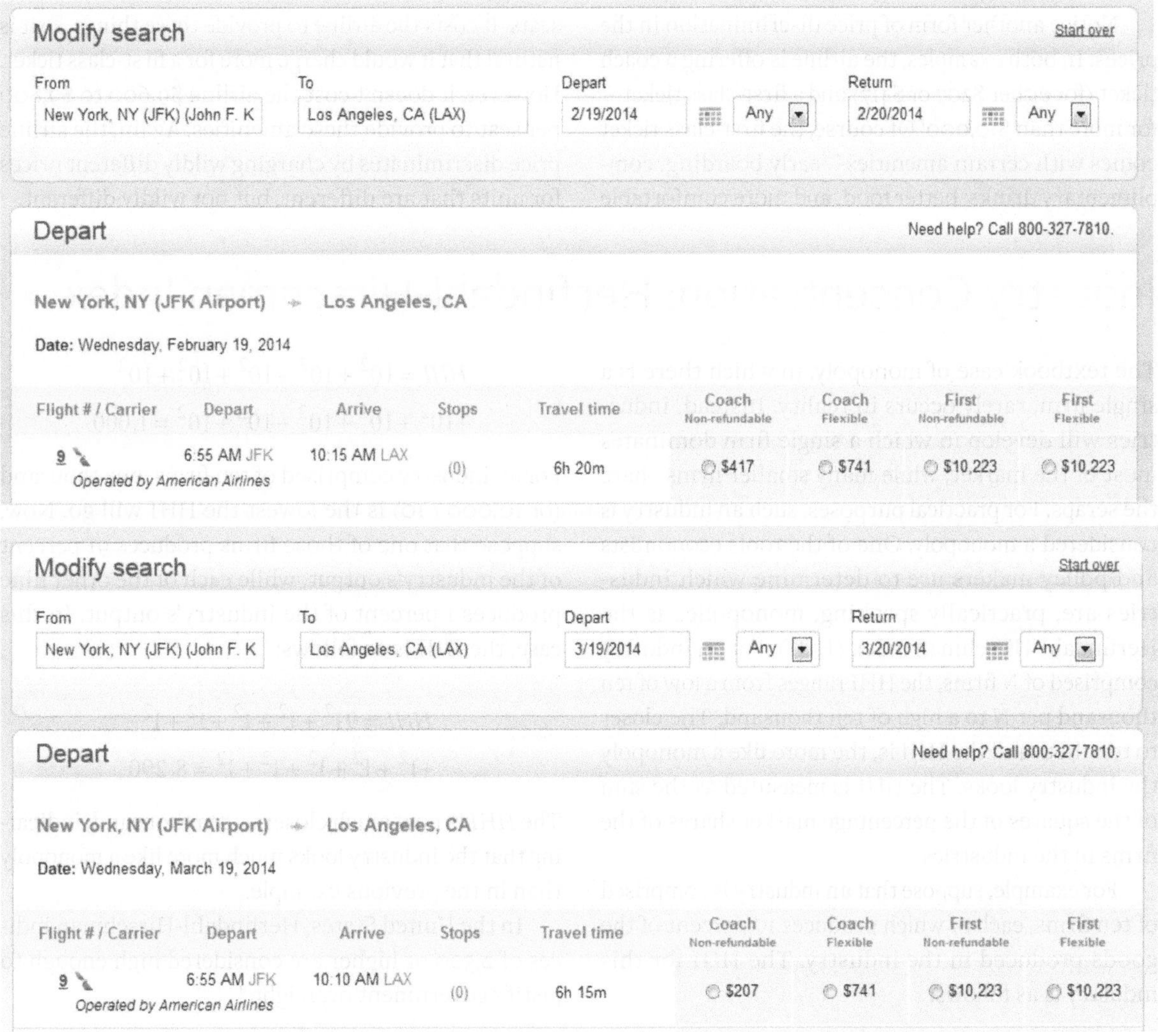

FIGURE 12.3 Price Quotes from an Airline

pay for depreciation on the aircraft, and it has to pay takeoff and landing fees at the airports. It has to pay for all of these things *regardless* of whether it sells one more ticket or not. Given that the February 19 flight would be departing in only three days, it seems that the airline would want to make sure that it filled any remaining empty seats while it could. In turn, this means that the airline should be charging a lower price for the flight that departs in three days. But it is actually charging more than 100 percent more. Why?

The answer is that the airlines knows that, on average, people who wait until three days before their departure to buy a ticket either have an urgent

---

PRICE DISCRIMINATION occurs when a firm charges different prices for different units of a product.

---

need to travel, or they can afford to wait until the last moment to purchase (perhaps because their employers are paying for the ticket). The airline takes *when* you purchase as an indicator of how much you can afford to pay. So, it charges more for the flight that departs in three days because it believes that the customers who wait until the last minute to purchase can, on average, afford to pay a higher price. This is price discrimination.

Notice another form of price discrimination in the prices. In both examples, the airline is offering a coach ticket (for either $207 or $417) and a first-class ticket— for more than $10,000! Of course, the first-class ticket comes with certain amenities—early boarding, complimentary drinks, better food, and more comfortable seats. It costs the airline to provide these things, so it is natural that it would charge more for a first-class ticket. However, it doesn't cost the airline $9,600 to $9,800 per seat to provide these amenities. Again, the airline price discriminates by charging wildly different prices for units that are different, but not wildly different.

Industry Concentration: Herfindahl-Hirschman Index

The textbook case of monopoly, in which there is a single firm, rarely occurs in reality. Instead, industries will develop in which a single firm dominates most of the market, while many smaller firms share the scraps. For practical purposes, such an industry is considered a monopoly. One of the tools economists and policy makers use to determine which industries are, practically speaking, monopolies is the Herfindahl-Hirschman index (HHI). For an industry comprised of N firms, the HHI ranges from a low of ten thousand per N to a high of ten thousand. The closer to ten thousand the HHI is, the more like a monopoly the industry looks. The HHI is measured as the sum of the squares of the percentage market shares of the firms in the industries.

For example, suppose that an industry is comprised of ten firms, each of which produces 10 percent of the goods produced in the industry. The HHI for this industry is as follows:

$$HHI = 10^2 + 10^2 + 10^2 + 10^2 + 10^2$$
$$+ 10^2 + 10^2 + 10^2 + 10^2 + 10^2 = 1,000$$

For an industry comprised of ten firms, one thousand (or 10,000 / 10) is the lowest the HHI will go. Now, suppose that one of those firms produces 91 percent of the industry's output, while each of the other nine produces 1 percent of the industry's output. In this case, the HHI is as follows:

$$HHI = 91^2 + 1^2 + 1^2 + 1^2 + 1^2$$
$$+ 1^2 + 1^2 + 1^2 + 1^2 + 1^2 = 8,290$$

The HHI is now much closer to ten thousand, indicating that the industry looks much more like a monopoly than in the previous example.

In the United States, Herfindahl-Hirschman indices of 2,500 or higher are considered high enough to justify government oversight.[8]

Regulating Monopolies

Jean Tirole won the Nobel Memorial Prize in economics in 2014 for his research on monopolies and regulation. Tirole argues that markets that are dominated by a small number of firms can impose negative consequences on society by keeping prices higher and output lower than they would be in a competitive market by preventing potential competitors from entering the market.

In the United States, unregulated private monopolies are illegal and so they must be either regulated or government-run. Regulated monopolies, like electric and cable companies, cannot raise their prices like non-regulated firms can. Instead, they must apply to the body that regulates them and request a price increase. The regulatory body will consider things like changes in the number of the firm's customers, changes in the firm's costs of labor, materials, and capital, and changes in overall market conditions. For example, if other employers start offering higher wages, the monopoly may find that it needs to increase the wages it pays in order to keep talented labor. In turn, this increases the monopoly's cost of production and the

---

8 US Department of Justice, "Herfindahl-Hirschman Index," n.d., http://www.justice.gov/atr/public/guidelines/hhi.html.

monopoly might use this fact to argue that it should be allowed to increase the price of its product.

How does the regulatory body decide what price the monopoly should be allowed to charge? One approach is marginal cost pricing, in which the regulator sets the price of the monopoly's product to be equal to the marginal cost of producing the last unit. Marginal cost pricing, at least in theory, appears to be desirable. For example, suppose the marginal cost to the monopoly of producing the last unit of output is $5. If the regulator sets the monopoly's price at $5, then the monopoly receives exactly enough money to compensate it for producing that last unit. But there are a couple of problems with this approach. First, it can be difficult to determine what the marginal cost is. Second, marginal cost only measures the cost of producing one more unit. It ignores fixed costs (which don't change as the firm increases its output). Because of this, even if the regulator could measure the monopoly's marginal cost, setting the price equal to the monopoly's marginal cost might not compensate the monopoly for its fixed costs. This could leave the monopoly with a loss, which would eventually put it out of business. Examples of this include public transportation and mail delivery. Monopolies that are required to use marginal cost pricing also require on-going government subsidies to remain in operation.

A more practical alternative to marginal cost pricing is average cost pricing (also called, "cost-plus" pricing). With average cost pricing, the monopoly's price is set equal to its average total cost – that is, its average total accounting cost plus an extra amount representing opportunity cost. The benefit of average cost pricing is that the price is set to a level at which the firm makes zero economic profit, and so the monopoly would not require on-going subsidies to remain in operation.

Figure 12.4 shows a monopoly with MC and ATC curves that are higher relative to the demand curve the monopoly faces. In this example, the marginal cost price is $6. At this price, consumers purchase 1,100 units of output per day, and the price is equal to the marginal cost of the 1,100th unit the monopoly produces. But, because the MC and ATC curves are relatively high compared to the demand curve, it costs the monopoly $7 per unit to produce its product. At the marginal cost price of $6 per unit, the monopoly is losing $1 per unit, or $1,100 per day. In this example, the average cost price is $7.10. At this price, consumers purchase 1,000 units of output per day, and the monopoly's average total cost is $7.10 per unit – the monopoly is making zero economic profit.

Figure 12.5 shows a monopoly with MC and ATC curves that are lower relative to the demand curve the monopoly faces. In this example, the marginal cost price is $7. At this price, consumers purchase 1,000 units of output per day, and the price is equal to the marginal cost of the 1,000th unit the monopoly produces. Because the MC and ATC curves are relatively low compared to the demand curve, it costs the monopoly only $5.50 per unit to produce its product, and so the monopoly is earning an economic profit of $1.50 per unit. In this example, the average cost price ($6 per unit) would be the regulator's preferred price. At $6 per unit, consumers purchase 1,100 units of output per day, and the monopoly's average total cost is $6 per unit – the monopoly is making zero economic profit.

Notice that in both cases, average cost pricing has the advantage of ensuring that monopoly earns zero economic profit – which means that the regulated monopoly charges a high enough price that it does not require on-going government subsidies to remain in operation, but a low enough price that it does not earn excess profit. The downside in both cases is that the monopoly is not producing at the efficient output level. Of course, since the unregulated monopoly would also not be producing at the efficient output level, the regulator would consider average cost pricing to be an improvement over having an unregulated monopoly.

One might ask, why doesn't the government just take over the private monopoly and run it for public interest or break it up into small firms and let them compete with each other? The taking over option requires the government to have the expertise and incentives to be an effective manager of a company, which is unlikely. The breaking up option is counterproductive in the case of natural monopoly. As discussed previously in this chapter, natural monopolies emerge due to significant economies of scale, giving them a cost advantage over the competition. Breaking up a natural monopoly into smaller firms would increase

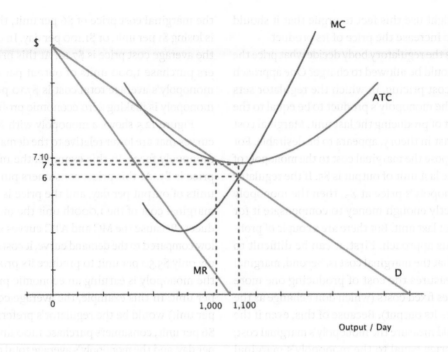

FIGURE 12.4 Marginal and Average Cost Pricing (higher MC and ATC curves)

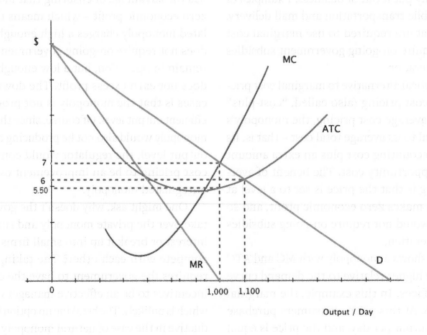

FIGURE 12.5 Marginal and Average Cost Pricing (lower MC and ATC curves)

their costs and the price that consumers pay. Again, the better option is for the government to regulate the price that a natural monopoly can charge.

As shown in figure 12.6, an unregulated natural monopoly enjoys significant economies of scale (continually decreasing average cost and constant marginal cost) and produces a socially inefficient level of output at Q* as indicated by the presence of deadweight loss or DWL (lower, purple-shaded triangle). It would also earn positive economic profit (turquoise-shaded rectangle) by charging the price (P*) that exceeds

its average cost (AC). In this case, consumer surplus (upper, yellow-shaded triangle) is lower than it could be. If the government uses marginal cost pricing (P = MC), this natural monopoly will be efficient but also incur a loss by producing at Qmc, where average cost exceeds price. If the government uses average cost pricing (P = AC), this natural monopoly will earn zero economic profit by producing at Qac, but it will still be a bit inefficient (DWL now is the little purple triangle between Qac, Qmc, and below demand).

CONCLUSION

Unlike perfectly competitive firms, a monopoly can pursue profits in two ways. First, like competitive firms, a monopoly can adjust its output so as to

influence its average total cost. Unlike competitive firms, a monopoly can also adjust the price of its product. By reducing its output, it creates a shortage and

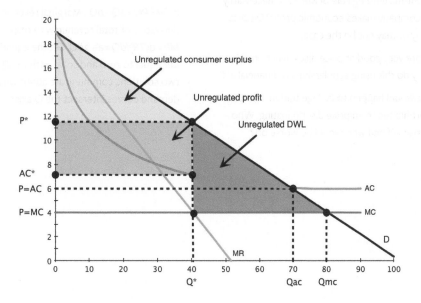

FIGURE 12.6 Marginal and Average Cost Pricing in a Natural Monopoly

the price of its product rises. By increasing its output, it creates a surplus and the price of its product falls. This means that, when the monopoly decides how much output to produce, it considers not just the effect on the average total cost of producing its product, but also the effect on the price at which it sells its product.

In addition, a monopoly can engage in price discrimination by attempting to segment its customers into those who are willing and able to pay a higher price and those who are not. By charging a higher price to the customers who are willing to pay a higher price, the monopoly can further increase its profits.

DISCUSSION QUESTIONS AND PROBLEMS

1. Make a list of monopoly (or near-monopoly) firms that existed at any point during the 1800s, and note how many of these firms exist today. Discuss whether it is possible for a monopoly to exist over a long period of time, and why.

2. An argument that non-economists often make against monopolies is that monopolies "can charge any price they like and still earn profit." Is this true?

3. Does the profit-maximizing rule of MR = MC necessarily imply that a company makes economic profit? Discuss when this may or may not be the case.

4. Universities are very good at price discrimination. Discuss how they do this using scholarships or financial aid.

5. Discuss what would happen to college tuition if universities were prohibited from price discriminating. Who would be better off and who would be worse off?

6. Provide an example of an artificial monopoly that exists today. Discuss whether it would continue to be a monopoly and, if not, what industry type would emerge if the government removed the barriers that prevent firms from competing with the artificial monopoly.

7. Suppose the monopoly's demand curve is $P = a - bQ$, where P is the price of the product and Q is the quantity demanded (a is the vertical intercept of the demand curve and b is the slope). The monopoly's total revenue is $TR = PQ = aQ - bQ^2$. Marginal revenue is the partial derivative of total revenue with respect to output: $MR = d(TR)/dQ = a - 2bQ$. Set the equations for P and MR equal to zero and solve each for Q. What do the two solutions communicate about where the MR and demand curves intersect the Q axis?

Oligopoly

13

The most famous (or infamous) oligopoly of the modern age is the oil industry. A handful of large firms conduct most of the oil exploration and extraction throughout the world. The capital and technology required for oil exploration and extraction is high enough that very few companies can earn enough profit to justify the startup expense. But the cost is not so high that there is only space for a single firm. The result is that the oil industry faces far less competition than perfectly competitive industries. There are interesting incentives among firms in oligopoly that can give rise to cartel or chiseling. Firms behave as a cartel when they collude to drive prices up. When oil producing nations get together and decide to cut back on oil production, the price of oil rises and the oil producing nations earn more profit. Consumers may see this in a sudden increase in the price of gasoline. Firms "chisel" when they break the cartel agreement. No cartel agreement lasts forever, largely because firms that cheat on the cartel agreement stand to make even more profit than they do in the cartel. Often, when the price of gas suddenly drops, it is because one or more oil producing nations cheated on a cartel agreement. Once one nation cheats, others do as well, and the cartel falls apart. While cartel behavior is illegal in the United States, other countries tolerate or even encourage it.

Attributes

The oligopoly industry has the following attributes: (1) there are few firms, (2) firms are large, and (3) there are significant barriers to entry.

ATTRIBUTES OF AN OLIGOPOLY INDUSTRY

1 There are few firms.
2 Firms are large.
3 There are significant barriers to entry.

What constitutes "few" firms is open to debate. Let us say simply that "few" is more than "one" and less than "many." Typically, oligopoly industries are comprised from anywhere from two to fifteen firms. Because all the firms in an oligopoly industry are large, each firm can affect the market. However, because there is more than one firm, no single firm can completely control the market. These two attributes make for very interesting interactions among the firms.

Consider four major players in the airline industry: Southwest, US Air, Continental, and Delta. Suppose that all of the firms charge $400 for a roundtrip ticket from New York to San Francisco. Let us assume that the firms do not negotiate any deals among each other. If Southwest decides to increase its price to $450, what should the other firms do? Nothing. When Southwest increases its price, many of its customers switch to the other airlines (because Southwest is large, the other airlines cannot accommodate *all* of Southwest's customers). As long as the other firms hold their prices at $400, their unit sales will increase, as will their profits. If one of the firms raises its price to $450 also, that firm, like Southwest, will lose many of its customers. Thus, in an oligopoly industry, when one firm raises its price, the best response of the other individual firms is to do nothing.

Suppose that Southwest lowers its price to $350. Because Southwest is large, it can accommodate a significant number of customers who will leave other airlines because their prices are higher. Any firm that matches Southwest's price cut will keep its customers plus pick up some of the customers of the firms that do not cut their prices. Thus, in an oligopoly industry, when one firm lowers its price, the best response of the other individual firms is to lower their prices also.

Recall that the slope of a firm's demand curve reflects, in part, the degree of control the firm has over the market price of its product. When the single oligopoly firm raised its price, the other oligopoly firms did nothing, so the market price did rise but not by much. When the single oligopoly firm lowered its price, the other oligopoly firms lowered their prices also, so the market price dropped significantly. In short, the degree of control the single oligopoly firm has over the market price varies depending on whether the firm is increasing or decreasing its price—when the firm increases its price, it exhibits little control over the market price; when the firm decreases its price, it exhibits much control over the market price. This means that the oligopoly firm's demand curve must have two slopes—steep for when the firm exhibits much control and flat for when the firm exhibits little control. What is true is that the oligopoly firm actually has two demand and marginal revenue curves—one that is applicable for a price increase and one that is applicable for a price decrease.

Figure 13.1 shows the two firm demand curves that every oligopoly firm has. The curves marked D_1 and MR_1 are the demand and marginal revenue curves the oligopoly firm faces when it attempts to raise its price above that of its competitors. The curves marked D_2 and MR_2 are the demand and marginal revenue curves the oligopoly firm faces when it attempts to lower its price below that of its competitors. In equilibrium, all oligopoly firms will charge the price that is found at the intersection of the two demand curves (point A). At point A, all the oligopoly firms are charging the same prices for their products.

Because the oligopoly firm is sometimes on the flat set of demand and marginal revenue curves and sometimes on the steep set of demand and marginal revenue curves, the oligopoly firm does not use the entirety of either curve. The oligopoly firm is never on D_2 or MR_2 when the price rises above the price at point A. Similarly, the oligopoly firm is never on D_1 or MR_1 when the price falls below the price at point A.

In figure 13.2 we redraw figure 13.1, leaving out the sections of the demand and marginal revenue curves that the oligopoly firm does not use. The result is what is called a *kinked* demand curve, but it is actually portions of two different demand curves. Similarly, the marginal revenue curve appears to be broken, but it is in fact two separate marginal revenue curves. We can think of the two marginal revenue curves as being joined by the dotted vertical line segment at the break. It turns out that the oligopoly firm's marginal

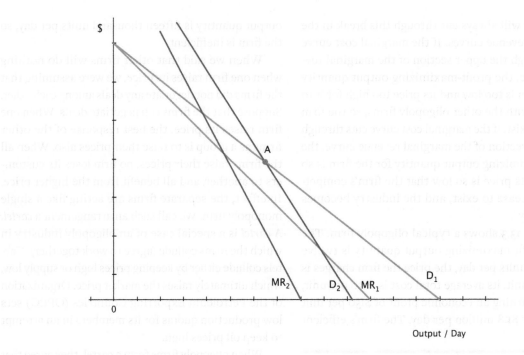

FIGURE 13.1 Oligopoly Firm Demand

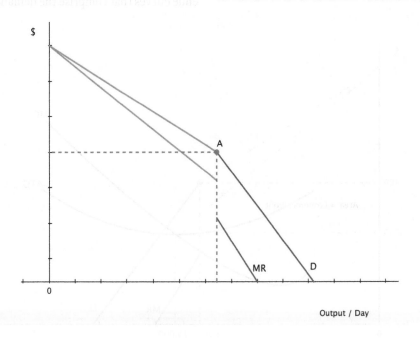

FIGURE 13.2 Oligopoly and the Kinked Demand Curve

cost curve will always cut through this break in the marginal revenue curves. If the marginal cost curve cuts through the upper section of the marginal revenue curve, the profit-maximizing output quantity for the firm is too low and its price too high for it to compete with the other oligopoly firms, so the firm ceases to exist. If the marginal cost curve cuts through the lower section of the marginal revenue curve, the profit-maximizing output quantity for the firm is so high and its price is so low that the firm's competitors will cease to exist, and the industry becomes a monopoly.

Figure 13.3 shows a typical oligopoly firm. The firm's profit-maximizing output quantity is twelve thousand units per day, the price the firm charges is $400 per unit, its average total cost is $250 per unit, and it is earning an economic profit of $150 per unit per day, or $1.8 million per day. The firm's efficient

---

A CARTEL is a special case of an oligopoly industry in which the firms collude.

---

output quantity is fifteen thousand units per day, so the firm is inefficient.

When we said that other firms will do nothing when one firm raises its price, we were assuming that the firms did not negotiate any deals among each other. Suppose that the firms can negotiate deals. When one firm raises its price, the best response of the other firms as a group is to raise their prices also. When all the firms raise their prices, no firm loses its customers to another, and all benefit from the higher price. In effect, the separate firms are acting like a single monopoly firm. We call such an arrangement a *cartel*. A *cartel* is a special case of an oligopoly industry in which the firms collude (agree to work together). Cartels collude either by keeping prices high or supply low, which ultimately raises the market price. Organization of the Petroleum Exporting Countries (OPEC) sets low production quotas for its members in an attempt to keep oil prices high.

When oligopoly firms form a cartel, they agree that when one firm raises its price, all others will raise their prices also. Recall the two demand and marginal revenue curves that comprise the demand curve that the

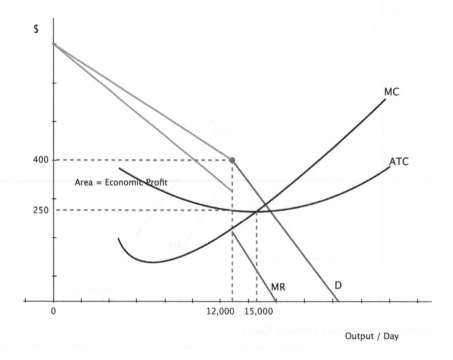

FIGURE 13.3 Profit Maximization in Oligopoly

oligopoly firm faces. We said that if a single oligopoly firm raises its price above that of its competitors, the competitors do nothing, the average market price rises only slightly, and therefore the oligopoly firm has exhibited little control over the market price, which puts it on the flatter of the two demand curves. Now, if the firms collude, when one firm raises its price, the other firms match the price increase, and the average market price rises significantly, which means that the single firm exhibited much control over the market price, putting the firm on the steeper of the two demand curves. In short, when oligopoly firms form a cartel, the firms' flat demand and marginal revenue curves no longer apply.

Figure 13.4 shows our oligopoly firm, which has colluded with the other firms and is now a member of a cartel. Because the flat demand and marginal revenue curves no longer apply, we find the firm's profit-maximizing output where MC and the steep MR curve intersect (point C). We follow this point up to the steep demand curve (point A) to find the price the cartel firm will charge. From this analysis, we see that, as a cartel, the firms are producing fewer units

(ten thousand per day instead of twelve thousand per day), they are charging a higher price ($450 per unit instead of $400 per unit), and their average total costs have risen from $250 to $260. The firm's profits have risen from $1.8 million per day to $1.9 million per day ($1.9 million per day = [$450 per unit – $260 per unit] ×10,000 units per day).

It would seem that because oligopoly firms make more profit when they enter into a cartel arrangement, all oligopolies would become cartels. This is not the case. Suppose that ten oligopoly firms enter into a cartel agreement. Each of the firms agrees to restrict its output and to charge a higher price for its product. Because all of the firms raise their prices, no firm loses its customers to another firm, and all receive the higher price for their products. What now should a single firm do? A single firm should cheat on the cartel. By lowering its price just slightly below that of the cartel, a single firm can greatly increase its unit sales by taking away customers from the other firms. This behavior is called *chiseling*. *Chiseling* is the breaking of a cartel agreement.

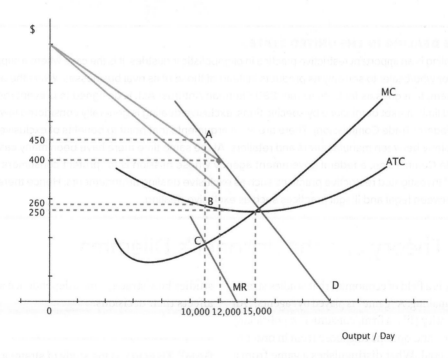

FIGURE 13.4 Oligopoly and Collusion

CHISELING is the breaking of a cartel agreement.

There are three levels of economic profit that a firm in an oligopoly industry can earn. A firm in a standard or competitive oligopoly (no collusion) earns positive but relatively low economic profit. A firm in a cartel earns more economic profit than it would have in a competitive oligopoly. A firm that breaks from a cartel earns more economic profit than it would have if it stuck to the cartel agreement. These three profit levels make the cartel unstable. When firms form a cartel, each one has incentive to chisel (cheat) on the others. In fact, when one firm does chisel, not only does that firm make much economic profit; the other firms' profits fall considerably. Thus, even if a firm, on its own, would not consider chiseling, it has incentive to do so just to avoid being chiseled on by another firm. Once one firm chisels, other firms will join in the chiseling. When this happens, all firms have broken the cartel agreement, and the industry is back to the standard (competitive) oligopoly case.

In figure 13.4 we see that while the profit-maximizing output quantity for the firm in a standard oligopoly

FIRMS in a competitive oligopoly make economic profit and are inefficient. Firms in a cartel make more economic profit and are more inefficient than firms in a competitive oligopoly.

is to the left of the efficient output quantity (i.e., the oligopoly firm is inefficient), the profit-maximizing output quantity for the firm in a cartel is even further to the left (i.e., the cartel firm is more inefficient). Cartels are illegal in the United States because of this inefficiency (for the same reason that monopolies are regulated). In fact, cartels are so illegal that it is illegal even to discuss forming a cartel. In the early 1990s, the price of airline tickets dropped by half over a period of a few days. The Justice Department investigated this and discovered that the major airlines had formed a cartel (which had escaped the notice of the authorities). The drop in the prices of airline tickets was triggered by members of the cartel chiseling. The Justice Department filed suit and won an award of several millions of dollars. People who could prove that they flew one of the airlines during the period that the cartel was in effect could apply to receive part of the settlement.

EXCLUSIVE DEALING IN THE UNITED STATES

Exclusive dealing is an important restrictive practice in oligopolistic industries. It is the case where a supplier arranges for a retailer or wholesaler to sell only its products instead of those of its rival businesses. While the antitrust law of the government, that goes as far back as the 1890 Sherman Antitrust Act, is designed to prevent restrictive trade practices and limit market dominance by specific firms, exclusive dealing is generally considered lawful with some limitations (Federal Trade Commission). There are even arguments that point to benefits of exclusive dealing contracts particularly between manufacturers and retailers. At the same time there have been many cases where the Federal Trade Commission, a federal government agency whose mission is to "protect consumers and promote competition," investigated restrictive practices such as exclusive dealing arrangements. Hence there seems to be a fine line between legal and illegal practices such as exclusive dealing.

Game Theory and the Prisoner's Dilemma

Game theory is a field of economics that studies strategic decision-making. A "game" is played by "agents." An agent is an entity (like a firm, consumer or politician) that has a goal and options to choose from in order to achieve that goal. What distinguishes a game from a mere decision is that one agent's choice may impact the other agents' choices. In other words, game theory studies how strategic interdependence among agents affects their decisions.

GAME THEORY is the study of strategic decision-making.

Cartel is a special case of a class of problems in game theory called the *prisoner's dilemma*, which is a simultaneous-move game where two (or more) agents can reap large rewards by working together (cooperating or colluding) and even greater rewards by reneging (defecting or cheating) on their agreement.

PRISONER'S dilemma is a canonical game where rational agents may fail to cooperate even if it is in their collective interest to do so.

In the classic prisoner's dilemma game, two suspects are detained and accused of jointly committing a crime. The problem is that the prosecutor does not have enough evidence to convict either of the people of robbing the bank, but hopes to jail them on a lesser charge. The prosecutor comes up with a plan. He separates the two people and offers each of them the same deal: If you confess that you and your friend robbed the bank, but your friend does not, you will go free and your friend will go to jail for 10 years. If you do not confess, but your friend does, your friend will go free and you will go to jail for 10 years. If you both confess, you will each go to jail for 2 years. The prosecutor has enough evidence to convict both of them on the lesser charge. So, if neither one of them confesses, they both go to jail for 1 year.

We can represent this game with the following payoff matrix. The columns represent Prisoner A's options. The rows represent Prisoner B's options. The body of the table shows the payoffs that result from their choices. For example, if Prisoner A chooses to deny all charges, then we are on the right column of the table. If Prisoner B denies all charges, then we are on the bottom row of the table. When Prisoner A and Prisoner B deny all charges, the two people receive the payoffs that are in the bottom right square of the table: each goes to jail for 1 year. Clearly this is the best outcome for the two suspects, combined.

	Prisoner A Confesses	Prisoner A Denies
Prisoner B Confesses	A goes to jail for 2 years B goes to jail for 2 years	A goes to jail for 10 years B goes free
Prisoner B Denies	A goes free B goes to jail for 10 years	A goes to jail for 1 year B goes to jail for 1 year

Unfortunately, the two prisoners (players) cannot communicate with each other, so neither one of them knows which option the other person will choose. First, let's see what Prisoner A should do. If Prisoner B chooses to confess, then Prisoner A is playing on the top row of the table. Prisoner A either confesses and goes to jail for 2 years or denies all charges and goes to jail for 10 years. Confessing appears to be the best strategy for Prisoner A in this case. But, if Prisoner B denies all charges, then Prisoner A is playing on the bottom row of the table. Then, Prisoner A either confesses and goes free or denies all charges and goes to jail for 1 year. Again, Prisoner A's best strategy is to confess. Now, you should be able to demonstrate that the same logic applies to Prisoner B's decisions: her best strategy is to confess as well. In other words, the dominant strategy for each player in this game is to confess, regardless of what the other player might do.

DOMINANT STRATEGY is the decision that yields the largest payoff for a player no matter what the other player does.

If each player pursues his or her dominant strategy, we can predict the game's outcome. Named after John Nash, Nobel Prize-winning economist, the *Nash equilibrium* is a game's solution that occurs when each player takes into account the actions of the other players when formulating his or her best strategy. In the prisoner's dilemma game we just solved, the Nash equilibrium is the top let quadrant: both players end up serving 2 years in jail each by pursuing their best strategies.

Herein lies the dilemma. No matter what Prisoner B decides to do, Prisoner A is better off confessing. Similarly, no matter what Prisoner A decides to do,

NASH EQUILIBRIUM is a solution concept where each player makes the best decision possible, taking into account the other players' best decisions.

Prisoner B is better off confessing. The end result is that they each end up spending 2 years in jail, which is not the best available outcome for both of them! The irony is that the two players would have been better off if they had not confessed – each would have spent only 1 year in jail. Because the two players in the game cannot coordinate and verify their actions, doing what is best for them individually leads to a less desirable outcome for them collectively, as a group.

A good example of the prisoner's dilemma game appeared on a National Geographic television program some years ago. Two scientists had partially tranquilized a lion and were trying to restrain it. The lion was awake and dangerous, just a bit groggy. Each scientist managed to get a rope around the lion's neck and stood to either side of the lion holding the rope. The arrangement was this: scientist A was on the left holding a rope around the lion's neck, which prevented the lion from moving to the right and devouring scientist B; the lion was in the middle; and scientist B was on the right holding a rope around the lion's neck, which prevented the lion from moving to the left and devouring scientist A.

The two scientists had, unwittingly, gotten themselves into a prisoner's dilemma. Suppose that the scientists have the following preferences: subduing the lion and studying it is good; not subduing the lion but avoiding being eaten is nothing to write home about, but is not particularly bad, either; but being eaten by the lion is definitely bad. Scientist A thinks, "Scientist B might accidentally drop his rope, which means I'll be eaten—this is bad. I can avoid the chance of being eaten by dropping my rope first—the lion will eat scientist B, and I shall escape! Bahahahaha!" Simultaneously, scientist B thinks, "Scientist A might accidentally drop his rope, which means I'll be eaten—this is bad. I can avoid the chance of being eaten by dropping my rope first." The game-theory solution is that both scientists immediately drop their ropes and run.[1]

An interesting version of the prisoner's dilemma game occurs in the final round of the popular British TV game show *Golden Balls*, where two players decide independently to either "split" or "steal" the winnings. The decisions and their respective payoffs (percentage of winnings taken home) are summarized in the table below. If both players choose to steal, they go home with nothing. If both players choose to split, they go home with an equal share of the winnings. If one player chooses to steal and the other chooses to split, the stealer goes home with all the money.

	Player A Steals	**Player A Splits**
Player B Steals	Player A gets 0 % Player B gets 0 %	Player A gets 0 % Player B gets 100 %
Player B Splits	Player A gets 100 % Player B gets 0 %	Player A gets 50 % Player B gets 50 %

Can you deduce the dominant strategy for each player and the Nash equilibrium for this game? If Player B chooses to split, then Player A's best strategy is to steal. However, if Player B chooses to steal, then Player A is indifferent between stealing and splitting because

he gets zero either way. In this case, economists say that stealing is a weakly dominant strategy, which basically means that stealing is still the prevailing strategy. Considering that the same logic applies to Player B's decisions, it is not surprising that the game

1 In the program, neither scientist dropped his rope. The true scenario was more complex than this example—the added complexity changes the outcome. For instance, the scientists were probably friends (or at least concerned about keeping their jobs as scientists), which means that there was a cost to each scientist from having the lion eat the other scientist. Because this cost was greater than the expected cost of being eaten (given the probability of the other scientist's dropping the rope), the problem was no longer a prisoner's dilemma—the benefit of chiseling was actually less than the benefit of the cartel agreement.

show typically keeps the winnings (otherwise the show would not last). However, what makes the show exciting is the possibility for multiple Nash equilibriums (all cells except the 50/50 split). If *Golden Balls* had conventional prisoner's dilemma payoffs, the game would have been too predictable (everyone would steal) and no fun to watch. By not punishing a player too much for choosing to split, the game show offers a small probability that at least one player may choose to split the winnings.

The travesty with the prisoner's dilemma game is that it can prevent rational individuals from cooperating, which is undesirable (<u>in</u>efficient) for them

---

PARETO efficiency is a situation where it is impossible to make someone better off without making someone else worse off.

---

as a group. Economists invoke the concept of *Pareto efficiency* to describe a socially desirable outcome, which is considered to be efficient for the group if it is impossible to make someone better off without making someone else worse off. Consider the payoffs in *Golden Balls*, for example. The Pareto inefficient outcome for both players occurs when both choose to steal and go home with nothing. In contrast, the other three outcomes in the game are Pareto efficient because either one or both players go home with money. The way to prove that these three outcomes are efficient is to show that it is impossible to help one player without harming the other. It is very easy to *Pareto improve* upon the outcome where both players get zero: simply move to any other outcome (cell) in the table and you will see that it makes at least one player better off. Once there, it becomes apparent that it is no longer possible to make one player better off without harming the other. You may notice that while the three outcomes are Pareto efficient, they are very different: either one player gets all the winnings or both players get an equal share of the winnings.[2]

One of the best-known Pareto <u>in</u>efficient outcomes occurs when people have free access to a common

resource or property, in which case the dominant strategy is to abuse that resource. The consequence

---

PARETO improvement is an action that harms no one and helps at least one person.

---

is the all too familiar problems such as overfishing, deforestation, and pollution. This type of problem is called *the tragedy of the commons* and it arises due to the lack of private property rights. One of the ways to ensure the efficient outcome is to make individuals bear the costs and benefits of their actions, which can be done through privatization of common resources or through corrective taxes and subsidies (Pigouvian solution). Otherwise, will prisoner's dilemma situations unequivocally fail to achieve a socially efficient outcome? Not necessarily. While game theorists still debate about the Nash equilibrium in finitely and infinitely repeated games (i.e. games with more than one round), it is likely that in an infinitely repeated prisoner's dilemma game, the two players can develop trust and choose a cooperative strategy (i.e. collude). Iterated or repeated games can be very complex, but one of the simplest yet effective strategies is *tit-for-tat*, where players may choose to trust each other and play "nice" (i.e. cooperate) in the first round and copy the opponents move in the next round.

You might be wondering by now that while game theory is cool, how does it relate to oligopoly? Firms in oligopoly end up playing variations of the prisoner's dilemma game as shown in the table below. Imagine a

---

TIT-FOR-TAT is a strategy of replicating an opponent's previous action in repeated games.

---

duopoly, an oligopoly with only two firms, where the two companies choose either to cooperate (collude) or defect (cheat). The two companies would make more profit, $5 million each, if they could act as a cartel (i.e. collude to keep output low and price high). Once the cartel is formed, however, each firm can make even

---

2 While Pareto efficiency seeks to maximize collective wellbeing, it has nothing to say about how this wellbeing should be distributed. Thus, a Pareto efficient outcome can be very unequal.

more profit by breaking the cartel agreement and stealing the other firm's market share (i.e. cheating). The dominant strategy for each firm is to cheat on the cartel agreement by lowering the price unilaterally. Again, herein lies the dilemma: if each company pursues its

dominant strategy, then both end up with lower profits ($1 million instead of $5). The first known version of this Nash equilibrium was articulated in 1838 by a French philosopher and mathematician, Antoine Cournot.[3]

	Company A Cheats	Company A Colludes
Company B Cheats	A's profit = $1 million B's profit = $1 million	A's profit = $0 B's profit = $10 million
Company B Colludes	A's profit = $10 million B's profit = $0	A's profit = $5 million B's profit = $5 million

It is possible, however, that in an infinitely iterated game, the two firms can develop implicit trust and pull off a collusive outcome (i.e. monopoly profit). In reality though, the game may not be infinite and new firms might be lured into the industry by monopoly profits. Thus, collusive agreements or cartels will be difficult to sustain. The inability of OPEC to stop the decline

in oil prices in recent years suggests that a competitive outcome might be more prevalent in oligopolistic industries.[4] Combining game theory predictions with Sherman (1890) and Clayton (1914) Antitrust Acts, we can conclude that oligopolies in the United States are likely to stay competitive.

FALLING OIL PRICES TEST OPEC UNITY

In November 2014, global crude oil prices fell significantly, cutting significantly into oil-producing nations' profits. In response, Venezuela's foreign minister (Venezuela is a major oil exporter) requested a meeting with Saudi Arabia's top oil official to request that the two countries cut their oil production so as to drive the price of oil back up.

Since 1984, the oil-producing nations' cartel has cut output 11 times in response to falling oil prices. Today, the oil cartel faces a new threat. If they agree to cut oil production, thereby causing the price of oil to rise, the increased price of oil would encourage the U.S. to invest in shale oil production. In turn, that would increase competition and drive down oil prices in the future – possibly further than they would fall if the cartel did not cut output.

CONCLUSION

An oligopoly industry exhibits attributes of both monopoly and competition. On one hand, each firm

(just like a monopoly) is large enough to influence the market price. If a single oligopolist increases its

---

3 A. Cournot, *Researches on the Mathematical Principles of the Theory of Wealth* (1838).

4 B. Faucon, S. Said, and A. Peaple, "Falling Oil Prices Test OPEC Unity," *The Wall Street Journal*, November 16, 2014, www.wsj.com/news/article_email/falling-oil-prices-test-opec-unity-1416188605-lMyQjAxMTAoMDE2OTYxNzk1Wj.

output, it creates a surplus and the market price falls. If a single oligopolist decreases its output, it creates a shortage and the market price rises. On the other hand, each firm (just as in a competitive industry) faces competition from other firms in the industry. The hybrid nature of the oligopoly industry leads to interesting interactions among the firms. If the firms work together, they can jointly cut back on their output thereby driving the market price up and (if they do it correctly) can increase their profits. We call this, cartel behavior. The problem is that, once they form a cartel, each individual oligopolist can make even more profit by cheating on the cartel and increasing its output. Because each oligopolist has this profit motive to cheat on the cartel, cartels tend to be short-lived.

QUESTIONS AND PROBLEMS

1. Identify a cartel industry not mentioned in the chapter. Discuss whether the firms in that industry ever engaged in cartel behavior.

2. Suppose an oligopoly is comprised of four equally sized firms, one of which is located in the U.S. and three of which are located abroad. Suppose the three that are located abroad form a cartel. Because cartel formation is illegal in the U.S., the one U.S. firm does not participate in the cartel agreement. Discuss what the cartel formation would do to the price, output, and profit of the U.S. firm.

3. Your professor promises to curve the grades on the next exam as follows: The student (or students) who earn the highest grade receives a 100%. The other grades get scaled down from this proportionally. For example, if the student with the highest grade answered 6 questions correctly, then answering 6 questions correctly is worth 100%. A student who answers 5 questions correctly earns 5 out of 6 points, or 83%. Your professor has, perhaps inadvertently, created a prisoner's dilemma. Discuss the students' cartel and chiseling behaviors

– specifically, how many questions should a student attempt to answer correctly if the students behave as a cartel, and how many should the student attempt to answer correctly if he chisels on the cartel. What effect will the student's chiseling have on the other students? In the end, how will all the students end up behaving?

4. Which is preferable for society, monopoly or oligopoly, and why?

5. Are all oligopolies the same, and why?

6. What are some cases when exclusive dealing helps or hurts businesses and markets? How is exclusive dealing treated in the U.S. antitrust law? How does the U.S. compare to Europe in terms of exclusive dealing?

14 Monopolistic Competition

Introduction

Imagine companies that compete with one another by trying to convince you that their product is better. Fast food restaurants, like McDonalds and Burger King, try to convince you that their food is fresher than that of their competitors. Retailers, like Wal-Mart and Target, try to convince you that they have more selection and lower prices than their competitors. Car dealerships try to convince you that they provide better "service after the sale" than their competitors. These are monopolistically competitive firms – firms that offer products that are similar but not exactly the same. The same behaviors that you'll observe among monopolistically competitive firms also occurs among monopolistic competitors who aren't firms. Politicians compete for your vote by trying to convince you that they care more about you than their opponents. Singles in a bar compete for your attention by trying to convince you that they are funnier, more attractive, or richer than the other singles.

In the United States, most industries are monopolistically competitive. Monopolistic competition can be thought of as partially monopoly and partially pure competition (despite the fact that the two types are polar opposites). Like a perfectly competitive industry, the monopolistically competitive industry contains many small firms. Each firm, however, produces a product that is slightly different from those produced by the other firms. For example, there are many different brands of beer—each slightly different from the other. If consumers regard different beer brands as interchangeable, the beer industry looks more like perfect competition—there are many firms producing the same product. But if consumers regard individual brands as being different from each other, the beer industry looks more like a collection of monopolies—each brand has only one producer.

Attributes

The monopolistically competitive industry has the following attributes: (1) there are many firms, (2) all the firms are small, (3) the firms produce a heterogeneous product, and (4) there is free entry and exit to and from the industry.

ATTRIBUTES OF A MONOPOLISTICALLY COMPETITIVE INDUSTRY

1 There are many firms.
2 All the firms are small.
3 The firms produce a heterogeneous product.
4 There is free entry and exit to and from the industry.

Notice that the attributes of the monopolistically competitive industry are identical to those of the perfectly competitive industry, with the exception of item 3—the products produced by the monopolistically competitive firms are heterogeneous. Recall that the perfectly competitive firms produced homogeneous products—the output of one firm was perceived by consumers to be identical to the output of all the other firms. Monopolistically competitive firms produce the same basic product but with some relatively minor variations. The variation (or the perception of variation, whether or not it actually exists) is the source of the heterogeneity. Consider, for example, the jeans industry. Jeans are, essentially, identical. There are, however, slight variations across manufacturers. Some have distinctive stitching, some come in different cuts than others, and so on. Beyond these objective differences, some jeans—for no other reason than the brand name—are perceived to be of higher quality than others.

How the firms in the monopolistically competitive industry behave depends on how the consumers perceive the firms' products. The more similar the consumers perceive the products to be, the more like perfectly competitive firms the firms will behave. The more distinctive the consumers perceive the products to be, the more like monopolies the firms will behave.

The monopolistically competitive firms do have some control over the prices of their products, but not as much as do monopolies. The reason is that the higher a single firm prices its product, the more consumers will discount the variations between the firm's product and other firms' products. For example, suppose that Levi's prices its jeans at $35 each, and Jordache prices its jeans at $45 each. Because consumers perceive Jordache jeans to be of higher quality than Levi's, both firms sell the same number of units per day. Now, if Jordache were to raise its price to $75, consumers may rethink their evaluation of Jordache jeans. They may find that Jordache jeans are not really higher quality, or they may find that they are higher quality, but that the higher quality is not worth the $40 price difference. Thus, consumers will now tend to disregard the differences in the products and will buy Levi's—the less expensive of the two. In short, Jordache does have control over the price of its product, but only so long its price does not deviate too significantly from the price offered by Levi's.

Figure 14.1 shows a typical monopolistically competitive firm. The firm's profit-maximizing output quantity is four hundred units per day (found by locating point A, where MR and MC cross). The firm charges $35 per unit for its product (found by locating point B, where profit-maximizing output intersects the firm's demand curve). The firm's average total cost is $35 per unit (found by locating point B, where profit-maximizing output intersects the average total cost curve). The firm's efficient output quantity is five hundred units per day (found by locating point C, where average total cost is minimum). Like the monopoly firm, the monopolistically competitive firm is inefficient. However, notice that the monopolistically competitive firm is making zero economic profit (its price and its average total cost are the same).

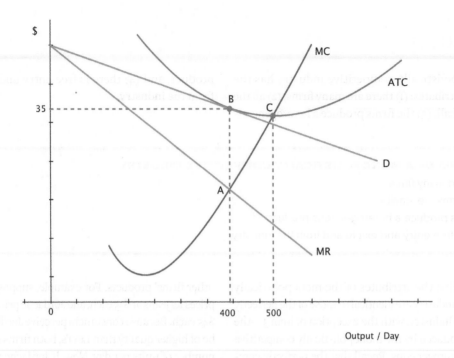

FIGURE 14.1 Monopolistically Competitive Firm in the Long Run

A perfectly competitive industry can become monopolistically competitive if the firms establish brand names and then advertise their products. The brand-name advertising creates the perception of heterogeneity among the products, which is the distinction between a perfectly competitive industry and a monopolistically competitive industry. What is required to make this transition from pure competition to monopolistic competition?

Firms must create brand names and logos, conduct market surveys to determine where their advertising would have the greatest impact, and then create and conduct an advertising campaign. All of this requires a substantial investment. Recall that the perfectly competitive firms make zero economic profit. According to figure 14.1, the monopolistically competitive firm is also making zero economic profit. Why would a firm

spend all the money and effort to establish and market a brand name, just to end up with the same zero economic profit it had before? The answer is that figure 14.1 is not the whole story. The diagram shows the monopolistically competitive firm in the long run. In the long run, the monopolistically competitive firm makes zero economic profit. In the short run, however, the firm can make positive economic profit.

The way the firm achieves this positive economic profit is through advertising. When the firm advertises, it attempts to alter the consumers' perceptions of its product.[1] This alteration of perception is a violation of the ceteris paribus assumption for demand requiring that consumers' preferences not change. The advertising causes the firm's demand curve to shift to the right, resulting in the diagram shown in figure 14.2. Notice that the average total cost and marginal cost

---

1 The intention is to *positively* affect consumers' perceptions of the product. There are some interesting examples of advertising that have actually had a negative impact on consumers' perceptions. For example, when Chevrolet marketed its compact car, the Nova, in Spain, sales were dismal. Finally, someone realized that in Spanish *nova* means "it doesn't go." Perdue had a similar problem when it mistakenly translated its slogan, "It takes a tough man to make a tender chicken," into Italian. The Italian translation read, "It takes a sexually active man to make a chicken scared." When Coca-Cola was first marketed in China, the Chinese mispronounced the name, placing the stresses on the second and the fourth syllables (coCA-coLA). Roughly translated, "coCA-coLA" means "bite the wax tadpole."

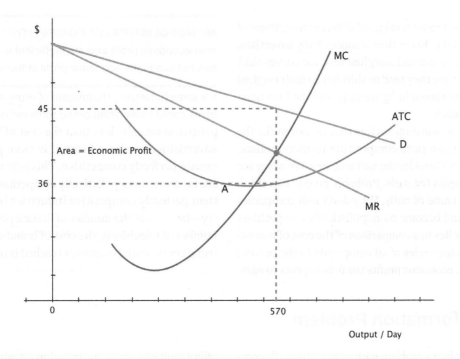

FIGURE 14.2 Monopolistically Competitive Firm in the Short Run

curves have not moved, but the advertising has caused the firm's demand and, hence, marginal revenue curve to shift to the right.[2] With the demand and marginal revenue curves shifted, the firm's profit-maximizing output quantity is now 570 units per day. The firm will charge $45 per unit for this output, and it will cost the firm $36 per unit to produce. Note that the firm earns an economic profit of $5,130 per day ($5,130 = [$45 per unit – $36 per unit] ×570 units per day).

The situation shown in figure 14.2 is only temporary. In the long run, (1) consumers will realize that there is no real difference between this firm's output

and the output of the other firms; (2) the consumers will determine that the difference, while real, does not warrant a higher price; or (3) other firms will incorporate the difference into their products. In short, in the long run, consumers' preferences for this firm's product will revert back to their normal state, and the firm will be back to making zero economic profit. Thus, figure 14.1 shows the monopolistically competitive firm in the long run, and figure 14.2 shows the monopolistically competitive firm in the short run. In order for the firm to continue to make economic profit, it must continually advertise and devise new reasons

---

2 If the firm has an ongoing and stable budget for advertising, the average cost curves will not shift when a new round of advertising comes out. If, however, the firm has never advertised before, or if it is increasing its expenditures on advertising, its average total cost curve would shift up and to the right (the advertising expense is not a function of the amount of output the firm produces; hence, it is a fixed cost).

for its product to be considered different from those of its competitors.[3] Every time it successfully advertises, the firm's demand and marginal revenue curves shift right. Over time they tend to shift left to their original locations (as shown in figure 14.1), and the firm must advertise again.

There are some industries that do not make the transition from pure competition to monopolistic competition. Consider the nail industry. We never see advertisements for nails. Probably no one can think of a brand name of nails. Why don't nail companies advertise and become monopolistically competitive? The answer lies in a comparison of the cost of mounting an ongoing series of ad campaigns to the present value of the economic profits the firm expects to earn.

> **MONOPOLISTICALLY COMPETITIVE** firms make zero economic profit and are inefficient in the long run, but can make economic profit in the short run.

For some industries, the amount of economic profit the firms could make from being monopolistically competitive is actually less than the cost of brand-name advertising. For these firms, it is more profitable to remain perfectly competitive. This tells us why there are far more monopolistically competitive industries than perfectly competitive industries in this country—because of the number of literate people and the number of televisions, the cost of brand-name advertising per potential consumer reached is relatively low.

The Information Problem

Consumers face a problem with monopolistically competitive industries that they don't face with the other industries: obtaining information about competing brands. To select well from among competing brands, consumers first need to know what brands exist, and then need to know each brand's attributes. For example, suppose that you want to select a cell phone plan. You first need to know what companies provide cell phone service in your area. You then need to know, among other things, the monthly price of each plan, the data restrictions of each plan, the additional fees associated with each plan, what phones are available with each plan, and how satisfied other customers are with each plan. Some attributes you may not care about, such as the colors in which the phones come. The attributes that consumers care most about are called *salient attributes*. Because the number of cell phone providers is small, even though each provider

offers multiple plans, information on what providers exist and what their salient attributes are isn't hard to obtain.

The problem is that, in the case of a monopolistically competitive industry, the number of competing brands is so large that consumers cannot obtain information on the salient attributes of every brand. Consequently, consumers are often forced to make purchase decisions based on incomplete information. For example, suppose that you want to select a brand of beer. There are thousands of beer brands, and each beer has slightly different salient attributes: taste, color, aroma, price, calories, availability. To collect information on the salient attributes of all beer brands would be extremely time-consuming—so much so that the benefit of having the complete set of information would outweigh the cost of obtaining the complete set of information. That means that every time a consumer

---

3 We see this clearly in the case of beer. First came slow-brewed beer, then fire-brewed beer, then beer brewed with mountain spring water, then ice-brewed beer, then cold-filtered beer, then draft taste out of a bottle, then bottle taste out of a can. None of these processes affects the taste of the beer in any appreciable manner; they are simply attempts to make the consumer perceive that one beer is better than another. In fact, the only appreciable factor that affects the taste of common American beers is that they are served "ice cold." American beers do not, strictly speaking, qualify as beers at all, given the extraneous cost-saving ingredients used (rice and corn instead of barley or wheat). These ingredients make the beer taste so bad that it is necessary to drink it ice cold, so as to stun the taste buds. Try this experiment: let a typical American beer and a German import (a real German import, not an American made beer with a German name) sit out overnight to become room temperature. Open and try both. Incidentally, the rice and corn additives contribute significantly to the headache and acidic taste associated with a hangover, as well as to the "skunky" smell some beers have when they are chilled and then allowed to come to room temperature.

chooses a brand of beer to purchase, he is doing so on the basis of incomplete information.

How can consumers make good purchase decisions if they don't have complete information about the brands and the attributes available to them? Consumer psychology research indicates that, in cases of incomplete information, consumers resort to *heuristics*—rules of thumb—to help them make better decisions. Consumers may not employ the heuristics consciously, but research shows that when consumers are faced with competing similar brands, they do employ the heuristics, at least on average, at a "gut level."

Brand Choice in a Monopolistically Competitive Market

In a perfectly competitive industry, firms' products are homogeneous—the output of each firm is qualitatively identical (or perceived to be identical) to the output of every other firm. In a perfectly competitive industry, if one firm develops a valuable improvement to its product, competing firms quickly adopt the improvement, leaving all the firms' products once again identical. In monopoly and oligopoly industries, although brands may differ from one another, the number of different brands is small enough that consumers can readily obtain information about the salient attributes of all the brands in the market.

With monopolistically competitive industries, because the brands are heterogeneous, consumers require information about the brands' salient attributes in order to make purchase decisions. But because the number of brands is large, the cost of obtaining all the information necessary to make fully informed purchase decisions is prohibitive. The heuristics that consumers employ involve using the information the consumers do have to infer information that the consumers don't have. We call this the *iterative choice process*.

The process begins with a *true brand universe*—the set of all brands and their salient attributes that actually exist. A consumer will not be aware of all brands that exist, nor will the consumer be aware of the salient attributes of all the brands. What is in the consumer's mind, the *estimated brand universe*, is the consumer's perceptions of the brands that he is aware exist. The consumer's perceptions of brands will differ from the true brand universe because *external uncertainty*. The consumer may not be aware that some brands exist, or may know that some brands exist but may not have tried the brand, or some brands' attributes may have changed since the consumer tried them last.

External uncertainty causes the consumer's knowledge of the brands to differ from the reality of the brands. An additional set of uncertainty is *internal uncertainty*. Internal uncertainty causes the consumer's knowledge about his preferences to differ from the reality of his preferences. The consumer has a true utility function—this tells us how the consumer will react to consuming a brand. But how the consumer believes he will react may differ from how he actually reacts. How the consumer believes he will react is determined by the consumer's *estimated utility function*. For example, based on the smell and the look, I might believe that I would like dark beer. But when I finally try it, I may realize that I don't like it, after all. The problem here is a disparity between my true utility function and my estimated utility function. True and estimated utility functions differ because of internal uncertainty.

Of course, there are some monopolistically competitive products about which consumers might care little, for example, bubblegum. The less engaged consumers are in the purchase decision, the more likely they are to behave either randomly (for example, selecting the first brand they see) or routinely (for example, selecting the brand they have selected in the past). However, as the consumer becomes more engaged in the purchase decision, the more likely the consumer is to follow the iterative choice process.

The Choice Process

The fact that there are many heterogeneous brands in a monopolistically competitive environment contributes to the external and internal uncertainties. The greater the uncertainties, the greater the differences are between the consumer's estimated brand universe versus the true brand universe, and the consumer's estimated utility versus his true utility. The consumer's problem is that he must make his purchase decision based on what he knows and believes—his estimated brand universe and estimated utility—not on what actually exists and how he will actually react.

In comparing and contrasting the information the consumer has, the consumer combines what he believes about the brands of which he is aware with what he estimates his reaction to those brands will be. We can construct a *perceived product market* to represent the consumer's mental arrangement of the brands. For example, suppose that a consumer is aware of eight brands of beer. For simplicity's sake, let's assume that the consumer cares only about affordability and taste. In the consumer's mind, the eight brands divide into two groups, or *clusters*. In the consumer's mind, the brands in the "affordability cluster" are similar in that the consumer rates them all low on taste but high on affordability. In the consumer's mind, the brands in the "taste cluster" are all similar for the reverse reasons: the consumer rates them high on taste but low on affordability.

Consideration

After the consumer has a mental picture of brands and estimates of their effects on his utility, making a decision can still be expensive, because the consumer must compare, contrast, and weigh tradeoffs among the attributes of the various brands. For example, if the consumer is aware of only eight brands of beer and only two attributes matter to the consumer (affordability and taste), as shown in figure 14.3, the consumer would need to consider fifty-six comparisons of affordability and taste in order to make a purchase decision from among the eight beers.

To streamline the decision-making process, the consumer will form a *consideration set*. That is, the consumer will eliminate all the clusters except for one. For example, in selecting a car, a consumer may immediately eliminate from consideration all cars that seat fewer than six people. In selecting a house, a consumer might eliminate from consideration all houses with fewer than three bedrooms. In our example, a poor college student might eliminate from consideration all the beers that are not in the affordability cluster.

Meanwhile, someone with more income might eliminate from consideration all the beers that are not in the taste cluster.

One of the heuristics the consumer will use to select his consideration set is the number of brands in the cluster. Remember that the consumer not only lacks knowledge of all the brands that exist; he also is aware of his lack of knowledge. On average, the larger the number of brands in a cluster is, the larger the number of consumers who also selected that cluster is. The larger the number of consumers who selected a cluster is, the happier consumers must be with the brands in that cluster. While the number of brands in a cluster does not determine which cluster the consumer will select, an increase in the number of brands in a cluster increases the probability of the consumer's selecting that cluster.[4]

---

4 There are several factors that influence the probability of a consumer's selecting a cluster and the probability of a consumer's choosing a brand, given that the consumer has selected the brand's cluster. We will consider only two of those factors here: cluster size and cluster frontier. For discussion of all the factors, see Frank Kardes, Thomas Cline, and Maria Cronley, *Consumer Behavior* (Mason, OH: Cengage, 2014).

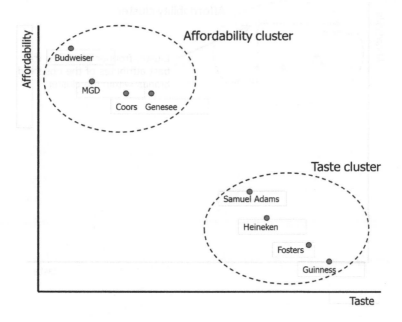

FIGURE 14.3 Affordability and Taste Clusters

WHEN THE NUMBER of brands a consumer perceives to exist in a cluster increases, the probability of the consumer's selecting that cluster to be the consumer's consideration set increases.

Choice-Given-Consideration

Once the consumer has selected a single cluster, the consumer will then compare, contrast, and trade off the attributes of the brands within the cluster. Eliminating clusters dramatically reduces the number of attribute comparisons the consumer needs to make. In this example, eliminating either the taste cluster or the affordability cluster reduces the number of comparisons of taste and affordability from fifty-six to six.

As the consumer examines the attributes of the brands within the consideration cluster, the consumer develops an idea of the "perfect brand." The perfect brand combines the best attributes of the individual brands. We call this the *cluster frontier*. For example, suppose that a consumer is more concerned with affordability than with taste and therefore selects the

affordability cluster as his consideration set. This is shown in figure 14.4. In the affordability cluster, the consumer perceives Budweiser to be worst for taste but best for affordability. The consumer also perceives Genesee to be best for taste but worst for affordability. Because the consumer knows that there are other brands out there of which he is unaware, he can imagine the existence of an "ideal brand" that combines the affordability of Budweiser with the taste of Genesee.

THE CLOSER a brand is to its cluster frontier, the greater the probability is that the consumer will choose that brand, given that the consumer selected the cluster as his consideration set.

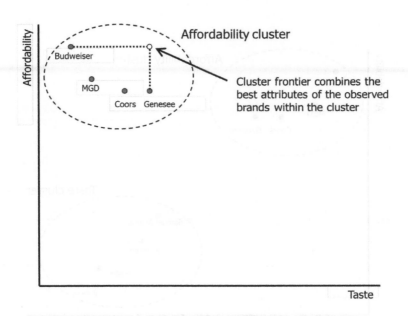

FIGURE 14.4 Cluster Frontier

Because the cluster frontier represents the consumer's ideal brand, the closer a given brand within the cluster is to the cluster frontier, the greater the probability is that the consumer will choose that brand, assuming that the consumer is considering the cluster in the first place. We call this *choice-given-consideration*.

For the consumer to choose a brand for purchase, two things must happen: first, the consumer must select the brand's cluster as the consideration set, then the consumer must choose the brand from among the brands in the cluster. Because each of these steps happens with some probability, we can describe the probability of the consumer choosing a particular brand as follows:

The first step is called the *consideration phase*. The second step is called the *choice-given-consideration*

PROB(CONSUMER will choose brand X) = Prob(-consumer will consider the cluster in which brand X is located) ´ Prob(consumer will choose brand X, given that the consumer will consider brand X's cluster)

---

phase. Finally, after the consumer purchases and consumes the product, the consumer updates his perception of the brand universe. Consuming the brand provides the consumer with information about the brand's true attributes and the consumer's true reaction to the brand's attributes. With this information, the consumer updates his mental map of the perceived brand universe.

EXAMPLE: THE PROBABILITY OF CONSIDERATION   In the mid-1990s, Miller Brewing Company introduced a new beer brand, Red Dog. At the time, market analysts said that Miller had erred in introducing the new brand because Red Dog was similar to Miller Genuine Draft (MGD), the company's flagship brand. Market analysts predicted that Red Dog would simply siphon off sales from MGD, leaving the company no better off than it was before Red Dog. In fact, sales of MGD increased significantly. Why? One factor was that, on its salient attributes, Miller positioned Red Dog within the same cluster as MGD. The accompanying ad campaign made consumers aware of the new entrant to the cluster. Because Red Dog was positioned close to MGD, it did not affect the cluster frontier. Consequently, the probability of consideration for MGD's cluster rose, while the probability of choice-given-consideration for MGD did not appreciably change. The result was an increase in sales of MGD at the expense of brands outside MGD's cluster.

EXAMPLE: THE PROBABILITY OF CHOICE-GIVEN-CONSIDERATION   As low-calorie foods became more popular, Ben & Jerry's, in an attempt to boost flagging sales, actually advertised that its ice cream was high in calories. Market analysts predicted doom for the company's sales, because it is inadvisable to draw customers' attentions to your product's undesirable attributes. Instead, Ben & Jerry's sales rose. Why? The consumer choice process provides some insight.

Ben & Jerry brands exist in the "high-taste" cluster—what some call "premium ice cream." Among the brands in this cluster, some had more taste but more calories, while others had less taste and fewer calories. Consumers who selected the "taste" compared taste and calories of the brands within the cluster and could imagine an ideal brand that, for example, had the great taste of Breyers but the lower calories of Haagen-Dazs. This ideal brand was the cluster frontier, as shown in figure 14.5. Other things being equal, the closer a brand is to the cluster frontier, the greater the probability is that the consumer will choose the brand (assuming that the consumer selected the brand's cluster for consideration). In its advertisements, Ben & Jerry's emphasized that high calories were the price of great taste. In other words, intentionally or not, they were convincing consumers that the ideal brand—something that combined the taste of Breyers with the calories of Haagen-Dazs—couldn't exist. Why? Because, according to the ads, better taste and lower calories are mutually exclusive. One way to interpret this is that Ben & Jerry's moved consumers' perceptions of the cluster frontier in toward the center brands—of which Ben & Jerry's was one. Consequently, the probability of choice-given-consideration for Ben & Jerry's ice cream rose at the expense of other brands within the cluster.

The Effect on the Firm's Demand Curve

The likelihood of consumers' choosing a given brand is a function of the probability of consumers' considering the brand's cluster and the probability of consumers' choosing the brand, given that they are considering the brand's cluster. When either of these probabilities increases, other things remaining constant, demand for the firm's brand increases. This is shown in figure 14.6.

When demand for the firm's brand rises, the firm is able to increase its output and its price and therefore earns an economic profit, as shown in figure 14.7.

Because the firms in the industry are monopolistically competitive, whatever the firm has done to increase demand for its brand can, eventually, be duplicated or counteracted by competing firms. When this happens, demand for the firm's brand falls until the firm is earning zero economic profit.

This means that monopolistically competitive firms earn short "bursts" of economic profit in response to their repositioning or advertising their brands. Eventually, the burst of economic profit subsides as other firms react. To earn another burst of economic profit, the firm must again advertise or reposition its brand. This is why, for example, beer companies spend millions of dollars on Super Bowl sponsorships and advertising—despite the fact that most people know the brands exist and are likely familiar with their attributes. The advertising provides a short burst in economic profit—until the next Super Bowl. So long as the bursts of economic profit exceed the cost of advertising, the firms have an economic incentive to continue advertising and repositioning their brands.

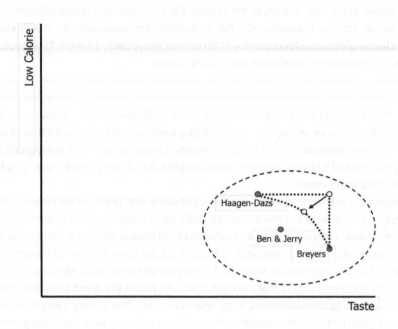

FIGURE 14.5 Low-Calorie versus Taste

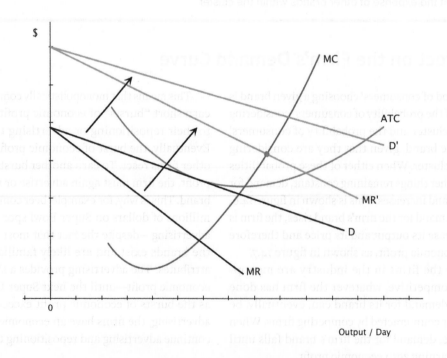

FIGURE 14.6 Demand Increase for a Firm's Brand in Monopolistic Competition

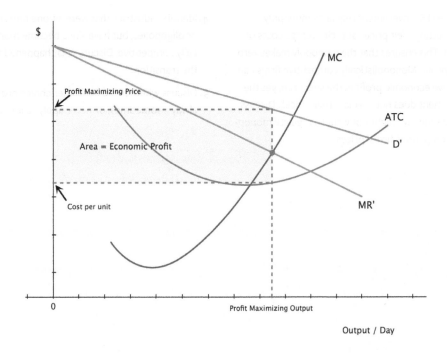

FIGURE 14.7 Demand Increase and Economic Profit in Monopolistic Competition

CONCLUSION

Monopolistically competitive industries present a problem not found in the other industries. As in a perfectly competitive industry, there are many firms. But unlike in a perfectly competitive industry, each monopolistically competitive firm produces a slightly variation on the product, which we call a *brand*. The many different brands present a problem for the consumer in that it can be too costly for the consumer to obtain enough information to decide which brand (out of all the brands) is best. The result is that the consumer makes the best choice possible using what limited information is available and with the knowledge that the information is incomplete. Like perfectly competitive firms, monopolistically competitive firms make zero economic profit in the long-run. Unlike perfectly competitive firms, monopolistically competitive firms are inefficient and can influence the price of their product in the short-run by advertising, earning positive economic profit in the short-run. One benefit of monopolistic competition though is product diversity.

DISCUSSION QUESTIONS AND PROBLEMS

1. Identify a monopolistically competitive industry not mentioned in this chapter. List as many competitors in the industry as you can. List the salient attributes on which most of the competitors compete.

2. Suppose that all firms in a perfectly competitive industry are considering whether to invest in name branding in an attempt to become monopolistically competitive and increase their profits. Discuss whether or not this will work.

3. One way the U.S. government regulates monopoly firms is by setting their prices at their average costs of production. This ensures that the monopoly makes zero economic profit. Monopolistically competitive firms can make positive economic profit in the short run, yet the U.S. government does not regulate their prices. Discuss why the government might not want to regulate monopolistically competitive firms' prices.

4. Identify industries that were, at one time, monopolies or oligopolies, but have since become monopolistically competitive. Discuss what happened to cause the transition.

5. Discuss whether the consumer choice process would always, sometimes, or never apply to impulse purchases.

Behavioral Economics and Experimentation

15

What can be thought of as a marriage of economics and psychology, behavioral economics is a field of economics that attempts to test economic theory in experimental settings. For most of the discipline's history, economists have been unable to conduct experiments due to ethical considerations and insurmountable expense. For example, to test whether a minimum wage hike causes an increase in unemployment would require repeatedly altering the minimum wage while holding all other factors constant and then observing changes in unemployment. There are several insurmountable problems here. First, experimenters can't change the minimum wage. That requires government action. Second, even when the government changes the minimum wage, it doesn't do so in a vacuum. Legislation that alters the minimum wage can also contain language that impacts employment in other ways. For example, a minimum wage bill might, in addition to raising the minimum wage, alter business taxes. The tax changes may also affect unemployment, thereby magnifying, mitigating, or even reversing the effect of the minimum wage. A third insurmountable problem is that experimenters can't control changes in other factors, like business cycles, prices of consumer goods, population migration, and education, that might also cause changes in employment.

The inability to impose policy changes prevents economists from conducting experiments. The inability to hold other relevant factors constant prevents economists from clearly identifying economic effects that result from policy changes. Consequently, economics is less like physics or chemistry and more like astronomy—largely unable to generate data in a controlled laboratory setting, economists mostly observe the data that the world makes available to them. Prior to behavioral economics, economics was a science based solely on thought experiments and field study, not controlled laboratory experiments.

Behavioral economics emerged following psychological experiments in the 1960s by Amos Tversky and Daniel Kahneman, who developed and experimentally tested theories about how people make decisions in the presence of risk.[1] Tversky and Kahneman's experiments provided an empirical critique of the neoclassical utility theory—the theory that forms the basis of most economic models.

Theory and Behavior

Neoclassical utility theory holds that, when presented with risk, people will make decisions based on expected outcomes. For example, suppose you have a choice between (at no charge to you) $5,000 cash or a lottery ticket that has a 50% chance of winning $10,000 and a 50% chance of winning $0. Expected utility theory says that you will choose between the lottery ticket and the cash based on two things: the expected payoff and your preference for risk. The lottery ticket's expected payoff is $5,000 ($5,000 = $10,000 × 0.5 + $0 × 0.5). The expected payoff of the cash is simply $5,000 because there is no risk. Since the expected payoffs are the same, when you choose between the lottery ticket and the cash, utility theory says that you will base your decision entirely on your preference for risk. If you are a risk-averse person (i.e., you generally dislike risk), you'll choose the cash. If you are a risk-loving person (i.e., you generally obtain a thrill from risk), you'll choose the lottery ticket. Finally, if you are a risk-neutral person (i.e., you neither like nor dislike risk), you'll be indifferent between the ticket and the cash.

Tversky and Kahneman set up a series of experiments like the following in which they asked subjects to imagine that they faced a choice between lottery tickets. First, they asked subjects to choose between two lottery tickets, A and B, where the payoffs were:

Ticket A: 80% chance of winning $4,000; 20% chance of winning $0.
Ticket B: 100% chance of winning $3,000; 0% chance of winning $0.

The expected payoff from ticket A is $3,200 ($3,200 = $4,000 × 0.8 + $0 × 0.2). The expected payoff from ticket B is, of course, $3,000. According to utility theory, and since the payoffs are rather similar, subjects who are risk averse will be more likely to choose ticket B, while subjects who are risk loving will be more likely to choose ticket A. As it turns out, 80% of the subjects chose ticket B. There's nothing remarkable about this—it simply shows that about 80% of the test subjects were risk averse.

But here is where Tversky and Kahneman's experiment becomes interesting. They then asked the same subjects to choose between two different lottery tickets, C and D, where the payoffs were:

Ticket C: 20% chance of winning $4,000; 80% chance of winning $0.
Ticket D: 25% chance of winning $3,000; 75% chance of winning $0.

The expected payoff from ticket C is $800 ($800 = $4,000 × 0.2 + $0 × 0.8), and the expected payoff from ticket D is $750 ($750 = $3,000 × 0.25 + $0 × 0.75). Here, 65% of the subjects chose ticket C.

Here's the remarkable thing about their results: In the choice between A and B, most of the subjects chose B. According to utility theory, a majority of the subjects believe that the utility they would gain from $3,000, which we can represent as "u($3,000)," is greater than an 80% chance at the utility they would gain from $4,000, which we can represent as "0.8 × u($4,000)." Mathematically, the majority believe that (for them):

Result #1:   u($3,000) > 0.8 × u($4,000).

In the choice between C and D, a majority of the same subjects chose C. According to utility theory, the majority believe that a 20% chance at the utility they

---

1   Daniel Kahneman and Amos Tversky, "Prospect Theory: An Analysis of Decision Under Risk," *Econometrica*, 47, No. 2 (1979): 263–292.

would gain from $4,000 is better than a 25% chance at the utility they would gain from $3,000. Mathematically, the majority believe that (for them):

Result #2:   0.25 × u($3,000) < 0.2 × u($4,000).

We know from the rules of mathematics that if we multiply both sides of an inequality by the same (positive) number, the inequality remains. So multiply both sides of Result #2 by 4, and you get a restatement of Result #2:

Result #2 (restated):   u($3,000) < 0.8 × u($4,000).

For proponents of utility theory, this is very disturbing. The restatement of Result #2 contradicts Result #1. That is, Tversky and Kahneman conducted two experiments with the same subjects and got what utility theory claims are contradictory results. In one experiment, a majority of the subjects said that $3,000 for certain is better than an 80% chance at $4,000. In the other experiment, a majority of the same subjects said that $3,000 for certain is worse than an 80% chance at $4,000.

Their results were not an aberration. Tversky and Kahneman repeated the experiment, changing the order in which the tickets were presented (A-B then C-D versus B-A then D-C), and the order in which the experiments were presented (A-B then C-D versus C-D then A-B), and drawing subjects from among Israeli students, then Swedish students, then American students. No matter how they altered the conditions of the experiment, the results came out the same. The subjects were not behaving the way utility theory predicts. These puzzling observations have lead to the development of "prospect theory" that seeks to provide a psychologically accurate description of actual decision-making. For this pioneering work, Daniel Kahneman won the Nobel Memorial Prize in Economic Sciences together with experimental economist Vernon Smith.

Tversky and Kahneman's results (which have been verified in subsequent studies) leave us with one of two conclusions. Either (a) there is a flaw in utility theory because it does not correctly predict how people make choices, or (b) people make irrational choices. Since rationality is a primary tenant of utility theory, if people make irrational choices, then utility theory is built on a false premise. Either way, utility theory appeared to be in danger of being thrown out.

Behavioral Premises

Early experiments like this gave rise to behavioral economics as economists sought to test whether the premises on which they base economic theory are realistic. Premises underlying utility theory include:

- *Rationality*. A person makes decisions in an attempt to maximize the person's utilities.
- *Completeness*. It is possible for a person to order a set of options according to the utility the person expects to obtain from each option.
- *Monotonicity*. Other factors constant, a person will prefer more of a thing to less of that thing. Monotonicity is also known as the "more is better" principle.
- *Convexity*. Other factors constant, a person will prefer more of a different thing to more of the

same thing. Convexity is also known as the "mix is better" principle.
- *Transitivity*. If a person prefers A to B and prefers B to C, then the person will also prefer A to C.
- *Discounting*. Other factors constant, a person will prefer to have a thing now to having that same thing later.

Whereas Tversky and Kahneman's experiments called into question the principles of rationality and transitivity, recent experiments call into question our understanding of the principle of discounting. Discounting is probably more familiar to students in finance courses, but the principle applies also in economics. In finance theory, future cash flows are worth less to you today because you must wait to receive them. While you are waiting, you are missing the opportunity to earn interest on the money you would otherwise earn if you had the cash now plus you are incurring the risk of the person who owes you the money not paying. Similarly, in economic theory, future consumption is worth less to a consumer today because the consumer must wait to consume.

For example, suppose a person has a subjective discount rate of 10%—in other words, each year he has to wait to consume something, the value of that consumption to the person today declines by 10%. A person who receives 100 utility from receiving a new car today, would receive 100 / (1 + 0.1) = 90.9 utility from receiving that same new car one year from now instead of today. The person would receive 100 / (1 + 0.1)² = 82.6 utility from receiving that same new car two years from now instead of today.

The discounting used in both finance and economics is called *exponential discounting* and looks like this:

$$\text{Present Value} = \frac{\text{Value received 1 period in the future}}{(1 + \text{discount rate})^1}$$
$$+ \frac{\text{Value received 2 periods in the future}}{(1 + \text{discount rate})^2} + \dots$$
$$+ \frac{\text{Value received } N \text{ periods in the future}}{(1 + \text{discount rate})^N}$$

Economists use this formula when talking about consumption over time. In finance, investors use this formula to price bonds, analysts use it in estimating the value of future dividends, and banks use it to calculate the interest they owe you on your savings.

The problem, behavioral economics tells us, is that this equation is likely incorrect. More specifically, when we observe people in experiments, they behave differently than this function predicts they would behave. For example, exponential discounting implies that intertemporal substitution is *time invariant*. Suppose you believe that waiting one year to get something makes that something half as good as it would have been had you received it sooner. Time invariance

means that this "halving in value due to a one-year wait" holds whether the one-year wait occurs now or later. Having the thing one year from now is half as good as having it now. Having the thing two years from now is half as good as having it one year from now. Having it ten years from now is half as good as having it nine years from now. Regardless of how far into the future you go, a one-year wait reduces your utility by half. This is time invariance, and it is what the exponential discounting function predicts.

However, experiments show that the discounting that people exhibit between a "very near future" and a "near future" is different from the discounting they exhibit between a "far future" and a "very far future."[2] That is, experiments show that people's preferences are not time invariant, so the exponential discounting function doesn't predict people's behavior. What we see in experiments is that people's behavior is better captured by an alternate formula called *hypergeometric discounting*. For example, suppose it was announced this year that Christmas is being pushed back from December 25 to December 30. Hypergeometric discounting predicts that you would be much more annoyed about waiting to open presents if the change were announced on December 24 than if the change were announced on July 24, but exponential discounting predicts that you'd be equally annoyed regardless of when the change was announced. Intuitively, many people would say that they'd be more annoyed if the change were announced closer to Christmas. We might describe the feeling as "not having time to prepare myself for the change," but what's going on is that we're behaving in a manner that is better described by hypergeometric discounting than by exponential discounting.

To make matters more complicated, experiments indicate that the way people behave is sometimes better represented by exponential discounting and sometimes by hypergeometric discounting, depending on how emotionally involved they are with the thing for which they have to wait.[3] A higher level of emotional involvement appears to cause people to behave more

2   George-Marios Angeletos, David Laibson, Andrea Repetto, Jeremy Tobacman, and Stephen Weinberg, "The Hyperbolic Consumption Model: Calibration, Simulation, and Empirical Evaluation," *The Journal of Economic Perspectives*, 15, no. 3 (2001): 47–68.

3   K. O'Malley, A. Davies, and T.W. Cline, "Do Psychological Cues Alter Our Discount Function?" *North American Journal of Psychology*, 12, no. 3 (2010): 469–480.

as hypergeometric discounting predicts, while a lower level of emotional involvement appears to cause people to behave more as exponential discounting predicts.

The problem here is not that people behave according to hypergeometric discounting or some other model yet to be discovered, but rather that people do not always behave according to the premises underlining the conventional economic theories of human behavior, and that calls into question the traditional conclusions and policy prescriptions that economists have put forth.

The good news is that behavioral economics might offer us new solutions that could work better than traditional command-and-control or market-based policies. In one of the best-selling books[4] in social sciences, Thaler and Sunstein have popularized a concept of behavioral economics known as "nudge,"

a subtle method of influencing individual behavior in a predictable way without the use of force or financial incentives. Perhaps the most frequently cited example of a nudge is the housefly image etched into the men's urinals at Amsterdam's Schiphol Airport with the inconspicuous intention of improving the aim. Both U.S. and U.K. governments have used behavioral economics in general and nudge theory in crafting public policy. Cuss Sunstein, for example, ran the Office of Information and Regulatory Affairs for Barack Obama, and his co-author Richard Thaler has been advising David Cameron's Behavioral Insight Team, dubbed the "Nudge Unit." Professor Thaler has also appeared in the 2015 movie "The Big Short" and was awarded the Nobel Memorial Prize in Economics Science in 2017 for his pioneering research into predictably irrational human behavior.

Give Economic Theory Another Chance

So far, all seems lost for the traditional economic theory. Behavioral economics has offered evidence that at least some of the premises (i.e., rationality) on which economic theory is based are not realistic. However, two important rejoinders save economic theory (at least until new and improved theories emerge).

The first rejoinder is that most behavioral experiments suffer from one of two flaws. Both of these flaws arise from the same problem: Conducting a proper economic experiment can be prohibitively expensive. For example, suppose you want to test whether an increase in the price of gas has an effect on the demand for hybrid cars. To actually test this, you'd have to give each subject enough money to buy a car. At $30,000 for each subject, an experiment involving just 100 subjects would cost $3 million. One way to get around this problem is to ask subjects to *imagine* that they are going to buy a car. Running the experiment this way makes the experiment nearly costless, but it means that the test results don't really show people's behavior. The results don't even show people's *beliefs* about their behavior. They show people's *self-reported beliefs*

about their behavior. Experimenters don't observe which cars people buy. They observe which cars people *claim* they *would* buy.

The problem here is that people's stated beliefs about their choices often diverge from their actual choices. Economists call this the difference between *stated preferences* and *revealed preferences*. People will often claim that they will do things that they wouldn't actually do when given the opportunity.

For example, students who turn in assignments late or perform poorly on a test will often say something like, "I wanted to spend more time on this, but I had to..." and then they list a bunch of things they actually did instead of studying, like pledging fraternities, working at a job, staying up with a needy friend, etc.

What the students don't realize is that (at least when they are talking to economics professors) they are *claiming* that studying is important, but in fact they are listing out all the things that they actually find more important than studying. In other words, the stated preference ("I wanted to spend more time on this") is irrelevant. What matters is the revealed

---

4   Richard Thaler and Cass Sunstein, *Nudge.* (New York: Penguin Books, 2008).

preference ("I pledged a fraternity, worked at a job, stayed up with a needy friend, ..."). In experiments, when subjects are asked to imagine their behavior, how they report they would behave may not be how they would actually behave. To the extent that this problem exists, it calls into question whether behavioral economics has actually demonstrated anything meaningful about economic theory.

The second rejoinder is that behavioral economics attempts to show us how individuals behave, but how individuals behave may be very different from how groups of people behave. For example, individual water molecules behave randomly and unpredictably. There is no law in physics that can predict the movement of a single water molecule. However, in large groups, the individual and unpredictable random movements average out so that what's left is so predictable that physicists give it a name—Bernoulli's law. The same appears to be true with people. While individual people may behave in seemingly irrational ways, in large groups and over time, the individual irrational behaviors average out so that what emerges is aggregate rationality. This means that the premises on which economists have built utility theory may not hold in individual cases but may well hold in the aggregate. To the extent that economics is concerned with aggregate behavior, the behavior of a particular individual may not matter. Yet behavioral economics tends to give us insights into individual, not aggregate, behavior.

Further criticisms of behavioral economics have been raised by both economists and psychologists but for different reasons. Psychologist Gerd Gigerenzer at the Max Planck Institute for Human Development argues that behavioral economics in general and "prospect theory" in particular can be criticized on the same grounds as the neoclassical utility theory. Even the simplest neoclassical models of expected utility maximization require some tedious mathematical calculations that most people would never do in their daily lives. Likewise, prospect theory, which offers a better fit for the choices observed in lab settings by weighing losses more than gains, requires even more complex mathematical gymnastics that a typical person would never do in the real world.

In other words, behavioral economics demonstrates that sometimes people make bizarre decisions, but it cannot explain why or how they make them. So far, behavioral economics as a field lacks a unified theory of human behavior. In contrast, traditional economics offers a unified and coherent, albeit imperfect, theory of how optimizing individuals ought to behave. Economists do not claim that individuals solve sophisticated optimization models every time they need to make a decision. Rather, economists develop these models to understand for themselves the incredibly fast and complex decision-making processes that take place in a human brain. Berg and Gigerenzer[5] have shown that people can devise heuristics to avoid making the complicated calculations required by many neoclassical models of rational behavior. For example, professional golfers may have no idea as to what equations describe the flight trajectory of a golf ball, and they certainly don't perform complex mathematical calculations before hitting a ball, but that does not prevent them from being able to hit a ball and have it land very close to where they intended it to land. For the golfers hitting balls as for consumers making purchase decisions, the mathematics attempts to describe *what* they do not *how* they go about doing it.

In a book titled *Predictably Rational*[6], University of California at Irvine economist Richard McKenzie offers a strong defense of the neoclassical utility theory, noting in particular that rationality may have an evolutionary advantage and that neuroscience offers evidence of human brains containing a utility function. Furthermore, he writes this in defense of rational individual optimization:

> Experimental economics does strongly suggest that animals, even rats and pigeons, will tend to consume preferred goods over less preferred goods. Field evidence has shown that ants and

5   Nathan Berg and Gerd Gigerenzer, "As-if Behavioral Economics: Neoclassical Economics in Disguise?" *History of Economic Ideas*, 18, no. 1 (2010): 133–165. *JSTOR*, www.jstor.org/stable/23723790.

6   Richard McKenzie, *Predictably Rational? In Search of Defenses for Rational Behavior in Economics*. (New York: Springer Science & Business Media, 2009).

termites appear capable of minimizing and maximizing behavior, within their limited capabilities (p. 13).

Traditional economists also raise concerns about the presence of systemic biases, lack of real incentives, and strategic behavior in experimental and survey-based techniques that are used extensively in behavioral economics.

CONCLUSION

Behavioral economics is a relatively new and rapidly evolving field of economics. As a fusion of psychology and economics, behavioral economics has brought to light numerous cases where individual behavior seems to deviate from the traditional economic perspective of rational individual optimization. Although not without its criticisms, behavioral economics can offer alternative models of human behavior that can be used to craft new (i.e. nudging) types of public policy that are arguably less intrusive or heavy-handed in comparison to the conventional government policies that often rely on coercion and control. In other words, behavioral economics, together with the newly emerging field of neuroeconomics, will probably augment rather than replace the insights into human behavior gained from traditional economic theory.

DISCUSSION QUESTIONS

1. Why is it hard for economists to conduct controlled scientific experiments?

2. How would you explain the field of behavioral economics to a friend?

3. What is "prospect theory" about?

4. What is the general conclusion of behavioral economics?

5. What are some of the criticisms of behavioral economics?